AN HISTORICAL AND SEMANTIC STUDY OF THE TERM 'ISLĀM' AS SEEN IN A SEQUENCE OF QUR'ĀN COMMENTARIES

HARVARD THEOLOGICAL REVIEW
HARVARD DISSERTATIONS IN RELIGION

edited by
Caroline Bynum
and
George Rupp

Number 1

AN HISTORICAL AND SEMANTIC STUDY OF THE TERM 'ISLĀM'
AS SEEN IN A SEQUENCE OF QUR'ĀN COMMENTARIES

by

Jane I. Smith

SCHOLARS PRESS
Missoula, Montana

AN HISTORICAL AND SEMANTIC STUDY OF THE TERM 'ISLĀM' AS SEEN IN A SEQUENCE OF QUR'ĀN COMMENTARIES

by

Jane I. Smith

Published by

SCHOLARS PRESS

for

Harvard Theological Review

Distributed by

SCHOLARS PRESS
University of Montana
Missoula, Montana 59801

AN HISTORICAL AND SEMANTIC STUDY OF THE TERM 'ISLĀM'
AS SEEN IN A SEQUENCE OF QUR'ĀN COMMENTARIES

by

Jane I. Smith
Harvard University
Cambridge, Massachusetts 02138

Library of Congress Cataloging in Publication Data

Smith, Jane I
An historical and semantic study of the term "islām" as seen in a sequence of Qur'ān commentaries.

(Harvard dissertations in religion ; no. 1)
Originally presented as the author's thesis, Harvard, 1970.
Bibliography: p.
1. Islām (The Arabic word) 2. Koran--Criticism, interpretation, etc.--History. 3. Islamic theology. I. Title. II. Series.
BP130.45.S59 1975 297'.2 75-22485
ISBN 0-89130-020-1 (Scholars Press)

Printed in the United States of America
1 2 3 4 5
Printing Department
University of Montana
Missoula, Montana 59801

CONTENTS

Transliteration xi
Abbreviations xiii
One: Introduction 1
Two: _Tafsīr bi'l-Ma'thūr_ and _Tafsīr bi'l-Ra'y_ 35
I. ^{c}Abd Allāh ibn ^{c}Abbās. 37
II. Muqātil ibn Sulaymān 48
III. Abū Ja^{c}far al-Ṭabarī 57
IV. ^{c}Alī ibn Ibrāhīm al-Qummī and Abū Ja^{c}far Muḥammad al-Ṭūsī. 76
V. Maḥmūd ibn ^{c}Umar al-Zamakhsharī. 89
VI. Fakhr al-Dīn al-Rāzī 101
Three: The Solidification of Traditionalism 119
VII. ^{c}Abd Allāh ibn ^{c}Umar al-Bayḍāwī. 120
VIII. Ismā^{c}īl ibn ^{c}Umar ibn Kathīr 127
IX. Jalāl al-Dīn al-Suyūṭī 134
X-XI. Muḥammad Abū'l-Su^{c}ūd al-^{c}Imādī and Muḥammad ibn Murtaḍá Fayḍ al-Kāshānī 141
XII. ^{c}Abd al-^{c}Azīz Walī Allāh al-Dihlawī. 159
XIII. Muḥammad ibn ^{c}Alī al-Shawkānī and Abū'l-Thanā Maḥmūd al-Ālūsī 172
Four: New Directions in _Tafsīr_. 181
XIVa. Muḥammad ^{c}Abduh and Muḥammad Rashīd Riḍā. . . 183
XIVb. Sayyid Quṭb 203
Five: Conclusion. 218
Bibliography. 235

فما فرح المسلمون بشيء بعد الاسلام
اشدّ مما فرحوا به

"Nothing else brings joy to the *muslimūn* as great as their joy in *al-islām*."

-- Aḥmad ibn Ḥanbal, *Musnad*, III, 168

FOR WILFRED CANTWELL SMITH

TRANSLITERATION

The transliteration of Arabic words is according to the following alphabetical substitution:

ا	- ' (omitted at the beginning of a word)	ض	- ḍ
ب	- b	ط	- ṭ
ت	- t	ظ	- ẓ
ث	- th	ع	- c
ج	- j	غ	- gh
ح	- ḥ	ف	- f
خ	- kh	ق	- q
د	- d	ك	- k
ذ	- dh	ل	- l
ر	- r	م	- m
ز	- z	ن	- n
س	- s	ه	- h
ش	- sh	و	- w
ص	- ṣ	ي	- y

The dipthongs are written: *ay* [شَيْ]
aw [شَوْ]

The three short vowels are represented by *a* for the *fatḥah*, *i* for the *kasrah*, and *u* for the *ḍammah*.

The long vowels are represented by *ā* for the *alif*, *ū* for the *wāw*, *ī* for the *ya'*.

The final *hā'* is represented by *ah* at the end of the word, *at* when in construct.

The following system of bracketing has been used:

a. Qur'ān verses: ﴿ . . . ﴾.

b. Transliteration and substitution of assumed material in translation: [. . .].

c. Parenthetical comment: (. . .).

ABBREVIATIONS

Abh. K. M.	Abhandlungen für die Kunde des Morganlandes
Beiträge	Beiträge zur Kenntnis des Orients
EI	Encyclopaedia of Islam (first edition)
EI_2	Encyclopaedia of Islam (second edition)
ERE	Encyclopaedia of Religion and Ethics
GAL	Geschichte der arabischen Litteratur (S = Supplementband)
Isl.	Der Islam
IC	Islamic Culture
IQ	Islamic Quarterly
JASB	Journal and Proceedings of the Asiatic Society of Bengal
JRAS	Journal of the Royal Asiatic Society of Great Britain and Ireland
MW	Muslim World
RO	Rocznik Orjentalistyczny
SEI	Shorter Encyclopaedia of Islam
SBKais. Ak.	Sitzungsberichte der Kaiserlichen Akademie der Wissenschaften
ZDMG	Zeitschrift der Deutschen Morganländischen Gesellschaft
ZS	Zeitschrift für Semitistik und verwandte Gebiete

ONE: INTRODUCTION

Many volumes have been written, especially over the past century, on the history of Islam. What these works generally are concerned with is a description of the Muslim peoples in their various historical situations. There is also an increasing interest in the study of islām as a term -- the verb s-l-m and its derivatives have been analyzed linguistically and semantically in an attempt to discover the specific meaning (or meanings) that they were intended to convey within the Qur'ānic context.

These two kinds of investigation represent what might be called the nominal and the verbal aspects of the word islām. Untroubled in Arabic with having to differentiate between capital and small letters, Muslims have been able to convey both of these aspects in a single term, namely the group or collectivity of those who call themselves muslimūn and the individual act of submission by which one responds to God and thereby declares himself a member of that group. What in Arabic consistently is called إسلام we must render in English either as Islam or islām, revealing by our very choice our understanding of the intent of its particular usage.[1]

The relationship between these two aspects has been expressed in several ways. We have just categorized them as verbal and nominal. Kenneth Cragg in a recent and very sensitive work has distinguished them as the general and the specific.[2] In the following essay I am combining the historical and the semantic approaches to the study of islām in order to show that in reality any attempt to distinguish between the communal and the personal aspects of this term, between Islam and islām, will be inadequate unless it takes into account the very fact that for the Muslim they have been traditionally indistinguishable. At the same time, however, I posit the thesis that within the Muslim community itself there has been a change in the understanding and interpretation of islām, i.e. that the word

---

[1] In the following essay I have given islām rather than Islam except in those cases in which its exclusively communal reference is obvious.

[2] The House of Islam, p. 5: "There is the general and the specific; the idea and its definitive expression, the thing in itself and the thing in its 'institution'. Islam organizes islām, enshrines and defines it."

connotes to Muslims of the current century something different from (or additional to) what it meant to those of the early centuries of Islam. In the broadest terms, I believe that I have shown that while *islām* originally meant at once the personal relationship between man and God *and* the community of those acknowledging this relationship, it often has come to be used as one *or* the other, with a greatly increased emphasis on the objectified systematization of religious beliefs and practices.[3]

I have chosen to investigate this question by considering the interpretations given to *islām* in the Qur'ān *tafsīr*[4] of centuries of Muslim commentators. There are other ways in which we might have undertaken this study, in many of which the results might have been more startlingly revelatory. One such possibility would have been an analysis of general works of theology representing a similar span of time. The value of this investigation lies in the discovery that even within the highly structured confines of Qur'ān commentary certain discernible changes in understanding have taken place.

The number of Muslim exegetes from whom one can choose is, of course, enormous and the total volume of their *tafsīr* monumental. It is therefore necessary to find some principle of selection. Working on a somewhat similar idea to the Muslim practice of selecting a *mujaddid* for each age, I have attempted to choose one appropriate *tafsīr* work from each of the fourteen Islamic centuries. (A few modifications in this pattern have been made with explanations offered in the text.) This has the double advantage of imposing a limit on what could be an endless number of possibilities, as well as providing a kind of bird's-eye view of the apparent historical development. The principle

---

[3]This process has been described by W. C. Smith in *The Meaning and End of Religion* as reification, a term which we will find useful in this essay.

[4]*Tafsīr*, the *maṣdar* of *fassara*, to explain, is and traditionally has been the term used by Muslims for explanation of a text. It has been applied to Greek and Arabic commentaries on works of philosophy, to interpretations of poetry, and in general to any kind of exposition or explanation. Specifically *tafsīr* has been used as the term for commentary on the Qur'ān, the usage to which we will refer in this essay. Originally *tafsīr* was synonymous with the term *ta'wīl*, both meaning exposition of a text, gradually limited specifically to the Qur'ān. Slowly *tafsīr* came to be applied more to the external philological exegesis of the Qur'ān, while *ta'wīl* took over the interpretive function. As the latter became more and more used to characterize the *tafsīr* of the *ṣūfīs* and the Shīʿah it took on the meaning of allegorical or symbolic interpretation.

of selection is the attempt to choose those *tafsīrs* most widely-read and highly esteemed by Muslims through the ages. This has had the happy result of providing a broad spectrum of theological and sectarian persuasions as well as giving a wide-spread geographical representation (following to some extent, of course, the historical vicissitudes of the centers of Muslim political domination). The authors and works to be considered are listed as follows according to the Islamic centuries:

FIRST: ʿAbd Allāh ibn ʿAbbās (d. 68/686), *Tanwīr al-miqbās*.

SECOND: Muqātil ibn Sulaymān (d. 150/767), *Tafsīr khams mi'ah āyah min al-Qur'ān*.

THIRD: Abū Jaʿfar Muḥammad ibn Jarīr al-Ṭabarī (d. 310/923), *Jāmiʿ al-bayān ʿan ta'wīl al-Qur'ān*.

FOURTH: ʿAlī ibn Ibrāhīm al-Qummī (d. 381-2/991), *Tafsīr al-Qummī*; Abū Jaʿfar Muḥammad al-Ṭūsī (d. 459/1067), *al-Tibyān fī tafsīr al-Qur'ān*.

FIFTH: Maḥmūd ibn ʿUmar al-Zamakhsharī (d. 538/1144), *al-Kashshāf ʿan ḥaqā'iq ghawāmiḍ al-tanzīl*.

SIXTH: Fakhr al-Dīn al-Rāzī (d. 606/1209), *Mafātīḥ al-ghayb*.

SEVENTH: ʿAbd Allāh ibn ʿUmar al-Bayḍāwī (d. 685?, 691?/1286?, 1291?), *Anwār al-tanzīl wa-asrār al-ta'wīl*.

EIGHTH: Ismāʿīl ibn ʿUmar abū'l-Fidā' Ibn Kathīr (d. 774/1373), *Tafsīr al-Qur'ān al-ʿaẓīm*.

NINTH: Jalāl al-Dīn al-Suyūṭī (d. 911/1505), *Tafsīr al-Qur'ān al-karīm*.

TENTH: Muḥammad ibn Muḥyi'l-Dīn Abū'l-Suʿūd, al-ʿImādī (d. 982/1574), *Irshād al-ʿaql al-salīm*.

ELEVENTH: Muḥammad ibn Murtaḍá Fayḍ al-Kāshānī (d. 1091/1680), *al-Ṣāfī fī tafsīr kalām Allāh al-wāfī*.

TWELFTH: Walī Allāh bin ʿAbd al-Raḥīm al-Dihlawī (d. 1176/1762), *Ḥujjat Allāh al-bālighah*.

THIRTEENTH: Muḥammad ibn ʿAlī al-Shawkānī (d. 1248/1832), *Fatḥ al-qadīr al-jāmiʿ*; Abū'l-Thanā' Maḥmūd Shihāb al-Dīn al-Ālūsī (d. 1270/1854), *Rūḥ al-maʿānī fī tafsīr al-Qur'ān al-ʿaẓīm*.

FOURTEENTH: Muḥammad ʿAbduh (d. 1323/1905) and Muḥammad Rashīd Riḍā (d. 1354/1935), *Tafsīr al-Qur'ān al-karīm, tafsīr al-manār*; Sayyid Quṭb (d. 1386/1966), *Fī ẓilāl al-Qur'ān*.

I have tried to ascertain from the selected *tafsīr* how the verses of the Qur'ān dealing with *islām* have been interpreted both in relation to previous commentary and in terms of their reflection of the peculiar historical circumstances in which each author wrote. Because my interest is in determining the point of intersection between the two aspects described above as personal and communal, I shall confine myself to a consideration of the fourth form maṣdar of the verb aslama, i.e. islām. The investigation is facilitated by the fact that this maṣdar occurs only eight times in the Qur'ān. It will very quickly become apparent, however, that it is impossible to appreciate the depth and breadth of the meaning of islām as expressed in the tafsīrs without seeing it in relation to two other crucial words whose occurrence is much more frequent in the Qur'ān itself: īmān and dīn.[5]

While the real understanding of what these last two terms have meant to particular writers can only be discerned by a careful consideration of their usage within the respective texts, it is safe to say that īmān generally is used as an expression of the internal response to and affirmation of God's revelation to man. A large portion of the succeeding tafsīr will be dealing with the involved and many-faceted question of the relationship of islām and īmān. With dīn (usually translated as 'religion') the problem is more intricate: in many ways the very issues we are discussing in connection with islām -- its several aspects of personal and group interpretation (the latter having both reified and non-reified elements) -- come immediately to the fore in considering dīn. With the recognition that an understanding of the dynamics of interaction between dīn, īmān and islām would be aided greatly by specific studies of the first two terms such as we are doing on islām, I hope that this investigation may help to shed more light on their meaning as they are seen to be coordinate with and/or distinguishable from islām itself.[6]

Basically, then, the concern of this essay is the endeavor to understand the meaning of islām in the richness of the historical development of its interpretation. The method is a consideration of the existing analyses of islām in the Qur'ānic context, examining both what the exegetes have said about the verses in question and the historical and sectarian situations out of which each wrote, in the attempt to indicate whether and how change has developed in the usage and implications of the

---

[5] Īmān is used forty-five times in the Qur'ān, dīn ninety-two times.

[6] Because the interpretation of these terms (particularly islām and dīn) is so highly dependent on their usage in the respective texts, I generally will give them in transliteration rather than translation, attempting to offer by accompanying analysis my understanding of their intended meaning.

term. The reward is a greatly increased understanding of its complex and truly dynamic nature. Inherent in the word itself is a flexibility that allows it to encompass not only historical diversity but what often appear to be extremes of understanding within the expressions of a single writer. Yet despite this variability, one can sense throughout these fourteen centuries of interpretation a very basic continuity of meaning, the essence of whose expression I hope to be able to communicate in the following pages of this essay.

* * *

Before considering the Qur'ān commentaries themselves it may be helpful to prepare in two ways. The first is by viewing together all of the Qur'ān passages in which islām is mentioned, as well as a series of traditions about islām that have served as primary source materials for most of the writers of tafsīr. Secondly, it will be useful to balance the characterizations or definitions of islām emerging from the commentaries against an historical background of interpretation and lexical analysis offered by both Muslims and orientalists.

II

Following are the eight passages of the Qur'ān in which the fourth form maṣdar of aslama is used, given first in Arabic then in my own translation. In several instances two or more verses are generally treated as a unit by the commentators. In the attempt to translate the words of the Qur'ān one becomes increasingly appreciative of the reasons why many Muslims so strongly have opposed rendering the Arabic words into any other language. Translation inevitably involves interpretation, a process that cannot help but jeopardize accurate understanding of the passages as they were originally intended. With the sincere hope that those instances in which misinterpretation may be possible have been held to a minimum, I offer these translations (following the Arabic passages) as the result of intensive study of many centuries of Muslim commentary on the verses in question.

سورة آل عمران

شَهِدَ اللّٰهُ أَنَّهُ لَا إِلٰهَ إِلَّا هُوَ وَالْمَلٰئِكَةُ وَأُولُوا الْعِلْمِ قَائِمًا بِالْقِسْطِ لَا
إِلٰهَ إِلَّا هُوَ الْعَزِيزُ الْحَكِيمُ ١٨ إِنَّ الدِّينَ عِندَ اللّٰهِ الْإِسْلٰمُ وَمَا اخْتَلَفَ
الَّذِينَ أُوتُوا الْكِتٰبَ إِلَّا مِن بَعْدِ مَا جَاءَهُمُ الْعِلْمُ بَغْيًا بَيْنَهُمْ وَمَن يَكْفُرْ
بِآيٰتِ اللّٰهِ فَإِنَّ اللّٰهَ سَرِيعُ الْحِسَابِ ١٩ فَإِنْ حَاجُّوكَ فَقُلْ أَسْلَمْتُ
وَجْهِيَ لِلّٰهِ وَمَنِ اتَّبَعَنِ وَقُل لِّلَّذِينَ أُوتُوا الْكِتٰبَ وَالْأُمِّيِّينَ ءَأَسْلَمْتُمْ
فَإِنْ أَسْلَمُوا فَقَدِ اهْتَدَوا وَّإِن تَوَلَّوْا فَإِنَّمَا عَلَيْكَ الْبَلٰغُ وَاللّٰهُ بَصِيرٌ بِالْعِبَادِ ٢٠

أَفَغَيْرَ دِينِ اللّٰهِ يَبْغُونَ وَلَهُ أَسْلَمَ مَن فِي السَّمٰوٰتِ وَالْأَرْضِ طَوْعًا وَكَرْهًا
وَإِلَيْهِ يُرْجَعُونَ ٨٣ قُلْ ءَامَنَّا بِاللّٰهِ وَمَا أُنزِلَ عَلَيْنَا وَمَا أُنزِلَ عَلَىٰ
إِبْرٰهِيمَ وَإِسْمٰعِيلَ وَإِسْحٰقَ وَيَعْقُوبَ وَالْأَسْبَاطِ وَمَا أُوتِيَ مُوسَىٰ وَعِيسَىٰ
وَالنَّبِيُّونَ مِن رَّبِّهِمْ لَا نُفَرِّقُ بَيْنَ أَحَدٍ مِّنْهُمْ وَنَحْنُ لَهُ مُسْلِمُونَ ٨٤
وَمَن يَبْتَغِ غَيْرَ الْإِسْلٰمِ دِينًا فَلَن يُقْبَلَ مِنْهُ وَهُوَ فِي الْآخِرَةِ مِنَ الْخٰسِرِينَ ٨٥

سورة المائدة

الْيَوْمَ يَئِسَ الَّذِينَ كَفَرُوا مِن دِينِكُمْ فَلَا تَخْشَوْهُمْ وَاخْشَوْنِ الْيَوْمَ أَكْمَلْتُ
لَكُمْ دِينَكُمْ وَأَتْمَمْتُ عَلَيْكُمْ نِعْمَتِي وَرَضِيتُ لَكُمُ الْإِسْلٰمَ دِينًا ۝

سورة الأنعام

فَمَن يُرِدِ اللّٰهُ أَن يَهْدِيَهُ يَشْرَحْ صَدْرَهُ لِلْإِسْلٰمِ وَمَن يُرِدْ أَن يُضِلَّهُ
يَجْعَلْ صَدْرَهُ ضَيِّقًا حَرَجًا كَأَنَّمَا يَصَّعَّدُ فِي السَّمَاءِ كَذٰلِكَ يَجْعَلُ اللّٰهُ الرِّجْسَ
عَلَى الَّذِينَ لَا يُؤْمِنُونَ ١٢٥

سورة التوبة

يَحْلِفُونَ بِاللّٰهِ مَا قَالُوا وَلَقَدْ قَالُوا كَلِمَةَ الْكُفْرِ وَكَفَرُوا بَعْدَ إِسْلٰمِهِمْ ٧٤

سورة الزمر

أَفَمَن شَرَحَ اللّٰهُ صَدْرَهُ لِلْإِسْلٰمِ فَهُوَ عَلَىٰ نُورٍ مِّن رَّبِّهِ فَوَيْلٌ لِّلْقٰسِيَةِ قُلُوبُهُم
مِّن ذِكْرِ اللّٰهِ أُولٰئِكَ فِي ضَلٰلٍ مُّبِينٍ ٢٢

سورة الحجرات

قَالَتِ الْأَعْرَابُ ءَامَنَّا قُل لَّمْ تُؤْمِنُوا وَلٰكِن قُولُوا أَسْلَمْنَا وَلَمَّا يَدْخُلِ الْإِيمٰنُ
فِي قُلُوبِكُمْ وَإِن تُطِيعُوا اللّٰهَ وَرَسُولَهُ لَا يَلِتْكُم مِّنْ أَعْمٰلِكُمْ شَيْئًا إِنَّ اللّٰهَ
غَفُورٌ رَّحِيمٌ ١٤ إِنَّمَا الْمُؤْمِنُونَ الَّذِينَ ءَامَنُوا بِاللّٰهِ وَرَسُولِهِ ثُمَّ لَمْ يَرْتَابُوا وَجٰهَدُوا
بِأَمْوٰلِهِمْ وَأَنفُسِهِمْ فِي سَبِيلِ اللّٰهِ أُولٰئِكَ هُمُ الصّٰدِقُونَ ١٥ قُلْ أَتُعَلِّمُونَ

اللهَ بدينكم والله يعلمُ ما في السمٰوٰتِ وما في الأرضِ والله بكلِّ شيءٍ
عليمٌ ۝١٦ يمنّون عليك أن أسلموا قل لا تمنّوا عليَّ إسلٰمكم بل
اللهُ يمنُّ عليكم أن هدٰكم للإيمانِ إن كنتم صٰدقين ۝

سورة الصف

ومن أظلمُ ممن افترى على الله الكذبَ وهو يدعى إلى الإسلٰم
والله لا يهدي القومَ الظٰلمين ۝ يريدون ليطفئوا نورَ الله
بأفواههم والله متمُّ نورِه ولو كره الكٰفرون ۝ هو الذي
أرسل رسولَه بالهدى ودينِ الحقِّ ليظهرَه على الدينِ كلِّه
ولو كره المشركون ۝٩

Surah Three:

God has borne witness that there is no God but He, likewise the angels and the people of knowledge; [He it is who] maintains justice; there is no God but He, the almighty, the wise. (18) Truly al-dīn with God [in God's sight] is al-islām; and those to whom the Book has been given did not differ until after knowledge came to them, out of envy among themselves; and whoever rejects the signs of God [will find] that God is quick to reckon. (19) And if they argue with you, say: 'I have surrendered myself to God, likewise whoever follows me.' And say to those to whom the Book has been given and to those who have no book, 'Have you surrendered?' And if they surrender then they have been guided, but if they turn away you are responsible only for conveying the message to them, for God is the observer of [His] servants. (20)

Do they seek other than [the] dīn of God, when to Him has submitted whosoever is in the heavens and in the earth, willingly or unwillingly, and to Him they will be made to return? (83) Say: 'We believe in God and what has been revealed to us and what has been revealed to Abraham and Ishmael and Isaac and Jacob and the tribes, and what was given to Moses and Jesus and the Prophets from their Lord; we make no distinction among them and we are submitters unto Him. (84) If anyone seeks other than al-islām as [a] dīn, it will not be accepted from him and he will be a loser in the hereafter. (85)

Sūrah Five:

Today those who reject despair of [doing harm to] your dīn; do not fear them, but fear Me. Today I have completed for you your dīn and fulfilled for you My blessing, and have chosen for you al-islām as [a] dīn. (3)

Sūrah Six:

Whomever God wills to guide, He expands his breast for al-islām; and whomever He wills to lead astray, He makes his breast narrow and tight as if he were climbing in a sheer ascent; thus does God lay abomination on those who do not have faith. (125)

Sūrah Nine:

They swear by God that they said nothing, but they did say the word of faithlessness [kufr], and rejected [Him] after their islām. (74)

Sūrah Thirty-nine:

Is he [the one] whose breast God has expanded for al-islām so that he follows a light from his Lord? Woe to those whose hearts are hardened to remembrance of God, for they are clearly in error. (22)

Surah Forty-nine:

The Arabs say: We have faith. Say: You do not have faith, but rather say 'We submit', for faith has not yet entered your hearts. But if you obey God and His Messenger, He will not keep from you [the reward of] your works. God is forgiving, compassionate. (14) The faithful are those who have faith in God and His Messenger and have not doubted but have striven with their goods and their lives for God's cause. These are the sincere. (15) Say: Would you teach God your dīn, when God knows whatever is in the heavens and in the earth? Truly God knows all things. (16) They deem it a favor to you that they have surrendered. Say: Do not deem your islām a favor, for it is God who bestows the favor on you by guiding you to have faith if you are sincere. (17)

Sūrah Sixty-one:

Who does greater wrong than he who invents a lie against God when he is called to al-islām? God does not guide the transgressors. (7) They wish to extinguish God's light with their mouths, but God will perfect His light however much those who do not have faith are averse. (8) It is He who has sent His Messenger with the guidance and the dīn of truth, that He may make it predominate over all dīn however much the polytheists may be averse. (9)

III

It will become apparent immediately in the succeeding chapters that the study of ḥadīth, tradition concerning what the Prophet said or did, has been one of the prime constituents of Qur'ān commentary. The following short survey of traditions dealing specifically with islām is presented both to acquaint the reader with this basic source material and to attempt a general summary of the understanding of the term islām as expressed in the ḥadīths of the first Islamic centuries. We will find many of these repeated or referred to in the tafsīrs themselves, sometimes with accompanying interpretation. For a collection of relevant traditions, the following sources have been consulted:[7] al-Bukhārī (Bu.), Ṣaḥīḥ; Muslim (Mu.), Ṣaḥīḥ; Abū Dā'ūd (A.D.), Sunan; al-Tirmidhī (Tir.), Ṣaḥīḥ; al-Nasā'ī (Nas.), Sunan; Ibn Mājah (I.M.), Sunan; al-Dārimī (Dā.), Sunan; Mālik ibn Anas (Mā.), Muwaṭṭa'; Zayd ibn ᶜAlī (Z.), Majmūᶜ al-fiqh; Aḥmad ibn Ḥanbal (A. b. Ḥ.), Musnad; and al-Ṭayālisī (Ṭay.), Musnad.

While this is not a complete compilation of every mention of islām in these important collections, it is certainly more than a random sampling. Using Wensinck's A Handbook of Early Muhammadan Tradition and Concordance et indices de la tradition musulmane I have considered a sufficient amount of material to be able to discern a number of categories into which particular traditions using the word islām can be placed. The following is an attempt at such a classification based on slightly over one hundred listings from the above collections.

It is clear that to a greater or lesser extent depending on the type of ḥadīths transmitted, the actual use of islām as the maṣdar form of aslama is often accidental. That is, in some cases traditions are cited in a form nearly identical, except that one uses islām and another uses a different form of the

---

[7] The abbreviation according to which each will be referred follows the name in parentheses. This practice is according to the suggestion of Wensinck's Handbook.

verb.[8] This is an interesting illustration of one of the basic points of this thesis, that particularly in the early centuries the maṣdar form was so clearly understood as verbal rather than (or as well as) nominal that such an interchange of forms was possible. In many instances the general content is the same in several traditions except that some specifically mention islām and others do not.[9]

Because it is the primary concern of this essay to attempt to ascertain an understanding of the maṣdar form, I have confined myself, as in the tafsīrs, to those traditions specifically mentioning islām. It might be noted that in Wensinck's English Handbook, in which he attempts a topical concordance, many of the traditions that he lists under the category ISLAM do not contain the maṣdar of the verb at all. In fact, in some instances, particularly those dealing with the duties of islām, no form of the verb aslama is present. Wensinck apparently is attempting to provide assistance for his readers who automatically associate the duties prescribed by the Prophet with the act of submission (or with what we have come to see as a designated system), although the advisability of such a practice might well be questioned in such a work as a concordance.

Here, then, are some of the categories into which the traditions seem naturally to fall. The largest grouping is that just mentioned which considers the duties [farā'iḍ] prescribed by the Prophet.

The most commonly cited tradition of this type[10] is that describing a man coming to the Messenger of God, very agitated, asking him about al-islām. The prophet enumerates the duties and the man asks if more is required. No, says the Prophet, except that you be obedient. This sequence occurs several times with more duties cited, and ends with the man saying: I will not increase this or decrease it, to which the Prophet replies: He is blessed if he is sincere [aflaḥa 'in ṣadaqa].

---

[8]Ayyu'l-muslimīn khair? Qāla man salima'l-muslimūn min lisānihi wa-yadihi. (Mu. I, 65) Ayyu'l-islām afḍal? Qāla man salima'l-muslimūn min lisānihi wa-yadihi. (Nas. II, 268)

[9]Most conspicuous here are the many ḥadīths that treat the five arkān or basic duties. Some list these as a response to the specific question, What is al-islām? while others suggest that they are to be enumerated when one meets one of the People of the Book, etc.

[10]Mu. I, 40-41; A.D., p. 93; A.b.Ḥ. I, 162; Nas. II, 297; Mā. I, 175; Bu. IV (pt. 2), 339.

In all of these narratives three duties specifically mentioned are five prayers day and night, fasting the month of Ramaḍān, and paying the alms-tax [al-zakāt]. In four they are enumerated in answer to the Messenger of God's having been asked about al-islām [yas'alu ᶜan al-islām]. In two instances (Bu. and Nas.) these three duties are referred to, but in answer to the question: What is the farḍ Allāh? In discussing zakāt the narrator says that the Messenger of God told the questioning man about the obligations of islām [sharā'iᶜ al-islām].

I have found four other examples of ḥadīths relating the duties of islām, all isolated examples in my collection. In Nas. I, 330 we read that there are in the call to al-islām three essential elements: witnessing (that there is no God but He) [al-shahādah], prayer [al-ṣalāt] and paying the alms-tax [al-zakāt]. And if after that anything is necessary it is the duty of fasting [al-ṣaum] and pilgrimage [al-ḥajj]. The narrator goes on to say that the arkān are five. Then in an interesting passage he says that the first three pillars are credal [iᶜtiqādī], physical [badanī] and financial [mālī], namely the shahādah, the ṣalāt and the zakāt. It is in terms of these three that one really answers the call to islām and the other two, ṣaum and ḥajj, are easy in comparison to these. "Islām is the basis [aṣl] and it is hard for the kuffār and prayer is hard because of its repetition and almsgiving is hard because of man's love of money." From this it appears that islām, as well as for the totality of the arkān, is used specifically for the shahādah, presumably because it designates "the act of" (whether becoming a Muslim, or committing oneself).

In A.b.Ḥ. IV, 200-201 we read that God commanded four things in al-islām; the performance of three of these does not suffice unless one observes them all: ṣalāt and zakāt and ṣaum Ramaḍān and ḥajj al-bayt. A.b.Ḥ. cites another tradition (I, 250) in which the Messenger of God says that the duties of islām are five with no increase. However he mentions only zakāt, ṣaum Ramaḍān and ḥajj. A final example is the instance cited by A.b.Ḥ. I, 264 of the mentioning by the Messenger of God of the duties of islām, specifically the zakāt and ṣaum and ḥajj and the obligations [sharā'iᶜ] of islām.

If we tally up the results of these examples we find that the prayers have been mentioned nine times (both as simply ṣalāt and specifically as five prayers day and night), the fast of Ramaḍān ten times, the zakāt nine times, the ḥajj four times and the shahādah once. As regards the last, however, in several of the narratives the questioner responds to the listing of duties by witnessing the two shahādahs (witness that there is no God but He and that Muḥammad is His Prophet). It should also be reiterated that there are as many occasions in the ḥadīth literature, perhaps more, in which the pillars [arkān] (or duties [farā'iḍ] as they have been more frequently called in our examples) are listed with no mention of islām as there are cases in which the term islām is actually used. What is of interest for the purposes of this essay is not the specifics of the duties as much as the fact that the listing of them was the response of the Messenger of God, as recorded in the traditions, to his having been asked about islām. We will consider the implications of this after having viewed other instances of the term islām as found in the ḥadīths.

Closely related to the above category is the group of traditions[11] which relate the statement of the Messenger of God that al-islām is built on five (things). In only one instance out of twelve is this cited as an answer to a question,[12] and here we know only that a group visiting the Messenger of God had previously been asking him about various matters. The results of these enumerations show more consistency than we saw above. All twelve mention that islām is built on ṣalāt, zakāt, ṣaum Ramaḍān and ḥajj al-bayt. It is only in regard to the first duty that there is some differentiation. Six mention the two shahādahs, four only the first shahādah, one says "to proclaim the unity of God" and one "to worship God and give the lie to all else". Two mention that the Messenger of God, having been asked about the jihād, indicates that it is good.

One of the most interesting groups of traditions mentioning islām is that in which the Prophet defines al-islām as distinct from al-īmān.[13] The most popular version tells the story of a man who comes to the Prophet of God while he is seated with some of the Companions. The man has a beautiful face and black hair and a white robe. He is unknown to the assembled group, and bears no marks of travel. After placing one knee over the other and putting his palm on his thigh he asks the Prophet,

---

[11]Tir. II, 100-101; Bu. I, 19; A.b.Ḥ. II, 26, 92-3, 120, 143 and IV, 363; Mu. I, 45; Nas. I, 268.

[12]A.b.Ḥ. II, 93.

[13]Tir. II, 101; Ṭay., p. 5; Bu. I, 48; Nas. II, 264-6; A.b.Ḥ. I, 27, 51, 52; II, 107, 426; and IV, 114, 164; I.M. I, 24, 25; Mu. I, 36-68, 39, 40.

What is al-islām [mā al-islām]? or, Tell me about al-islām [akhbirnī ᶜan al-islām]. The circumstances of the story are altered somewhat in the different narrations but this version is most common. Much to the surprise of the assemblage, after receiving the answer (which is that islām is certain duties, listed below) the man informs the Prophet that he, the Prophet, is correct. He then proceeds to inquire about al-īmān [faith], al-iḥsān [beneficence], and al-sāᶜah [the hour], indicating after each reply that the Messenger of God is correct. We find at the end of the narration that the beautiful stranger is indeed the angel Jibrīl who says he has come to teach the assembled group about their dīn [atākum yuᶜallimukum dīnakum].

Adding up the elements related in this sample of fourteen traditions we find that islām consists of the following elements (the numbers in brackets indicate frequency of mention in the various traditions): witnessing that there is no God but God and that Muḥammad is His Messenger (eight); submitting to God with no association [shirk] of anything else (six); doing ṣalāt (fourteen);[14] paying zakāt (fourteen);[15] ṣaum Ramaḍān (thirteen); making the ḥajj al-bayt if it be possible (nine); and cleansing of the major ritual impurity [janābah] (one). Īmān, on the other hand, means faith in the following: God (fourteen), His angels (fourteen), His Books (nine), His Book (three), His Messengers (twelve), His Messenger (one), the last day (seven), the decree [al-qadr] in its totality of good and evil (eleven), resurrection [baᶜth] after death (seven), the garden (four), the fire (four), meeting Him (four), death and life after death (one), reckoning [al-ḥisāb] (one), and the balance [al-mīzān] (one). In several of the traditions cited the Messenger of God is asked after the recital of the elements of islām and īmān: If I do that am I a muslim/mu'min? to which the reply is "yes".

In these traditions we seem to have a fairly distinct line drawn between islām and īmān: the former consists almost exclusively of performance of the (five) specific duties prescribed by God through His Prophet for the muslim; the latter is faith in (acceptance and affirmation of) the various elements proclaimed through the word of the Prophet as real and valid. This distinction is further supported by such ḥadīths as the following: In A.b.Ḥ. III, 134-5 it is related that the Messenger of God asserted that al-islām is overt [ᶜalānīyah] while al-īmān

---

[14] In several instances this is called al-ṣalāt al-maktūbah.

[15] In several instances this is called al-zakāt al-mafrūḍah.

is in the heart and pointing to his breast he said, piety [al-taqwá] is here. But in A.D. II, 523 a tradition is cited from al-Zuhrī that the explanation of Qur'ān 49:14 is that al-islām is the word [al-kalimah] and al-īmān is the deed [al-ᶜamal].

Such a clear distinction was not always made, however, and in several traditions we see that while islām and īmān were generally given different emphases, they were definitely seen as interrelated. In I.M. I, 34 we find the only instance of a form of āmana being used within the definition of islām. The Prophet tells ᶜAdī b. Ḥātim: If you submit you are preserved [aslim taslam]. When ᶜAdī asks, What is al-islām? the Prophet replies: Witness that there is no God but God and that I am the Messenger of God, and have faith in all foreordinations [al-aqdār kullihā], their good and evil, their sweetness and bitterness.

Then we have a group of traditions[16] in which the question, What [part] of islām is best [ayyu'l-islām khayr]? is given the reply that it is feeding food (presumably this means feeding the poor and hungry) and giving peace [salām] to those whom one knows and does not know. To the question, Which islām is virtuous? we find the answer that the Muslims (the other members of the community) are safe from what you say and what you do [an yaslimu'l-muslimūn min lisānika wa-yadika], i.e. that the true Muslim is he from whom other Muslims are safe. In one case the latter reply is given to the former question. However there is one ḥadīth[17] in which the Messenger of God is asked, What is al-islām? And to this question he replies that the muslims submit because of what you say and do. Then when asked which islām is more virtuous, he answers: al-īmān, which consists of faith in God and His angels and His Books and His Messengers and the resurrection [baᶜth]. This progression continues so that the most virtuous īmān is the emigration [al-hijrah], the most virtuous hijrah is al-jihād, and so on. Here īmān is a kind of subdivision of islām, an understanding which also may apply to the above-mentioned narratives in which Jibrīl inquires progressively about al-islām, al-īmān, al-iḥsān and al-sāᶜah.

Al-Bukhārī himself in introducing a ḥadīth concerning which islām is good says: The spreading out of peace [al-salām] is from al-islām; and ᶜUmar said, There are three things that whoever gathers together these has gathered al-īmān: being fair, giving peace [salām] to the world, and being generous. (I, 31)

---

[16]Tay., pp. 246, 300; Bu. I, 21, 32 and IV (pt. 2), 168; Nas. II, 268; A.b.Ḥ. II, 149-50, 195 and III, 372; Mu. I, 65.

[17]A.b.Ḥ. IV, 114.

Here again there seems to be no clear indication of where islām and īmān are distinct from one another. In several traditions[18] islām seems to consist of īmān plus works, as the Messenger of God upon being asked to discuss al-islām answers that one should say, "I have faith" and should walk the straight path.

Thus far we have been considering those ḥadīths which are generally concerned with defining al-islām. Several more traditions are relevant here. One group[19] deals with the signs of islām. A man comes to the Messenger of God and asks him: With what has your Lord sent you to us? The Prophet replies: With al-islām. Asked what are the signs of al-islām he answers: Al-ṣalāt (six), al-zakāt (six), submitting one's face to God and being sincere (four), two shahādahs (one), and submitting one's heart to God and turning his face to Him (one). In several cases it is added that God will not accept the one who does shirk after his islām.

A final ḥadīth on the defining of islām, of which I have a single example,[20] says that al-islām is eighteen portions. The narrator, who does not claim an isnād direct from the Prophet, lists some of the portions, of which al-islām itself is one. The other portions mentioned are al-ṣalāt, al-zakāt, al-ḥajj, ṣaum Ramaḍān, al-jihād, and command to what is fitting [al-amr bi'l-ma^crūf] and prohibition of the forbidden. If this tradition is seen in the light of others dealing with the arkān it would appear that islām in the larger sense consists of the usual elements, including jihād, and in the narrower sense probably refers to the act of submission itself in which is included the saying of the two shahādahs.

The traditions thus far considered, and they make up the great majority of those in which the term islām is used, have been concerned primarily with the elements which comprise the act of submission or are connected with it. And it is clear that by islām has been intended individual submission, regardless of how this was seen in relation to īmān. The rest of the ḥadīths in our collection are not directly dealing with the constituent elements of the act, but in a number of them it is still quite apparent that the act, rather than the group or community, is intended.

---

18 A.b.Ḥ. III, 413 and IV, 385; Mu. I, 65.

19 A.b.Ḥ. IV, 446 and V, 3-5; Nas. I, 331.

20 Ṭay., p. 55.

Three traditions[21] discuss what God will do if the servant submits and his islām is good. One says He will forgive all the evil done before, one that al-islām will be written ten-fold for him, and one that it will be increased ten to seven hundred times and the evil wiped away.

Islām as dīn is mentioned specifically in several traditions. In A.b.Ḥ. I, 318 it is related in reference to those whom a muslim may marry that all are forbidden to have a dīn other than the dīn al-islām. And the relationship of īmān and islām is again touched on in Tir. II, 103 where we read: He tastes the food of al-īmān who accepts God as his Lord and islām as his dīn and Muḥammad as his Prophet. In a reference to 49:14 of the Qur'ān, while not dealing specifically with īmān Bukhārī himself discusses true islām. (I, 30) He says that al-islām out of fear of being killed is not true or real [ḥaqqan], but is al-istislām (i.e. islām not because they are sincere but merely out of physical surrender). This accords with God's having said, "The Arabs say 'We believe'. Say: You do not believe, but say 'We have submitted'." And if it be true, says Bukhārī, it is in accordance with His having said, "Truly al-dīn with God is al-islām". (Qur'ān 3:19)

One interesting ḥadīth refers to the bonds [ᶜurwah, pl. ᶜurá] of islām.[22] The Messenger of God said, Let them destroy (pick apart) these bonds of islām one by one. Each time one bond is removed people cling to the remaining one (the one next to it). And the first of these likely to be destroyed is judgment [al-ḥukm] and the last is al-ṣalāt.

On another occasion,[23] the Messenger of God in discussing the Day of Resurrection says that the ṣalāt will come and say, Oh Lord, I am the ṣalāt, and He will say, You are correct. This sequence continues with the coming of the truth [al-ḥaqq] and the fast. Then the Messenger of God says: Then al-islām will come and say, Oh Lord, you are the salām and I am the islām. And God will say: You are right; today I accept you and by you this day I will give recompense. A.b.Ḥ. follows this by citing, "Whoever chooses other than al-islām as [a] dīn it will not be accepted from him and he will be a loser in the Hereafter." (Qur'ān 3:85) This is varied slightly in Ṭay. where it is the Lord who says: You are the islām and I am the salām. This

---

[21]Bu. I, 41-2; Nas. II, 267-8.

[22]A.b.Ḥ. IV, 2, 232 and V, 251.

[23]Ṭay., p. 324; A.b.Ḥ. II, 363.

interesting tradition, in which we may find an echo of Zarathustrian lore, lends itself to several possible interpretations and frequently is referred to in the commentaries.

While there is certainly room for more than one understanding of some of these last ḥadīths, it is, as we have said, quite clear that the intention of al-islām is the individual act of submission. There are a few traditions, however, in which it is less easy to understand just what is meant by islām; in some cases they seem to lend themselves more readily to an understanding of the community of muslims, although their metaphorical nature makes it difficult to determine this with any certainty. Centuries of Muslim scholars have debated the interpretation of some of these more ambiguous traditions. When such interpretation occurs in the context of the tafsīr to be studied in this essay we will consider it in more detail.

One group contains the familiar reference to islām as strange [gharīb].[24] All of these center on the phrase: al-islām began strange and it will return (as it began) strange, and blessed are the strangers. Several ask the question: Who are the strangers? The answer comes that they are those who are righteous when the people are corrupt.[25] What seems to be implied by gharīb here is that (sincere) islām is rare and will become rare, apparently another indication of personal submission. Finally we have the interesting assurance that islām will join (or seek shelter in) [ya'rizu] the two mosques (probably referring to those at Mecca and Madīnah) as the snake shrinks in its hole.[26]

Related to this eschatological prediction are the narratives that discuss the revolution of al-islām.[27] These are essentially the same in content and tell that the Messenger of God said that the millstone of islām will turn in a circle [tadawwara] for thirty-five or thirty-six or thirty-seven years, and those destroyed will have gone the way of destruction while the ones remaining will have their dīn set up for them for seventy

---

[24]Tir. II, 104; A.b.Ḥ. I, 398 and IV, 73; I.M. II, 1320; Mu. I, 130-131; Dā. II, 311-12.

[25]Tir. II, 104, A.b.Ḥ. IV, 74.

[26]The editor of this edition of Muslim (I, 131) suggests that ya'rizu means uniting [yanḍammu] or bringing together [yajtamiʿu].

[27]Ṭay., p. 50; A.b.Ḥ. I, 390, 383, 395, 451.

years. In two of the narratives (A.b.Ḥ. I, 395, 451) the word "disappear" [tazūlu] is used instead of tadawwara.

One story related by A.b.Ḥ. (III, 463) tells of ᶜUmar b. al-Khaṭṭāb in a mosque in Madīnah. Asked about al-islām he said that he had heard the Messenger of God saying that al-islām begins as a stem, then doubles, then quadruples, then is made six-fold, then splits into many branches. And ᶜUmar said, There is nothing after the branching [al-buzūl] except decrease.

In the most general terms, then, we see islām in the traditions interpreted primarily by means of its constituent requirements or duties, sometimes as these are compared with the elements which make up īmān. In some cases the ḥadīths present a metaphorical or allegorical picture, often with an eschatological intent. Frequent reference is made to these hadīths in the Qur'ān commentaries; we will find that the most common mention is of those that relate (or compare) islām and īmān rather than to those that simply enumerate the duties or arkān of islām.

There are more isolated instances of the mention of al-islām in the collections of traditions, but their inclusion here would not, I feel, add anything significant to our understanding of the intention of the term. Let two last examples here suffice to illustrate the positive nature of islām in the eyes of the ancestors. In the first we see that three are those things found in the sweetness of islām: that one love God and His Prophet more than anyone else, that he who loves a human being love him for God's sake, and that one avoid returning to faithlessness [al-kufr] as he would hate being thrown into the fire.[28] And in the second a man is talking with the Messenger of God, saying: I have not prepared for the hour with great works, but truly I love God and His Prophet. To this the Prophet replies: You are with him whom you love. And the narrator concludes: Nothing else brings joy to the muslimūn as great as their joy in al-islām.[29]

IV

If we take as a basic aim of this essay the attempt to find an answer to the simple question, "What is al-islām?", we are really trying to discover what it is (and what it has been)

---

[28] Nas. II, 264.

[29] A.b.Ḥ. III, 168.

considered to be. To a great extent this is an exercise in definition, how islām has been defined traditionally and what kind of definition it is now given. This task, generally with a much wider area of reference than we are considering in this specific study of tafsīr, has occupied many generations of Muslims and recently Western orientalists. Before beginning our own investigations, then, it seems worthwhile considering in a brief historical summary what have been the results of the lexical investigations of Arab writers and how the recent generation of Western writers has chosen to analyze and define this term.

One of the earliest of the notable Arabic lexicons is that of Ismāʿīl al-Jawharī (d. 398-400), a teacher and writer of Nīsābūr. His dictionary, the Tāj al-lughah,[30] provides for our purposes only the barest definition of islām. Quoting Qur'ān 2:208, "enter in al-silm all of you", he equates the meaning of al-silm with al-islām. Later he equates al-silm with al-istislām, and says one submits out of [because of] al-islām. (p.1951)

Writing about a century later, Abū'l-Qāsim al-Rāghib al-Isfahānī (d. c. 502/1108) enlightens us a bit more on the meaning of islām. His lexical al-Mufradāt fī gharīb al-Qur'ān[31] has enjoyed an excellent reputation. In this he says that islām is entering into al-salm,[32] meaning that each of those who enter it is safe from receiving pain from his companions [wa-huwa an yaslama kullu wāḥidin minhumā an yanālahu min alami ṣāhibihi]. Religiously [in al-sharʿ] islām is of two kinds. One is without faith [īmān], involving acknowledgement [iʿtirāf] with the tongue in order to avoid the spilling of one's blood (i.e. application of the sword for not submitting) regardless of conviction [iʿtiqād]. This is the intent of Qur'ān 49:14-17. The second meaning is beyond [fawqa] al-īmān and this involves both acknowledgement and conviction of the heart as well as fulfillment of deed [fiʿl] and total submission [istislām] to God. Here, in one of the earlier of the best-known lexicons, we have a full definition which in a few words covers a broad range of possibilities in the relationship of islām and īmān.

---

[30] Egypt: Maṭābiʿ Dār al-Kitāb al-ʿArabī, 1377 [1957].

[31] Egypt: Muṣtafá al-Bābī al-Ḥalabī, 1381 [1961]. All references are to pages 240-41.

[32] The pointing in this text as published indicates salm rather than silm.

The two most popular Arabic lexicons in use today are the Lisān al-ᶜarab[33] of Ibn Mukarram and the Tāj al-ᶜarūs of Sayyid Murtaḍá, the former of which is some five centuries older. Known generally as Ibn Mukarram, Abū'l-Faḍl Muḥammad ibn Manẓūr (d. 711/1214) was a qāḍī at Tarābulus who produced some five hundred volumes of historical and philosophical works.[34] In the Lisān he followed closely, as did Sayyid Murtaḍá in the Tāj, al-Azharī's Tahdhīb.[35]

The emphasis in the Lisān is also on the islām which is, he says, evidencing of submission [al-khudūᶜ] and of the sharīᶜah and of what is required because it was brought by the Prophet. The purpose of this islām is to avoid the shedding of blood. Ibn Manẓūr then quotes the Tahdhīb: "And how excellent is what was summarized by Thaᶜlab when he said al-islām is with the tongue and al-īmān is with the heart." (Lisān XV, 186-87) Then in a long passage from al-Azharī which is also cited in the Tāj, he discusses the meaning of 49:14. Again we find that islām is submission [khudūᶜ] and acceptance [qabūl] of what the Prophet brought; when to this are added conviction [iᶜtiqād] and confirmation [taṣdīq] it becomes īmān. "And the muslim perfect in al-islām is the one who evidences obedience, being faithful [mu'min] to it. And the muslim who evidences al-islām for protection is not truly a mu'min, although the rule of him in externals is the rule of the muslim [i.e. he should be treated as a muslim]." (XV, 187)

Even more enlightening is the work written some four centuries later by Muḥammad Aᶜlá b. ᶜAlī al-Tahānawī (d. 1185/1745). Edited by A. Sprenger, his dictionary of technical terms entitled Kashshāf iṣṭilāhāt al-funūn[36] contains a lengthy and comprehensive analysis of islām as a term.

Al-Tahānawī implies that islām and īmān have been viewed traditionally in three possible relationships. Linguistically islām is obedience [al-ṭāᶜah] with inqiyād of the internal being [al-bāṭin] regardless of works. "And according to this

---

[33] Cairo: al-Mu'assasah al-Miṣrīyah al-ᶜĀmmah, 1308 [1890].

[34] Brockelmann, GAL, II, 21.

[35] Strictly speaking it takes us out of chronological order to consider al-Azharī's work at this point (he died in 202/817), but since the authors of the Lisān and the Tāj both quote him extensively his thought can, of course, be seen to be representative of later periods.

[36] Calcutta: Lee's Press, 1862, 2 voll.

meaning [*al-islām*] differs from *al-īmān* and is separated from it." (I, 696) Then citing one of the *ḥadīths* in which is asked the question: "Which *islām* is more virtuous?"[37] al-Tahānawī concludes that "according to that, it [*al-islām*] is different from *al-īmān* but not separated from it." (I, 696) Finally he says that since in *sharᶜ* *īmān* is not found without *islām*, nor is the opposite true (since *al-islām* is *al-khudūᶜ* and *al-inqiyād* to the regulations, meaning acceptance of them and submitting [*idhᶜān*] to them, which is the essence of *taṣdīq* [confirmation]), they are therefore synonymous [*yatarādifāni*]. (I, 697) Referring to the apparent difference related in 49:14 he implies that by saying that *īmān* is *taṣdīq* and that *islām* is *inqiyād*, one simply uses different words to express different aspects of the same thing. Apparently very much of the understanding that *īmān* and *islām* are one in that they represent slightly varying aspects of the same, he adds to the insistence that *islām* is *taṣdīq* further proof that *īmān* also involves works. "[Works] are connected inseparably to the understanding [of *īmān* and *islām*]. And they two are *al-taṣdīq* and *al-inqiyād*." (I, 697) Consideration of this should be enough, he says, to ward off any doubt.

Contemporary with al-Tahānawī was Abū'l-Fayḍ al-Zabīdī al-Ḥanafī (d. 1205/1790), better known simply as Sayyid Murtaḍá, author of the popular *Tāj al-ᶜarūs*.[38] Compiling much of the work done in previous lexicons, this work is actually a commentary on or supplement to the *Qāmūs* of Fīrūzābādī (d. 817/1414).[39] Murtaḍá himself, who lived and wrote in Egypt, was an adherent of the Māturīdī school.

Although specific mention of it has not been made in this introduction, some have cited the application of various forms of the verb *aslama* to the meaning of advance monetary payment.[40] Sayyid Murtaḍá quotes a *ḥadīth* of Ibn ᶜUmar that stresses his distaste for using *al-islām* in this way. "And he said *al-islām* is to God, as though he begrudged the name of that which is the placing of obedience [*al-ṭāᶜah*] and submission [*al-inqiyād*] to God being used for anything . . . other than obedience." (VIII, 38) In other specific references to the *maṣdar* *islām* in his analysis of the forms of *aslama* Murtaḍá quotes verbatim the same

---

[37]See above, pp. 13-14.

[30]Egypt: al-Maṭbaᶜah al-Khayrīyah, 1306 [1888], 8 voll.

[39]Lane, *Lexicon*, I (pt. 1), xviii.

[40]Particularly al-Jawharī of the writers cited here.

material we read in the *Lisān* quoted from the *Tahdhīb* of al-Azharī which stresses that *islām* (*al-khudūʿ* and *qabūl* of what the Messenger of God brought) is external and that *al-īmān* (*iʿtiqād* and *taṣdīq*) is internal.

The following chart summarizes the foregoing conclusions concerning the meaning of *islām* as found in these lexicons:

al-Jawharī:

- *islām* = *silm* (no definition)

al-Iṣfahānī:

- *islām* = entering into *al-salm* (wholeness, security)
- *islām* in *sharʿ*
    1. *iʿtirāf* (acknowledgement) without *īmān*
    2. *iʿtirāf* & *iʿtiqād* & *fiʿl* & *istislām*

Ibn Mukarram:

- *islām* = evidencing *khudūʿ* & *sharīʿah* & *iltizām*
- *islām* external, *īmān* (*iʿtiqād* & *taṣdīq*) internal

al-Tahānawī:

- *islām* and *īmān* different and separate
- *islām* and *īmān* different but not separate
- *islām* and *īmān* synonymous (interpretation favored by al-Tahānawī)

Sayyid Murtaḍá:

- *islām* = *al-ṭāʿah* & *al-inqiyād*
- *islām* external, *īmān* (*iʿtiqād* & *taṣdīq*) internal

We see, then, that the primary concern of the lexicologists of the traditional period of Islam was the linguistic and legal definition of the word, usually in terms of its relationship to *al-īmān*, although they viewed the nature of this relationship in differing ways. In no instance is there evidence that the reified group Islam implying the particular community of *muslims* is intended.

When we consider a few of the modern definitions of the term, however, the case immediately appears to be quite different. One wishing an explanation in English might find any number of definitions along the lines of that given in *Webster's Third International Dictionary*:

> islam . . . [Ar *islām* submission (to the will of God), fr. *aslama* to surrender] 1: the religious faith of Muslims who profess belief in Allah as the sole deity and in Muhammad as the prophet of Allah . . . 2a: the cultural system or civilization erected in history upon the foundations of Islamic religious faith . . . b: the national political units of the modern world that share the Muslim religion . . . (p. 1198)

Here the distinction between the personal and the reified understandings of islām is immediately apparent. The question then arises, do we find the same kind of distinction in the Arabic lexicons and dictionaries themselves? A few examples will suffice to illustrate that such indeed is the case. As early as 1889 Saᶜīd al-Shartūnī in Aqrab al-mawārid[41] offered the following definition:

> (al-islām) obedience [al-ṭāᶜah] and being led [al-inqiyād] and surrender [al-taslīm] to the command of the One who commands [God] and His prohibition without resistance and -- a famous religion [dīn mashhūr] and its application with the meaning of the muslimūn, figuratively meaning the people of Islam [ahl al-islām]. (I, 537)

This definition was repeated almost verbatim a decade later by Louis Maᶜlūf in al-Munjid (p. 347).[42] Then in 1959 Aḥmad Riḍā gave the following explanation in Muᶜjam matn al-lughah:[43]

> al-islam: evidencing al-inqiyād and al-khudūᶜ to what the Prophet Muḥammad. . . brought, and the obligation [al-iltizām] of it; then it became the name for his dīn, which he brought and to which he called . . . (II, 201)

We shall see throughout the Qur'ān commentaries the interesting phrase dīn Allāh, and it will be one of the objects of our investigations to attempt to find a correct translation of that phrase. Here, however, it is clearly dīn Muḥammad that is intended, the definition itself indicating the distinction between this usage and the first given.

In the current decade two very interesting definitions have been given. The first by ᶜAbd Allāh al-ᶜAlāyilī in al-Marjaᶜ, muᶜjam wasīṭ[44] contrasts "oral" islām, which is al-iqrār by the tongue (and if joined by agreement of the heart is īmān) with "al-dīn al-Muḥammadī, and it is one of the great religions [al-adyān al-kubrá], leader in the battlefield of cultural history [al-qā'idah fī muᶜtarak al-ta'rīkh al-ḥadārī] . . ." (I, 160-61) In all of these instances the first meaning given has been islām as the personal act of submission, the second the group or reified usage of the term. This continues to hold in our last

---

[41]Beirut: Maṭbaᶜat Mursalī al-Yasūᶜīyah, 1307 [1889].

[42]Beirut: al-Maṭbaᶜah al-Kāthūlīkah, 1326 [1908].

[43]Beirut: Dār Maktabat al-Hayāt, 1379 [1959], 25 voll. in 5.

[44]Beirut: Dār al-Muᶜjam al-ᶜArabī, 1383 [1963].

example, al-Rā'id of Jibrān Mas^c ūd,[45] but the space given to explanation of the second far exceeds that of the first:

> 1. Aslama.
> 2. [A] divine religion of unity [dīn samāwī tawḥīdī] to which the Prophet Muḥammad called in Mecca at the beginning of the seventh century A.D. [li'l-mīlād], and it was not long before it extended to the farthest regions of the Arabian Peninsula and passed to adjacent countries and to distant regions. The basis of its instruction is the call to the good and avoidance of the forbidden. The number of Muslims in the world today has reached about 400 million. (p. 135)

The above works were selected more or less at random, their authors coming out of several religious persuasions. Without exception they indicate two distinct ways of understanding islām -- as personal submission and as the name of a religion -- which dual interpretation was not evident in any of the classical definitions. One of our tasks in the following essay will be to determine to what extent the Qur'ān commentaries reflect this lexical change between the classical and the modern understandings. Before proceeding with this investigation, however, we should analyze briefly what some Western writers of the late nineteenth and the twentieth centuries have had to say concerning the definition of [al]-islām.

* * *

Historically the religion of Islam and its theological foundations has been one of the least appreciated -- perhaps because it has been one of the least understood -- of the world faiths considered by Western theologians and writers. Over the past century, interest in studying Islam (to which as a religion the West has given a variety of names[46]) has greatly increased, often with an apparently corresponding increase in both sympathy and depth of appreciation for its constituent elements. Most orientalists include in their analyses some indication of how they understand the term islām, and some have gone into lengthy and detailed investigationsof its origins and linguistic implications, generally within the Qur'ānic usage.[47]

---

[45]Beirut: Dār al-^c Ilm li'l-Malāyīn, 1384 [1964].

[46]I recently received a Christmas card on which were pictured the traditional symbols of "Buddhism, Judaism, Christianity, Hinduism and Moslemism". See also W.C. Smith, Meaning and End of Religion, pp. 82-84, for a variety of names.

[47]Space does not permit a thorough presentation of the arguments leading to these conclusions; in many cases the writers

The great majority of writers have felt that the maṣdar of the fourth form of aslama is intended to convey the general meaning of submission or surrender. Tor Andrae[48] emphasizes that this submission is a willing one, to distinguish it from the necessary submission to God of all creatures in heaven and earth. " . . . religion is primarily a voluntary surrender in trust and faith." It was as designation of this voluntary act that Muḥammad used the term islām. While also indicating that islām means surrender, Theodor Nöldeke[49] stresses much more than some others, particularly Andrae, the "divine omnipotence and arbitrary sovereignty" of God which he feels is essentially the Old Testament conception. "Everything is done and determined by God; man must submit himself blindly . . ." One senses here a slightly different emphasis from that of voluntary surrender.

Goldziher[50] agrees that islām is the submission of the believer to God and says that better than any other word this term expresses the situation in which Muḥammad places the believer in relation to the object of his adoration. Above all, he says, islām is an indication of the feeling of dependence before the Almighty, to whom it is necessary to abandon oneself in abdicating one's own will completely. According to Goldziher this feeling of dependence is the main element in all forms of the Islamic religion and characterizes the mentality of its adherents. We find some of the same feeling that Goldziher expresses in the comments of Hubert Grimme.[51] Islām, he says, first of all expresses inclination and self-denying devotion to God ("Hinneigung und Hingebung an Gott"). In later sūrahs, however, when it is applied to the initiative of man, it carries more the idea of resignation than of hopeful inclination.

Josef Horowitz[52] goes into considerably more detail than Grimme in outlining what he sees as the development of the meaning of islām within the Qur'ān. Originally, such as in those

---

cited do not offer the reader much illustration of how and why they reached their stated conclusions. Complete references to the works cited are to be found in the bibliography.

[48] Muhammad, the Man and His Faith, (1946), p. 67.

[49] Sketches from Eastern History, (1892), p. 62.

[50] Le Dogme et la Loi, (Vorlesungen, 1910), p. 2.

[51] Mohammed, (1892-95), p. 108.

[52] Koranische Untersuchungen, (1926), pp. 54-56.

instances where aslama is used in connection with Abraham and Isaac, it connoted surrender to the will of God. This original meaning was gradually lost and the verb aslama came to be used, in distinction from āmana [to have or evidence faith], to mean attaching oneself externally to Islam ("sich äusserlich dem Islam anschliessen"). (p. 54) Horowitz discusses various differing interpretations of the original meaning of islām, such as that of Lidzbarski at which we shall look below, but concludes that the basic meaning must have been to surrender ("sich ergeben"). (p. 55) With Nöldeke[53] he feels that the word was not original in Arabic but was borrowed from the Aramaic.

In the Encyclopaedia of Religion and Ethics Edward Sell comments obliquely on the question referred to above concerning the degree of man's will involved in personal islām. The term itself, he says, means resignation of oneself; however, the attitude of some orientalists that it expresses "complete resignation to the will of God in all matters of faith and duty"[54] is too strong. He makes reference to the definition of Amīr ᶜAlī that islām is striving after righteousness.[55] We might note here that Sell goes on to comment that historically Muslim commentators have stressed the importance of the formal performance of outward duties in connection with islām. "It is doubtful", he says, "whether [islām] ever had an ethical meaning attached to it. The commentators seem to be unanimous in using it in a mechanical sense".[56] With Muṣṭafá ᶜAbd al-Rāziq I certainly must disagree with Sell on this point.[57] It hopefully will be

---

[53] Geschichte des Qorans, II, (1920), 20, n. 2.

[54] ERE, VII, (1915), 437.

[55] Amīr ᶜAlī in The Spirit of Islam (1891) takes issue with the general tendency among orientalists to define islām as submission or resignation. Noting that Christianity, Buddhism and the religion of Moses are named after their teachers he asserts that the religion of Muḥammad alone is distinctive in its appelation of Islam. Salāma, he says, means primarily to be tranquil, at peace, and only secondarily to surrender oneself. "The noun derived from [salama] means peace, greeting, safety, salvation. The word [islām] does not imply, as is commonly supposed, absolute submittion to God's will, but means, on the contrary, striving after righteousness." (p. 137)

[56] Sell, ERE, VII, 437-38.

[57] I am grateful for the translation of ᶜAbd al-Rāziq's al-Dīn wa'l-waḥy wa'l-islām (1945) done by L. H. Kenny (presented to the School of Oriental Studies of the American University at Cairo in June, 1967) available to me in typed manuscript. The following is from pp. 86-87 of that manuscript, 87-88 in the Arabic text. " . . . the attempt of Edward Sell to make every-

illustrated in the following pages that the writers of tafsīr felt and expressed the depth of islām to be far more than mechanical and that indeed it was precisely as an ethical expression that it very often was used. This has already been indicated to some degree in the preceding section on classical definitions of islām.

The above, with the different emphases noted, are in general agreement that the original intention of islām was submission or surrender. Other writers have arrived at somewhat different conclusions, some varying slightly and some more radically. For example, we find Karl Ahrens[58] stressing the idea of thanks. Stating first that one of the duties of men in return for God's evidencing of grace is thanks, he continues with the proposition that within this category belongs also that declaration of piety which has given the name to Muḥammad's religion, "das 'Sich-Gott-Ergeben' 'islām -- ".[59] Islām as thanks is also cited by Helmer Ringgren as one of the several supportable interpretations of the term: "Islam is an act of gratitude towards God . . . "[60]

Probably the most extreme interpretation of muslim, and thereby of islām, is that of D. S. Margoliouth.[61] He attempts to prove that muslim was used before Muḥammad to apply to the followers of the prophet Musaylimah, the word coming from that prophet's name. The verbal forms were, he says, simply derived from the participle. Striking as this theory is, in general it has been given little or no credence.

Reference was made above to the conclusions of Mark Lidzbarski.[62] His theory, which has found certain support, may be

---

thing that occurs in the Qur'ān regarding the term 'Islam' and its derivations give the meaning of outward submission and obedience with merely the physical members, is an attempt that has no basis . . . . As for the unanimity of the commentators in using the term 'Islam' with a mechanical meaning, this is not true, as is apparent to everyone acquainted with the various interpretations of the Qur'ān."

[58]"Muhammed als Religionsstifler" in Abhandlungen, XVIX (1935), 112.

[59]The idea of islām as thanks is an interesting parallel to Izutsu's analysis of the pre-Islamic meaning of kufr as thanklessness; cf. The Concept of Belief, p. 15, and God and Man in the Koran, p. 22.

[60]Islam, 'aslama, and Muslim, (1949), p. 29.

[61]"On the origin and import of the names muslim and ḥanīf" in JRAS, XXXV (1903), 467-483.

[62]"Salām and islām" in ZS, I (1922), 85-96.

seen here as an interesting variation on the usual interpretation of islām. Lidzbarski comments that Muḥammad apparently borrowed many words from other languages and that he also seems to have given new meanings to old Arabic words. The original meaning of aslama is really impossible to ascertain, but it is certain that to Muslim exegetes and philosophers it has meant giving oneself completely to God ("sich gänzlich Allah hingeben"). (p. 86) But, says Lidzbarski, the concept aslama (islām) means nothing in and of itself and one must see it as entering into a condition or state. This condition is that of salām, a holy state, the Greek sōtēria. Only a Muslim, he says, possesses salām or can arrive at it. Helmer Ringgren[63] concludes that while this interpretation may have validity for certain Qur'ānic passages, in most cases it is not applicable and cannot be accepted.

Another variant on the usual interpretation of islām is provided by David Künstlinger.[64] He too refers to the traditional Muslim understanding of the term as submission, "'Unterwerfung' des Menschen dem Willen Gottes gegenüber,'Ergebung, Abhängigkeit'". (p. 129) Basing his conclusions on parallels with Hebrew tradition, citing especially the work of Pederson, Künstlinger insists that by islām Muḥammad did not understand surrender (ergebung), not the submitting of oneself to the will of God, but rather the reciprocal relationship between God and man. Islām, he says, is the "Friedensbund" between them both, the pact resting on mutual obligation. (p. 133) God indicates to man his duties and man, accepting the conditions, expects from God well-being (Wohlergehen) in this world and beyond. "Dieser also abgeschlossene Vertrag -- zum Frieden beider Parteien -- wird Islām genannt. Es ist leicht begreiflich, das slm . . . 'ganz, unverletzlich, heil sein, sich friedlich verhalten' zu der Bezeichnung eines religiösen Verhältnisses geführt habe." (p. 133)

One of the most thorough and careful studies of the various forms of s-l-m as used in the Qur'ān and in pre-Islamic poetry is that already referred to of Helmer Ringgren entitled Islam, 'aslama, and Muslim. Besides a critical commentary on other work on the subject, Ringgren gives a clear linguistic analysis of the several forms of the verb, indicating both possible and probable meanings. It would only be an injustice to

---

[63] Islam, 'aslama, and Muslim, p. 4.

[64] "'Islām', 'muslim', 'aslama' im Kurān" in RO, XI (1935), 128-37.

Ringgren to attempt here to summarize his findings; let us rather note some of his general conclusions and refer the reader to his work for more detail. Considering first the forms of s-l-m other than the fourth (which latter would include aslama, islām and muslim) he summarizes the general meaning to be that of "wholeness, entirety, or totality", an unbroken and undivided whole, peaceful and harmonious. "The stress lies on totality, not on submission." (p. 13) In discussing the fourth form, he notes that it is difficult to ascertain the meaning in its Qur'ānic usages because usually aslama is a technical term for professing the religion of Muḥammad, which is islām. In some instances, however, we get clues as to the concept behind the word. Gleaning its meaning from a variety of Qur'ānic examples, Ringgren finds that islām ". . . means that [man] belongs entirely to God", (p. 25); ". . . is a relation to the God to whom everything belongs, who is Lord of all things . . . . Could the reaction of man towards Him be anything but humble submission?", (p. 25); ". . . is an act of gratitude towards God". (p. 29) In what I find to be a most sympathetic and appreciative expression of the meaning of islām as individual submission Ringgren concludes his technical and exacting study with these words:

> Submission and self-surrender are well known phenomena in religious life, and so is the feeling of total dependence upon God . . . we meet them also in modern Christian preaching. Submission is the true religious reaction towards a God, who is highly exalted beyond that which is earthly and human. And it is certainly a very natural reaction in a religion like that of Muḥammad, which stresses the distance between God and man, and in which God is conceived of as the exalted Lord, the severe Judge and Punisher of the sins of men. Fear and submission are characteristic features of that religion, but as true religion cannot exist without faith and trust in God, the relation to God in Islam has also these characteristics. In many cases submission and faith are even identified. Total surrender is total confidence. (p. 33)

Two scholars have raised serious questions about the interpretation of islām as submission. C. C. Torrey in The Jewish Foundation of Islam (1933) asks: "But why 'submission'? This was never a prominently appearing feature of the Muslim's religion. It is not an attitude of mind characteristic of Mohammed himself. It is not a virtue especially dwelt upon in any part of the Koran. It would not in itself seem to be an attractive designation of the Arabs' faith." (p. 102) Agreeing, however, that the correct understanding of islām indeed is submission, Torrey offers the explanation that the choice of this term by

Muḥammad was because of the doctrine that what he preached was the final form of the true revelation given to Abraham and Isaac. While not a dominant theme in the life of the Meccan Arabs, submission was associated with Abraham, as in Qur'ān 2:128: " . . . our Lord, make us submissive to Thee, and of our seed a nation submissive to Thee . . ."

D. H. Baneth, in an unpublished paper,[65] also questions the idea of islām as submission. "Is not a word expressing 'surrender', 'submission', 'resignation' as a name for the new religion far too spiritual for the social environment in which Muḥammad had to preach?" (p. 2) Basing his theories on the work of Ringgren, Baneth answers the question in a different vein from Torrey. He takes Ringgren's conclusion that "The stress lies on totality, not on submission"[66] and asks permission of the reader to go "one small, almost invisible step further." (p. 3) He insists that giving entirely really means giving exclusively, which difference is more significant theologically than semantically. What he attempts to prove is that the real meaning of islām is the devotion of oneself to God to the absolute exclusion of any other objects of devotion, i.e. the complete denial of polytheism. This rather external meaning of islām deepened, says Baneth, once polytheism was not one of the immediate concerns of the "Mohammedan religion", and then took on the implication of complete surrender to God.[67]

No survey of the linguistic analysis of islām could be concluded without consideration of the recent and very thorough studies of Toshihiko Izutsu. Three works are particularly relevant in this context;[68] we will consider his conclusions in the

---

[65] "The original meaning of islām as a religious term; a renewal of a medieval interpretation" in Proceedings of the Twenty-Third International Congress of Orientalists, Cambridge 1954, London, n.d. [available to me as a typed copy from the author].

[66] Ringgren, Islam, 'aslama, and Muslim, p. 12. It should be noted again, however, that this conclusion is based on Ringgren's analysis of the first three forms of the verb, not on the fourth form of which islām is the maṣdar. Baneth does make brief mention of this when he indicates that "also in dealing with aslama itself Prof. Ringgren often stresses the totality of the surrender." (Baneth, p. 3)

[67] In a personal correspondence with me (January 1969) Prof. Baneth indicated that Ringgren had concurred fully in this extension of interpretation from giving entirely to giving exclusively, with the ramifications indicated by Baneth.

[68] A fourth volume, The Concept of Belief in Islamic Theology (1965), is invaluable as an historical analysis of the understanding of īmān, and consequently sheds much light on

chronological order of their writing. To a degree unusual in orientalists, Izutsu exhibits an appreciation for, as well as an understanding of, the subtleties of the many constituent elements of the Muslim faith.

In The Structure of the Ethical Terms in the Koran (1959) Izutsu defines islām, as have many others, literally as submission, " . . . the act of surrendering one's self entirely to someone else's will." (p. 185) He then comments briefly on the relationship between islām and īmān in the controversial 49:14 passage, making the insightful observation that while the act of joining the community of Muslims does not guarantee inward belief, we cannot assume from this verse that there is a complete dichotomy between islām and īmān as external and internal. "This . . . does not in any way detract from the supreme religious value of islām as an inner act of the complete surrendering of one's self to God's will. In this latter sense, islām is no less an important element of Muhammad's religion than īmān."[69] (p. 186) Citing the same verse (2:128) that Torrey noted in connection with Abraham and submission, Izutsu says that here we find the deep religious meaning of 'surrendering'. "We see that the Surrender, far from being a lukewarm and superficial sort of belief, or the first fumbling step in the faith, is the very foundation on which the whole religion of Islam is to be based." (p. 187)

Izutsu continues his emphasis on the internal aspect of islām in God and Man in the Koran (1964) when he says that " . . . islām, as an inner personal religious experience of each individual person, means the occurrence of an important event that marks the initial point from which real obedience and humbleness begins." (p. 200) He feels that all of the other Qur'ānic terms used for obedience and submission are vague and ambiguous, not implying what he calls the existential decision involved in islām. Islām, then, is something new, in its original sense denoting a clean break from the jāhilī period in the community meaning and "the birth of a new nature" individually.

---

traditional interpretation of islām. It will be referred to elsewhere in this essay but does not, I think, add anything substantial to Izutsu's own understanding of islam apart from what is dealt with in his other works.

[69]We have already viewed some classical Muslim statements on this relationship; it will be interesting to keep Izutsu's statements in mind in the coming historical investigation of the exposition of this verse.

In a very interesting discussion Izutsu outlines what he sees as the smooth transition from pre-Islamic ḥilm (in which are included elements of iḥsān [kindness], ᶜadl [justice], the forbidding of ẓulm [wrongful violence], the control of passion, the criticism of arrogance, etc.) to the concept of islām. (p. 216) "From the Koranic point of view, islām in the sense of absolute submission and self-surrender was not a simply downright negation and rejection of ḥilm; it was rather a continuation and development of ḥilm." (p. 218)

Izutsu enlarges somewhat on his previous definition(s) of islām in his Ethico-Religious Concepts in the Qur'ān (1966) when he discusses in detail the "old Arab virtues" which he feels came to be active constituents of the post-jāhilī faith. Specifically he refers here to generosity, courage, loyalty, veracity, and patience. Emphasizing again that Qur'ān 49:14 does not mean that islām is not an inner act of complete surrender to the will of God, he stresses that it is equally as important as īmān. The difference lies, he says, in the inclusion in the semantic structure of the former of those virtues just enumerated. (p. 190) But first and foremost he maintains here, as in his other works, that the deep religious meaning of islām is humble submission and surrendering.

The inadequacies of many of the above-summarized conclusions about the meaning of islām stand out immediately. The very fullness of some of the definitions makes other more limited ones suffer by comparison. The objections to a kind of superficial or external understanding such as that proposed by Sell have already been indicated. In addition there is a recurring implication, seen especially in Goldziher, Andrae and others, that it was Muḥammad rather than God who chose this term as the name for his religion, an idea which is misleading in several ways. The basic objection that I feel can be made to these statements as a whole is that, with few exceptions, while pointing correctly to different aspects of the meaning of islām they fail adequately to present the range and variety of its understanding for Muslims.

We will return to consider the validity of this charge in the conclusion, after having had the opportunity to view the way in which different Muslim peoples, in different times and places and with different orientations, have through tafsīr of the Qur'ān expressed their interpretation of this interesting and often controversial term islām.

* * *

In this twentieth century we have entered a period in which that characterized as "dogma" is at best often uninteresting or seemingly irrelevant, and the adjective "dogmatic" rather specifically perjorative. It is not surprising, therefore, that the student of the history of religious consciousness is sometimes initially put off by tafsīr, finding it not only detailed and repetitious, but dogmatic in the negative as well as the technical sense. Certainly it is true that while the style may differ from the exegesis of one group to another and one age to another, there is a certain underlying defensiveness characterizing much of Qur'ān tafsīr, be it in terms of a reaction to meeting other cultures or to the varying interpretations of those within the community of Islam.[70]

To see little more in tafsīr, however, than a dry reiteration of centuries of polemic is to do both the writings and oneself a great disservice. One of the greatest benefits of the study undertaken for this essay has been the discovery that through the formal and often pre-set structures of Qur'ān commentary can come the deepest, most personal expression of the meaning of God's word to those who have accepted the call to islām. If the first step toward understanding another religious community is the consideration of its traditional patterns of expression, surely the next step must be the sensitive appreciation of how individual men have used these patterns to convey the meaning of their own relationship to God. In no place can this better be illustrated than in a study of what it means to enter a state of submission, islām, and it is to an understanding of this that we now turn.

---

[70] It is hardly necessary to note, however, that such defensiveness is confined neither to tafsīr nor to Muslim writing; Christian as well as Jewish theological works abound in this kind of apologetic.

TWO: "TAFSĪR BI'L-MA'THŪR" AND "TAFSĪR BI'L-RA'Y"

> It should be known that the Qur'ān was revealed in the language of the Arabs and according to their rhetorical methods. All Arabs understood it and knew the meaning of the individual words and composite statements. It was revealed in chapters and verses, in order to explain the oneness of God and the religious duties according to the (various) occasions.[1]

This straightforward statement of Ibn Khaldūn with which he begins his short discursus on Qur'ān interpretation gives simply and clearly the classical Muslim position regarding the revelation of God's word. The fact that all Arabs understood it, however, has really never throughout the centuries of Muslim history deterred pious men from attempting to comment on and elucidate the Holy Book. In a sense one can even call the Prophet himself the first commentator, for as Ibn Khaldūn says: "He used to explain the unclear statements . . . and to distinguish the abrogating statements from those abrogated by them, and to inform the men around him in this sense."[2] These explanations were passed down as tradition and along with the earliest biographies of Muḥammad[3] were incorporated into the tafsīr of the following centuries.

The fact that commentary of the Qur'ān has existed since the earliest times does not mean, however, that such activity was acceptable in all circles. In the beginning those who attempted to comment on the Book were severely criticized. Imām Aḥmad (ibn Ḥanbal) is famous for his remark that tafsīr is one of three things having no basis or foundation.[4] Rashīd Aḥmad[5] quotes the well-known question of Abū Bakr: "What earth would bear me and what heaven would protect me if I say concerning the

---

[1] Ibn Khaldūn, The Muqaddimah, II, 443.

[2] Ibid., II, 443.

[3] Nabia Abbott, The Rise of the North Arabic Script, p. 45.

[4] "Three [things] have no foundation: al-tafsīr and al-malāḥim and al-maghāzī." (al-Suyūṭī, al-Itqān, II, 178) Much of this opposition was due to fear of misinterpreting the Qur'ān, expressed in such traditions as the following: "The Messenger of God said, Whoever speaks concerning the Qur'ān without knowledge [bi-ghayr ᶜilm] will occupy a place in the fire." (Ibn Ḥanbal, Musnad, I, 269).

[5] "Qur'ānic exegesis and classical tafsīr" in IQ, XII (1968), 79, from al-Ṭabarī's Jāmiᶜ al-bayān, I, 78.

Book of God what I do not know?", indicating how this illustrates the reticence of the Companions to comment on the Qur'ān for fear of falling into error.[6]

Because of the conviction that the Qur'ān was not inspired but revealed, the literal word of God existing in the Arabic language from all eternity, the only critical study accepted by the pious was in connection with the various recensions of the text. Research on sources for the Qur'ān, i.e. consideration of possible Jewish, Christian and oriental influences, served to disparage the divine authenticity of the text. On the other hand, however, there were doctors of tafsīr seeking philological and historical sources to aid in understanding the precise sense of the verses, an activity that earned the censure of many in the the early Muslim community. We have increasing evidence that despite the opposition, tafsīr of the Qur'ān on one level or another did exist in the first century and increased greatly in the second.[7]

It has been argued that in its attempt to maintain the intention of the Prophet and the Companions, traditional tafsīr was concerned less with the progress of textual study than with defense against any commentary that was not, in the traditionalist definition, orthodox. In any case, orthodox tafsīr (often called tafsīr bi'l-ma'thūr)in the first centuries was characterized particularly by the repetition of ḥadīth materials transmitted through an acceptable chain of authority. It should be noted that this pre-set pattern did not preclude varying interpretations of any one verse; as long as these interpretations

---

[6]Goldziher, Muhammedische Studien, II, 206. Harris Birkeland ("Old Muslim opposition against interpretation of the Koran" in Avhandlinger [1955], pp. 16-19) makes the point that to those who objected to tafsīr, knowledge was identical with tradition; "Opposition against tafsīr was an opposition against ra'y. To the representatives of this opposition originally every tafsīr signified tafsīr bi-r-ra'y. . . "

[7]Nabia Abbott, in an excellent analysis of early tafsīr and ḥadīths, (Studies in Arabic Literary Papyri, II, 106-113) places much less emphasis on the strong opposition to tafsīr than does Goldziher, supporting Birkeland's conclusion that even Ibn Ḥanbal in the statement quoted above was referring not to the content [matn] but to unsoundness or lack of isnāds. Summarizing her findings she says that there was a rapid increase in widespread Qur'ān commentary, that the ḥadīth and opinions of second generation Muslims were definitely in excess of that of the Prophet and Companions, that formal isnāds appeared late and that opposition to tafsīr of the ambiguous verses [al-mutashābihāt] among the pious was strong.

had the support of a respectable isnād their variety was used to prove the superiority and versatility of the Qur'ān. For the traditionalists, that which was rendered unacceptable was the exercise of personal opinion [ra'y] in interpretation. Many of the Sunnī writers, however, beginning with some of the Companions, did attempt intelligent understanding and commentary on such elements as the conditions of revelation [asbāb al-nuzūl] as well as straightforward elucidation of the text of the Qur'ān. Most distinguished among these was Ibn ᶜAbbās, whose commentary we will study as representative of the first century.

The degree to which pure traditionalism has dominated the writing of Qur'ān commentaries, and indeed all of Muslim scholarship, has been analyzed and debated by a variety of competent scholars. Wherever appropriate we will refer to some of the conclusions of these analysts. Concerning the commentaries chosen in this essay as representative of their respective centuries, however, several things can be observed. As we might expect from the foregoing, traditionalism was obviously predominant and in many ways culminated in the great tafsīr of al-Ṭabarī in the third century hijrī. Yet we will see particularly throughout the first six centuries an increasing tendency toward the use of personal opinion and interpretation as well as philosophical speculation. With the close of the sixth Islamic century we come almost abruptly to the end of the period in which individual initiative and expression, seemingly, were allowed a place. From that point on we will discover very little not already presented by the writers of tafsīr of this first era of Qur'ānic scholarship. (That situation changes, of course, with the modern period.) In this following section, then, we will trace the development of the themes of interpretation that are to become standard up to the latter part of the thirteenth/nineteenth century.

I

In the first Islamic century, in which tafsīr was at best a questionable activity, one figure stands out as worthy of special attention, a venerated collector of traditions and very often quoted commentator on the Qur'ān. This figure is ᶜAbd Allāh ibn ᶜAbbās, Abū'l-ᶜAbbās. Known in the West as the "father" or even the "übermensch" of tafsīr,[8] he is repeatedly referred

---

[8] Goldziher, Richtungen, p. 65.

to in Muslim chronicles and biographies as the sea [al-baḥr][9] and the religious authority of the community [ḥibr al-ummah].[10]

Genealogically Ibn ᶜAbbās is of great importance as he was the first cousin of the Prophet, the son of Muḥammad's father's brother al-ᶜAbbās, who was the progenitor of the ᶜAbbāsī dynasty. It is generally accepted that he was born three years before the hijrah, although different traditions raise some question about this.[11] We know that early in his life Ibn ᶜAbbās devoted himself to collecting material about the Prophet and was, of course, in an advantageous position to do so.[12] He was thus quickly recognized as an authority[13] and soon had a large circle of students. His lectures covered a variety of topics from details of the life of Muḥammad to points of law, history and poetry as well as exegesis of the Qur'ān.

As he became better known in public circles his fame for settlement of apparent contradictions in the Qur'ān increased. Several sources relate that his predecessor Ibn Masᶜūd recognized his ability in exposition by saying, "Indeed, Ibn ᶜAbbās is tarjumān al-Qur'ān!"[14] He was fond of quoting lines of old Arabic poetry to illustrate his exegesis, a habit which did much to perpetuate the importance of this verse and to illustrate his own literary sensitivity.

Much has been made of the supposed relationship between Ibn ᶜAbbās and the khalīfah ᶜUmar centering on ᶜUmar's attitude toward Qur'ān commentary. Muslim sources contain frequent references to the high esteem in which the khalīfah held this

---

[9]Ibn Ḥajar, al-Iṣābah, p. 809; Ibn al-Athīr, Usd, III, 193; al-Dhahabī, Ta'rīkh, III, 30.

[10]al-Dhahabī, (Ibid., III, 32) relates a ḥadīth in which the angel Jibrīl tells Muḥammad to take care of Ibn ᶜAbbās, for he is ḥibr ummatika, or ḥibr min al-aḥbār.

[11]In some ḥadīths he is reported to have been ten years old at the time of the Prophet's death and in others fourteen or fifteen. Cf. Ibn Ḥajar, al-Iṣābah, p. 802; al-Dhahabī, Ta'rīkh, III, 30-31.

[12]At ten he is said to have gathered the clear facts [al-muḥkam] and detailed information [al-mufaṣṣal] concerning the age of the Prophet. (al-Dhahabī, Ibid., III, 31.)

[13]An often cited story relates that the Prophet himself prayed concerning Ibn ᶜAbbās: Oh God, teach him al-dīn and instruct him in al-ta'wīl." (Ibn al-ᶜImād, Shadharāt, I, 75; al-Dhahabī, Ta'rīkh, III, 31).

[14]Ibn Ḥajar, al-Iṣābah, p. 807; al-Dhahabī, Ta'rīkh, III, 30.

exegete[15] and orientalists have generally recognized that whatever ᶜUmar's objections may have been to the pursuit of exegesis, he apparently had some appreciation for the excellence of Ibn ᶜAbbās' tafsīr. Although Ibn ᶜAbbās did collect material for a codex of the Qur'ān,[16] this was probably in his youth; his exegesis itself was from the redaction of ᶜUthmān. It was apparently later in his career that he developed an interest in Jewish and Christian material. One of his best-known sources of instruction was the Yamanī Jewish convert Kaᶜb al-Aḥbār, although we are unsure whether or not the two actually had personal contact.[17]

The political importance of Ibn ᶜAbbās, while worthy of mention, is too controversial to be detailed here,[18] and is not really germane to our purposes. On a pilgrimage to Mecca at the time of ᶜUthmān's assassination, he returned to pay homage to ᶜAlī and later was appointed by ᶜAlī as governor of Baṣrah. He is perhaps best known to students of Islamic history as a signatory in the arbitration between ᶜAlī and Muᶜāwiyah at Ṣiffīn in 37 hijrī.[19] After a falling-out with ᶜAlī, Ibn ᶜAbbās left the governorship and returned to a private life of study and teaching in the Ḥijāz. Some feel that his income during this period was handsomely subsidized by the Banū Ummayah for what was considered a betrayal of the family of the Prophet.[20]

---

[15] See al-Dhahabī (Ibid., III, 33) and Ibn al-ᶜImād (Shadharāt, I, 75) for a ḥadīth in which ᶜUmar refers to the young Ibn ᶜAbbās as mature with a questioning tongue and intelligent heart and as having knowledge not possessed by others.

[16] Jeffrey, Materials, p. 193.

[17] According to Goldziher the conversion of the Jews with whom Ibn ᶜAbbās was in contact raised them above suspicion to a position of real influence as sources of knowledge and information. (Richtungen, p. 67) Less charitable in his analysis, Aloys Sprenger felt that Ibn ᶜAbbās changed the legends he received to accord with his own opinions and with Muslim tenets, ". . . und nöthigte seine Lehren mit despotischer Macht seinen Zeitgenossen, ja selbst seinem Lehrer Kaᶜb auf." (Das Leben, pp. cix-cx).

[18] Conclusions on this range from that of Veccia Vagliere (EI_2, 1, 40): "The truth is that Ibn ᶜAbbās did not enter political life until after ᶜAlī came to power, and took an active part in it for only three or four years at the most . . ." to Nöldeke (Geschichte, II, 163): "Politische spielte er nie eine Rolle."

[19] See Wellhausen, The Arab Kingdom, pp. 102-105 for a discussion of the differing versions of the Muslim chronicles.

[20] See Nöldeke, Geschichte, II, 164.

Whatever the exact reasons for his split from ᶜAlī, they probably were based on certain political events such as the continuing claim of ᶜAlī to be khalīfah despite the decision at Ṣiffīn, as well as Khārijī massacres. Ibn ᶜAbbās died at al-Ṭā'if in 68/687. It is related that when he was buried it was said of him, "Today has died the godly man [rabbānī] of this community . . .",[21] and that a white bird came and settled in his shroud.

The chronicles are replete with tales of the excellence of Ibn ᶜAbbās' tafsīr, in which he is said to have surpassed all others in knowledge and understanding of the fundamentals of the religious sciences.[22] While undoubtedly he merits real recognition for his achievements, however, this commendation must be seen in the light of historical fact. Since he was between the ages of ten and fifteen when the Prophet died, one supposes that his direct information was to some extent limited. In addition, it was no doubt to the political benefit of the ᶜAbbāsī family to promulgate and perhaps enlarge upon the knowledge and devotion of their forerunner as well as the blessings of the Prophet upon him. These considerations, plus the fact that the pure volume of the traditions handed down from Ibn ᶜAbbās arouses suspicion, have led most scholars to conclude that a great many of the sayings in his name are either exaggerations or are falsely attributed.[23] Indicating that there is really no doubt left that very little of what we have from Ibn ᶜAbbās is genuine, Goldziher says that a chain of tradition leading back to him can almost automatically be characterized as a chain of lies.[24] Harris Birkeland,[25] while agreeing that there is little doubt that "very few, if any, of the traditions attributed to him, can be genuine", disagrees with the severity of Goldziher's accusation, saying we must recognize that most of those who transmitted traditions in the name of Ibn ᶜAbbās did believe that he was of the opinion expressed in those traditions. In a discussion of the Codex of Ibn ᶜAbbās, Arthur Jeffery comments that one would

---

[21] al-Dhahabī, Ta'rīkh, III, 32.

[22] See Ibn al-Athīr, Usd, III, 193; al-Dhahabī, Ta'rīkh, III, 43; Ibn Ḥajar, al-Iṣābah, pp. 809-10.

[23] Rashīd Ahmad tells the story that so numerous were the fabrications in the name of Ibn ᶜAbbās that Imām Shāfiᶜī asserted that only one hundred traditions from him were valid. ("Qur'anic exegesis" in IQ, XII [1960], 80).

[24] Richtungen, p. 74.

[25] "The Lord guideth" in Skrifter, II (1956), 7.

have expected it to be as well-known among Muslims as that of Ibn Masʿūd. "The rarity of its mention in his case serves as an argument for its genuineness, for had it been an invention we should have found it running wildly through the Commentaries as his supposed School of exegesis."[26]

It is difficult to determine just how the *tafsīr* that we have in Ibn ʿAbbās' name came into being. Quite early his exegetical comments were gathered into collections with *isnāds* going back to his own pupils,[27] the authenticity of which has been seriously questioned.[28] A *tafsīr* attributed to him, without title, is cited by Ḥājjī Khalīfah[29] as condensed [*mukhtaṣar*] and compounded [*mamzūj*], a description which fits the edition we are using here. Speaking particularly about the redaction of *tafsīr* notes which Mujāhid, ʿAṭā and others transmitted in the name of Ibn ʿAbbās, Goldziher says it is considered one of the oldest collected writings of Muslim literature.[30] He then discusses a coherent *tafsīr* work existing in several manuscripts and repeatedly published in the Orient which carries the name of Ibn ʿAbbās. It is this *tafsīr* that we have under the title *Tanwīr al-miqbās*,[31] and from which we will take the following analysis of his understanding of the term *islām*.

It is difficult, then, to come to an accurate assessment of the *tafsīr* we have in the name of Ibn ʿAbbās. "The full extent of Ibn ʿAbbās' literary activities, especially in the field of *tafsīr* . . . is still uncertain despite all that has been written about them for over a century."[32] It seems likely that he himself never wrote *a* specific *tafsīr*. Whether all or indeed any of the material attributed to him is truly the work of Ibn ʿAbbās (or even a faithful reproduction of his opinions) is impossible to determine at this stage; we certainly would be aided in our assessment by the discovery of more first- and second-

---

[26] *Materials*, p. 193.

[27] Ibn al-Nadīm, *Fihrist*, p. 50.

[28] In a recent (1961) study, *al-Tafsīr wa'l-mufassirūn* (I, 82), Muḥammad al-Dhahabī says that the *tafsīr* was collected by Muḥammad b. Marwān al-Saghīr from Muḥammad b. al-Sā'ib al-Kalbī from Abū Ṣāliḥ from Ibn ʿAbbās, a chain so weak that the work can hardly be considered authentic.

[29] *Kashf*, II, 348.

[30] *Richtungen*, pp. 76-77.

[31] On the margin of Jalāl al-Dīn Suyūṭī's *al-Durr al-manthūr*. Teheran: al-Maktabah al-Islāmīyah, 1377 [1957], 6 voll.

[32] Abbott, *Studies*, p. 112.

century papyri. (One issue that must be dealt with by anyone undertaking a specific study of this question is why so little of the material concerning specific passages of the Qur'ān attributed to this man by later writers of *tafsīr* is not to be found, or is found in different form, in his own *tafsīr*.) The work done by Miss Abbott, Birkeland and others on the intricate and as yet hazy questions of authenticity and authorship of the traditions and exegesis of Ibn ᶜAbbās, although an excellent beginning, are really only first steps toward a clarification of the problems involved. A detailed study of the material attributed to this influential thinker is greatly needed: one hopes that in the near future we may be able to discuss these questions armed with fewer opinions and more facts.

* * *

With these problems in mind, and with the understanding that the following may or may not represent the real thought of Ibn ᶜAbbās or even of the first century (although it probably is among the earliest available to us), let us consider some of what is contained in *Tanwīr al-miqbās*.

A great many of the commentaries from the third century al-Ṭabarī on consider the relationship of 3:19 ‹Truly *al-dīn* with God is *al-islām*› to the preceding verse in which God bears witness that there is no God but He. Many of these *mufassirūn* include a discussion of the preference of al-Kasā'ī for *anna* over *inna* to begin the clause of 3:19, a choice which he felt would indicate clearly that the latter verse is a direct continuation of the former rather than a new sentence. Ibn ᶜAbbās does not make a particular point of this issue, but it seems from his *tafsīr* of the two verses that unlike the majority of his predecessors he may well have agreed with al-Kasā'ī on the usage of *anna*. Here is his commentary on the verses in question:

> ‹God has borne witness› even if no one other than He witnesses ‹that there is no God but He, likewise the angels› witness to that ‹and the people of knowledge› and the Prophets and those who have faith witness to that. ‹[He it is who] maintains justice› fairness; ‹there is no God but He, the almighty› with vengeance to whomever does not have faith in Him ‹the wise›; He commanded that one not serve [*lā yaᶜbuda*] other than Him ‹that [or: truly] *al-dīn*› that approved [*al-marḍiy*] ‹with God is *al-islam*›; and it is said that God witnessed that *al-din* with God is *al-islām* first [*muqaddam*] and last [*mu'akhkhar*], and the angels and the Prophets and those having faith witness to that. (I, 160)

It appears that in Ibn ᶜAbbās' understanding the basic witness of God has been to two facts: that there is no God but He and that the dīn of which He approves is al-islām. Aside from the grammatical issue, the real point is that the two verses are clearly seen as a unit. The words "He commanded that one not serve other than Him" followed immediately by the assertion that the approved dīn is al-islām make it quite evident that this dīn is service or worship[33] of God by the profession of His oneness. That the two (God's unity and man's dīn) are related is shown in the tradition given by Ibn ᶜAbbās that this sign [āyah] was revealed to two men from the North who had asked the Prophet what testimony is considered the greatest in the Book of God. (I, 160-61) Presumably not just 3:19 would be considered the greatest, but rather the testimony of God's oneness in terms of which man's acceptable response is determined.

Discussing those Peoples of the Book who have differed after knowledge came to them (3:20), Ibn ᶜAbbās makes clear to whom this verse refers: ". . . meaning the Jews and the Christians concerning al-islām and Muḥammad" and "He indicated their dispute with the Prophet concerning dīn al-islām." (I, 161) Although he does not give any detail here, he apparently is referring (as do several of the later commentators in greater detail) to the fact that the Christians claimed a divine trinity and the Jews allegedly claimed that ᶜUzayr is the son of God. In other words, their dispute concerning al-islām is a dispute with a dīn understood to be the recognition of God's oneness. While he does not use the term tawḥīd in the tafsīr of 3:19, he does so in explaining 3:83-85, a commentary which fully supports the above understanding of islām:

> Then He mentioned the opposition of the Jews and the Christians and their having asked the Prophet, Which of us is according to the dīn of Ibrāhīm? And the Prophet said, Both groups have given up the dīn of Ibrāhīm. And they said, We are not content with that. Whereupon God said [this verse] ❬Is it other than the dīn of God❭ al-islām ❬they are seeking❭ are demanding of you ❬when to Him has submitted❭ has confirmed al-islām and the affirmation of God's unity [al-tawḥīd] ❬whosoever is in the heavens❭ among the angels ❬and the earth❭ among those who have faith ❬willingly❭ the inhabitants of the heavens in voluntariness ❬or unwillingly❭ the inhabitants of the earth unwillingly; or it is sometimes said, the pure-hearted willingly and the hypocrites unwillingly. Another view is that those who were born in al-islām [is meant] by "willingly" [al-ṭawᶜ] and those who entered into al-islām by the sword [is meant] by "unwillingly" [al-karh]. (I, 188-89)

---

33 See below, p.

Again we see that islām means for Ibn ᶜAbbās the affirmation of God's unity [al-tawḥīd]. This is repeated when immediately preceding 3:85 ⁅and if anyone seeks other than al-islām as [a] dīn . . . ⁆ he says that ⁅we are submitters unto Him⁆ means we are affirmers of Him in servanthood [al-ᶜibādah] and in al-tawḥīd. (I, 189) This, then, has been the consistent stress in his commentary thus far, with one interesting exception. At the end of the passage quoted above explaining willing and unwilling submission he adds that some feel that the correct interpretation is that the willing refers to those born in al-islām and the unwilling to those made to enter al-islām by the sword. That Ibn ᶜAbbās did not necessarily hold this view is suggested by the way he presents it as a variant opinion. Yet it is very interesting as the first instance seen in his tafsīr where islām apparently is used to refer to the group of muslimūn. One could scarcely be born into tawḥīd; he is rather born into a group which acknowledges and professes the oneness of God. Certainly one might be made to give this profession by the sword, and indeed that is what did occur during the early days of the Muslim community, but the phrase "dakhalū fī'l-islām" also seems to connote entrance into that community. We shall see frequent instances in the subsequent commentaries, particularly in ḥadīth materials, in which there seems to be no distinction made between the act of submission (to God) required to join the group and the group itself.

One final point should be mentioned in connection with the tafsīr of 3:83-85. Talking about the Qur'ān's discussion of the Prophet to whom the word of God has been revealed, he says that the passage ⁅we make no distinction among them⁆ means "we do not disavow any of the Prophets, and it is said [this means] we do not differentiate between them and God in [statements about] prophethood and al-islām." (I, 189) Again, while it is offered as one interpretation, there is no evidence that Ibn ᶜAbbās does not agree with this understanding that there is no differentiation between what the Prophets have said and what God says concerning the matter of prophethood and of al-islām. The implication here is that the Prophets since the time of Ibrāhīm have been concerned with islām and have spoken the truth about it. In this case he is not referring to the community of Muḥammad, that into which some have been made to enter by the sword, but to the dīn of Ibrāhīm and of all of the Prophets sent by God to the Peoples of the Book.

There is, perhaps, no verse of the Qur'ān among the eight considered in this essay about which there is as much general consensus of understanding among the *mufassirūn* as 5:3 ❛Today I have completed for you your *dīn* and fulfilled to you My blessing, and have chosen for you *al-islām* as [a] *dīn*.❜ This is the clearest reference among the eight verses to the idea of *dīn* as a set of specific practices and regulations and it is with this understanding that it usually is discussed. This interpretation of *dīn* was common among the Arabs even before Muḥammad, and in fact may have been the most generally understood meaning of the word at that time.[34] Ibn ᶜAbbās' comments are not lengthy here, but he does say, as will be said frequently by his successors, that the completion of *dīn* by God means the clarification of the laws of *al-dīn* concerning what is permissible [*al-ḥalāl*] and what is forbidden [*al-ḥarām*] and what is commanded [*al-amr*] and what is prohibited [*al-nahy*]. (I, 319) God's fulfilled blessing is that the *muslimūn* shall not be joined by the *mushrikūn* during the ritual practices of the pilgrimage; there is no further explanation of the choosing of *al-islām* as *dīn*, the third part of this verse.

In this case *dīn* (which from the above we can assume means *islām* for him) is given a somewhat different emphasis from the understanding of man's response to God's oneness. Here the specifics of that response are spelled out and while there is no indication of reification, there is a suggestion of the idea of group *islām* insofar as these regulations are incumbent upon all the members of the *muslim* community.

As we will see to be the practice of many of the commentators, Ibn ᶜAbbās leaves the "*islāmihim*" of 9:74 as self-explanatory, precluding any further analysis here. In verses 6:125 and 39:22, however, guided by the structure of the verses he gives his understanding of *islām* clearly as the internal response of the individual.

> ❛Whomever God wills to guide❜ to direct to *dīn* of Him ❛He expands his breast❜ his heart ❛for *al-islām*❜ for acceptance of *al-islām* so that he submits . . . (II, 58)

> ❛Is he [the one] whose breast God has expanded❜ God gently widened his heart ❛for *al-islām*❜ and by the light of *al-islām* ❛so that he follows a light from his Lord?❜ continues according to the generous gift [*karāmah*] and clarification [*bayān*] of his Lord. (V, 15-16)

There is, of course, no hint here of entering *islām* unwillingly. Submission is by the heart, out of acceptance [*qabūl*]

---

[34]See Izutsu, *God and Man*, pp. 219-229.

of al-islām. The phrase concerning 39:22, "by the light [bi-nūr] of al-islām", is interesting; we see the direct relationship between what man does and what God is and does. The light is clearly from God, yet it is also seen as the light of man's personal submission. We will see expressed throughout the tafsīrs, particularly from the early centuries, an understanding that man's response cannot in its deepest sense be separated from the apprehension of the being and nature of God Himself. This has been shown clearly in Ibn ᶜAbbās' affirmation of the relationship of man's islām to God's oneness expressed in tawḥīd.

We now come to the tafsīr of one of the most controversial passages of the Qur'ān, 49:14-17. The text itself seems to make a clear distinction between islām and īmān on the basis of the external nature of the former and the internal aspect of the latter. It will be very interesting to note how the tafsīr writers from century to century deal with this in relation to their other comments on islām. We will find in several instances what appear to be real contradictions or inconsistencies of thought. A resolution of this seems to come only in the recognition that islām apparently did (and does) for most writers have what we might call a series or variety of levels and meanings. We have seen this already in the work of Ibn ᶜAbbās. While some commentators, like Fakhr al-Dīn Rāzī in the sixth century, have made a concerted effort to be consistent, most apparently have not been troubled by inconsistency or indeed even seen it as such.

Thus Ibn ᶜAbbās identifies the Arabs who claimed to have faith as the Bani Asad who had been hit during a year of hardship and therefore entered al-islām, abundant in family and progeny, coming to the Prophet in order to obtain his bounty (and causing some trouble there). He refers to them as hypocrites [munāfiqūn], requesting favors from the Messenger of God for their true and sincere īmān when in reality they were hypocrites in their dīn, lying in their hearts. (V, 246-47) Earlier Ibn ᶜAbbās clearly indicated islām is of the heart (on 6:125 and 39:22) and here, in the context of a verse saying that these Arabs should be said to have submitted, he calls them hypocrites. Following the framework of the Qur'ān he supports the distinction between this kind of submission and true faith by repeatedly emphasizing the sincerity of the men of faith. (V, 249) The kind of islām described in these verses, he says, is no favor to God; it is God who has favored man by calling him to the confirmation of faith [li-taṣdīq al-īmān]. (V, 250) The point in all this, seemingly, is not that islām is exclusively external or characterized by a lack of conviction while īmān is of the heart and involving sincere affirmation. It is rather that what characterizes these Arabs, while it cannot be called īmān, is nevertheless islām. That is, Ibn [c]Abbās is not saying that islām is not or cannot be a matter of conviction, merely (by implication) that it need not be.

In his commentary on 61:7-9 Ibn [c]Abbās comes back to his repeated assertions that the call to islām is a call to tawḥīd. Again this is made with specific reference to the fabrications of the other Peoples of the Book in claiming for God a son or a female companion. Particularly interesting is his understanding of dīn at the end of this section:

> ❨It is He who has sent His Messenger❩ Muḥammad ❨with the guidance❩ with al-tawḥīd and it is said with the Qur'ān ❨and the dīn of truth❩ the witnessing that there is no God but God ❨that He may make it predominate over all dīn❩ over all the religions [al-adyān]. And the hour will not come until there does not remain any except he have entered into al-islām or pay to them the poll-tax [al-jizyah]. (VI, 62-63)

Again it is clear that the true dīn, the acceptable way of acknowledging and responding to God, is through the witness of His oneness. What is particularly noteworthy is that Ibn [c]Abbās suddenly changes the singular usage of dīn given in the Qur'ān [li-yuẓhirahu [c]alá'l-dīn kullihi] to the plural [. . . [c]alá'l-adyān kullihā]. Since we scarcely can suppose that such a switch was unintentional, a slip or mistake, it seems that the author here was pointing to something different from the dīn (al-islām) of the previous verses. Especially interesting in this context is the specific equation of al-islām with a group of people when he says, ". . . except he enter into al-islām or pay to them the jizyah." By clearly indicating that one who pays the head-tax is distinguished from the one who enters al-islām and by using the pronoun "them" for islām, Ibn [c]Abbās is obviously referring to something other than the personal submission of tawḥīd which has been preached and practiced by the Prophets since Ibrāhīm. Islām here apparently refers to the specific group of those who formed the community of the Prophet.

The contrast between the kind of interpretation given to this verse and that which has generally characterized the tafsīr of the preceding verses is great enough to lead one to suspect that very possibly at least this last series of comments was written by another hand. The use of al-adyān, which is not to this writer's knowledge even to be found two centuries later in such a commentator as al-Ṭabarī, might well indicate that this material was composed some time after the death of the first century Ibn ʿAbbās.[35]

We see in the *Tanwīr al-miqbās*, as might certainly be expected, a kind of archetypal understanding of the several facets of *islām* which will be repeated, with differing emphases, by most of the succeeding *mufassirūn*. *Islām* is personal submission in response to the word of God that He alone is God, yet at one or two points we have seen the suggestion that it is also the name of the group of those who have accepted the call to submission. It is the light received into the expanded breast, but it is also applicable to the hypocrites [*munāfiqūn*]. Yet the theme of *islām* as *tawḥīd* so dominates the commentary of Ibn ʿAbbās that we are left in no doubt but that this was primary in his understanding. Many of the seeming contradictions we shall also find to a greater or lesser degree in the commentary of the following centuries. Whether it is indeed contradiction, or whether it is rather illustration of the fascinating depth and breadth of the concept of *islām*, we hopefully shall discover as we consider the major succeeding works of *tafsīr*.

II

We saw in the introduction to this chapter, in viewing the general development of Qur'ān commentary in the first several centuries after the Prophet, that without question there *was* *tafsīr* of one kind or another; the exact nature of this material is elusive because so little is extant in any form. Most of what we have is to be found in the traditions already examined, which are repeatedly given in the commentaries of the centuries to come.

Three writers cited by Nabia Abbott[36] as outstanding leaders in the field of second century *tafsīr* literature are Ismāʿīl

---

[35]Such a conclusion at this stage of investigation of course can be no more than a hypothesis. While not used in the *tafsīrs* under consideration in this essay until the fifth century, the plural *adyān* was not unknown in the collections of traditions. However, the listing of *ḥadīths* mentioning *dīn* in Wensinck's *Concordance* (II, 163-68) gives only three usages of the plural: (1) "the people of the religions" [*ahl al-adyān*] (A.D., p. 18; A.b.Ḥ. I, 396, IV, 408 and VI, 1990); (2) "which of the religions is the most desirable to God?" [*ayyu'l-adyān aḥabbu ilá'llāhi*] (A.b.Ḥ. I, 236); and (3) "your religion is (has become) the most desirable of the religions" [*inna dīnaka aḥabbu'l-adyān* or *inna aṣbaḥa dīnuka aḥabba'l-adyān*] (A.b.Ḥ. II, 247, 452).

[36]*Studies*, II, 95.

ibn ᶜAbd al-Raḥmān al-Suddī [?] (d. 127/744), Muḥammad ibn al-Sā'ib al-Kalbī (d. 146/763),[37] and Muqātil ibn Sulaymān al-Balkhī (d. 150/767). It is the last of these on whom we shall concentrate in our consideration of the second century; we are fortunate that at least some of his writing has survived.

On the whole the sources report far more derogatory comment about Muqātil's scholarship in general and his tafsīr in particular than appreciation of him, although the latter is not entirely lacking. His value for us lies primarily in the fact that he obviously was considered important and influential enough to refute, given the numerous and sometimes lengthy passages devoted to him in a variety of references. Too, sketchy as the material we have from him is, it remains one of the few sources available to us of second century Qur'ān interpretation. What, then, do we know about this man?

Opinions about him are abundant; facts concerning his life are not. Abū'l-Ḥasan Muqātil b. Sulaymān b. Bashīr al-Azdī came originally from a family of Balkh, lived in Marv, and went from there to Baghdād and Baṣrah where he died.[38] He spent most of his career in ᶜIrāq, though there are reports that he travelled as far as Beirut. He is noted as a traditionist, despite the fact that the severest criticism of his tafsīr is based on the allegation that he inadequately documented his traditionist material. According to Brockelmann he belonged to the oldest school of Qur'ān expositors, closely related to the qaṣṣāṣ [story-teller], who tried to bring the text of the Qur'ān into harmony with the traditions of the Jews and Christians.[39] He was politically a Zaydī, though theologically he tended toward the understanding of the Murji'ah.

It appears that while Muqātil did enjoy a certain amount of prestige among his associates,[40] nonetheless certain accusations

---

[37] Abbot (Ibid., II, 105) calls al-Kalbī "the one contemporary scholar who could challenge his [Muqātil b. Sulaymān's] leadership in the field of tafsīr." For reasons which we shall see below Muqātil suffered heavy censure, while al-Kalbī continued to be respected in the eyes of the community.

[38] Ibn Khallikān, Wafayāt, III, 408-9; Ibn Ḥajar, Tahdhīb, X, 284.

[39] Brockelmann, GAL, S I, 332.

[40] Al-Khaṭīb al-Baghdādī (Ta'rīkh Baghdād, XIII, 160-66) cites several traditions that praise his ability at tafsīr and his great knowledge, though with qualifications to be noted below; Ibn al-ᶜImād (Shadharāt, I, 227) mentions a ḥadīth in which he is called excellent [nabīl]; al-Dhahabī (Mīzān, III, 196) quotes the statement that "He is truthful and his knowledge

were levelled against him which seem to fall into three categories. In the light of the strong emphasis on traditions current in the subsequent Muslim community it is not surprising to find Muqātil strongly censured because he had failed adequately to support his statements with the corresponding isnāds. The comments about Muqātil range from complete condemnation of his tafsīr to admission of its acceptability, in some cases excellence, were it more thoroughly documented.[41]

In the second place, as was suggested by Brockelmann, Muqātil was later strongly suspect for his apparent association with the Jews and the Christians.[42] Goldziher cites him as one of the prime examples of those "curious scribes" who filled the gaps of their understanding of the Qur'ān with supplementary stories taken from the Christians and the Jews.[43]

The third accusation later levelled with some consistency against Muqātil is that he was a strong advocate of anthropomorphism [tashbīh]. Abū Ḥanīfah is supposed to have said that from the East have come two offensive sights [ra'yān khabīthān], Jahm[44] the one who denies God's attributes [muᶜaṭṭil] and Muqātil the one who ascribes human characteristics to God [mushabbih].[45] He was frequently accused of likening God to the creatures.[46]

Aside from these specific accusations the sources are replete with straightforward allegations that he was a liar, that his tafsīr is nothing but falsehood, and that he was actually a bit of a fool in giving ludicrous answers to questions posed to

---

is like a sea." Both al-Baghdādī and al-Dhahabī mention that al-Shāfiᶜī considered him to be an outstanding leader in the area of tafsīr. (Ta'rīkh XIII, 161 and Mīzān, III, 197).

[41] Ibn Ḥajar (Tahdhīb, X, 279) quotes Mubarrak as saying concerning Muqātil's tafsīr: "Oh what a learning that would be if only it had isnād!"

[42] See al-Dhahabī, Mīzān, III, 197 and Ibn Ḥajar, Tahdhīb, X, 284 for examples of such accusation.

[43] Goldziher, Richtungen, pp. 57-59.

[44] Jahm b. Ṣafwān (d. 128/745-6) shared the Muᶜtazilī conviction that no anthropomorphic attributes can be predicated of God.

[45] Al-Khaṭīb al-Baghdādī, Ta'rīkh, XIII, 164. Al-Dhahabī (Mīzān, III, 197) quotes a tale in which Muqātil is supposed to have said that on the day of resurrection one may pass through the rows of angels until he sits on the throne of God touching His knee.

[46] Ibn Ḥajar, Tahdhīb, X, 284.

him.[47] He may have had some ascetic tendencies, as it is related that he never wore a shirt unless he had something woolen under it,[48] but we have little or no specific information about this. According to Brockelmann[49] he had some knowledge of philosophical methods and his use of the homonym in exegesis was adopted by al-Shāfiᶜī.

One of the most recent and detailed studies of Muqātil is that by Nabia Abbott,[50] in which she debates the possibility of his authorship of a particular manuscript. She brings out a number of interesting facts about this exegete, in particular shedding light on the question of the form of his own Qur'ān tafsīr. According to Miss Abbott, the twelve works listed by al-Nadīm in his Fihrist[51] all can be considered tafsīr. She says that four of these are possibly extant either as individual works or as extracts in works of other authors.[52] These are Tafsīr khams mi'ah āyah min al-Qur'ān, al-Wujūh wa'l-naẓā'ir, al-Tafsīr fī mutashābih al-Qur'ān and al-Tafsīr al-kabīr. Two of these are available for our study.

The work with which we shall be dealing is the Tafsīr khams mi'ah āyah which was obtained on microfilm from the British Museum.[53] As Miss Abbott indicates, an extract of the third work, al-Tafsīr fī mutashābih, is contained in a work of Malaṭī (d. 377/987).[54] Unfortunately this section does not contain more than two or three brief references to islām; in no case are they sufficient to aid in our investigation. The biographers and chroniclers do not make clear which of Muqātil's works of tafsīr is being discussed; in some cases the references could as easily be to spoken comments quoted from one person to another.

---

[47] One instance in which his reply was not dull-witted is related by several chroniclers, including al-Khaṭīb al-Baghdādī (Ta'rīkh, XIII, 160). Abū Jaᶜfar al-Manṣūr was sitting in a yard, exceedingly annoyed by flies lighting on him. Seeing Muqātil he attempted to have some fun by asking him to explain why God created flies. It was, replied Muqātil, so that He might bring the great ones to humility!

[48] Ibid., p. 162.

[49] GAL, S I, 332.

[50] Studies, II, 92-113.

[51] Fihrist, pp. 253-54.

[52] Studies, II, 96.

[53] OR. 6333, British Museum Photographic Service, London.

[54] Kitāb al-tanbīh wa'l-radd.

We do know, however, that there were copies of his tafsīr works circulating and that through them, to a great extent, he earned the reputation discussed above.

It is unfortunate that so little of Muqātil's work is actually available, as he was unquestionably a most interesting, if controversial figure in early Muslim literature. Miss Abbott concludes her introduction of his works with this appraisal:

> Kalbī and his extensive Tafsīr notwithstanding, Muqātil with his several and varied tafsīr works emerges as not only the most prolific but also the leading Qur'ānic commentator of his day. His knowledge and initiative were put to use in the development of the various specialized branches in that field, and his works came to be widely used but for the most part without formal or public acknowledgment, largely out of deference to the sentiments of powerful orthodox circles.[55]

* * *

In the case of Muqātil's tafsīr, because so little of his original commentary is available to us, we shall make an exception to the general practice of viewing the interpretation of the eight verses of the Qur'ān in which the maṣdar islām is mentioned. The tafsīr of five hundred verses actually contains specific reference to only one of these eight, Qur'ān 5:3. Therefore to attempt to get a fuller picture of Muqātil's understanding of islām, all of the places in the tafsīr where he uses the word have been examined. The following is a summary of the ways in which it has been presented. The manuscript itself consists of 104 double pages and one single page: on only sixteen of these double pages is the word islām used.

Since we are not dealing with given verses, it seems easiest to attempt to present a picture of Muqātil's conception of islām by categorizing the general ways in which he uses the term. Without doubt in some cases he is using it to refer to that which is the opposite of kufr, i.e. that which involves an internal acceptance and affirmation. At other times the reference is apparently only to the external prescriptions and commandments incumbent upon the muslim. In several cases it is not totally clear whether he is referring to an individual personal act or to the group phenomenon. Finally, in a few instances Muqātil clearly is referring to the group of people themselves who have become muslims, and in some of these instances it seems obvious that he intends the specific group constituted by the

---

[55] Abbott, Studies, II, 106.

Prophet and having its concrete and recognizable beginning with him.

The first instance of *islām* as an individual internal act comes when Muqātil is discussing the meaning of ❛and whoever repents❜ (Q 25:70):

> A revelation occurred about this [the matter previously under discussion], such that He indicated an exception: ❛and whoever repents❜ meaning from idolatry [*al-shirk*] ❛and has faith❜ meaning he confirms [*ṣaddaqa*] the *tawḥīd* of God ❛and does a good deed [*ʿamila ʿamalan ṣāliḥan*], those God will change❜ meaning God will turn ❛their evil deeds into good❜ meaning He will put for them *al-islām* in place of *al-shirk* and the cessation [of killing] in place of killing and sexual purity in place of adultery. (35^{r})

It is apparent here that repentance means the confirmation of *tawḥīd*, which means that *islām* has now replaced *shirk* in man's heart affecting his conduct. The relationship between the outward act and the inward affirmation is given again by Muqātil on 94^{r} in a very interesting parallel: "The pilgrimage [*ḥijjah*] of *al-islām* is more virtuous than ten raids", but "the proof [*ḥujjah*] of *al-islām* is more virtuous than ten pilgrimages [*ḥijjāt*]." One would assume from this that he feels the evidence that one's *islām* is sincere is worth more than any external indications he might give. (Unfortunately Muqātil does not elaborate on what is meant by 'proof'.)

In Q 9:29 God has enjoined the faithful with regard to the *ahl al-kitāb* to ❛fight those who do not put their faith in God . . . ❜. Muqātil, in what seems to be the last clear example of an understanding of *islām* as internal, says that this means:

> . . . those who do not have faith in the unicity of God [*lā yuṣaddiqūna bi-tawḥīdi'llāhi*] ❛and in the last day [*yawm al-ākhir*] and do not forbid that which God and His Prophet have forbidden❜ i.e. of wine and pigs. ❛And they do not take as *dīn* the *dīn* of truth [*lā yadīnūna dīn al-ḥaqq*]❜ meaning *dīn al-islām*. For any *dīn* other than *dīn al-islām* is false [*bāṭil*]. (97^{v})

Here again the recognition of God's oneness and affirmation of it are said to constitute *islām*. Unfortunately the *tafsīr* of 3:19 ❛Truly *al-dīn* with God is *al-islām*❜ is not included in this manuscript, but one can easily imagine that the above would constitute his understanding of that verse. There is no other way in which man can respond, both to God and to his fellow man (as implied in following the commandments of God and the Prophet) that can be considered valid or true *dīn*. In a less direct but still obvious understanding of *islām* as personal submission, giving oneself exclusively, on 85^{r} Muqātil says, "The *muslim* man does not call his brother *muslim* with the name he had before *al-islām*." This is apparently a reference to the practice still observed throughout the Islamic world whereby one changes one's name on conversion. *Islām* here thus means the act of submission by which this individual earned the name of *muslim*.

Of the eight Qur'ān verses dealing with *al-islām*, the one most consistently interpreted by the exegetes over the subsequent centuries to be a reference to the duties prescribed by God is 5:3 ﴾Today I have completed for you your *dīn* and fulfilled for you My blessing, and have chosen for you *al-islām* as [a] *dīn*﴿. We are fortunate to have Muqātil's comments on this verse, and he proves to be no exception to the general pattern. Concerning the first clause he says that God made incumbent upon [*faraḍa*] the *muslimūn* at Mecca the following duties: the two parts of the *shahādah*, faith [*īmān*] in the resurrection and the garden and the fire, prayer with two kneelings, etc., as well as many others later in Madīnah. These duties were finalized on Friday of the Yawm al-^{c}Arafah -- after this there would come no further commandments or prohibitions. (98^{v}-99^{r})

> And He said to them, ﴾I have completed to you My blessing﴿, which means *al-islām*, when you performed the pilgrimage with no *mushrik* with you. ﴾And I have chosen﴿ meaning I have *selected* ﴾for you *al-islām* as [a] *dīn*﴿ and there is no *dīn* more acceptable with God than *al-islām*. (99^{r})

Again we see that the blessing of God, which is *al-islām*, is cited in the context of duties and commandments. It is interesting to note that Muqātil does not say, as he indicated above, that a *dīn* other than *islām* is unacceptable; rather he says that no *dīn* is more acceptable [*arḍá*] than *al-islām*. The emphasis on *islām* as God's blessing comes also in the context of a discussion on divorce in which he quotes Q 2:231: "﴾Recall﴿ meaning remember ﴾the grace of God to you﴿ meaning *al-islām* and remember ﴾what was revealed to you of the Book﴿."(61^{r}) The implication seems to be that men should be gracious and considerate to their wives as God has extended His grace to them, that they should communicate *al-islām* to their wives by the remembrance and practice of it.

On 37^{v} Muqātil mentions those who were killed in the period of ignorance [*al-jāhilīyah*] before *al-islām*. To the modern reader this would seem to be a clear reference to the historic age preceding the establishing of Muḥammad's *dīn*, thus implying a reified concept of *islām*. We must remember, however, as Izutsu points out in *God and Man*,[56] that in the early period *jāhilī*

---

[56] p. 201.

generally referred not to an historical period but to the personal state of an individual before his own *islām*. Here again, then, is an apparent reference to individual submission.

In several cases Muqātil has used *islām* in a context difficult to categorize, that involving apostasy from *islām*. On 35^{v} he mentions those who after becoming *muslims* apostasized [*irtaddū*] from *al-islām*. Then he mentions another who, after he became *muslim* [*aslama*] and killed in *al-islām*, then became *mushrik* [*ashraka*] and joined the rejectors [*kuffār*]. Muqātil could mean either that these departed from their personal acceptance of God's *tawḥīd* or that they left the community of *islām*. The point really seems to be, however, that there is no distinction in his mind between these two possibilities -- each necessarily involves the other.

There remain six instances of Muqātil's having used *islām* in his *tafsīr*, and these six can be said to refer in a general sense to group *islām*. One is particularly interesting in that it speaks of the "*ḥaqq al-islām*" in a way we have not seen before. There are three *ḥuqūq* (which in this case seem to mean rights in the sense of prerogatives) between one and his fellow: (1) that of relationship [*ḥaqq al-qarābah*], (2) that of neighborliness [*ḥaqq al-jiwār*], and (3) that of *islām* [*ḥaqq al-islām*].[57] (20^{r}) The *muslim* neighbor has two *ḥaqq*s upon you -- that of neighborliness and that of *islām*, while he who is not of your religion [*min ghayr ahli dīnika*] has only the *ḥaqq* of neighborliness. In this case rather than actually meaning group in the sense of a community, the reference to *islām* is as the plural of *muslim* and thus does not carry the suggestion of reification.

In another place (85^{v}) Muqātil quotes Q 16:93 ❨If God wished, He would have made you one community [*ummah wāḥidah*]❩, saying that the "you" refers to the *mushrikūn* and the *muslimūn*, and the one community means the *millah* of *islām*. "But He leads astray whomever He wills from His *dīn* and they are the *mushrikūn* and He guides whomever He wills and they are the *muslimūn*." It might be argued that this usage has certain overtones of reification, but they do not seem as strong as those found in the remaining four passages to be discussed.

These four deal with *islām* as a group phenomenon with specific regulations and characteristics and with a specific beginning. That is, the *islām* referred to here could not possibly be

---

[57] Cf. A.b.H. IV, 34, who cites a tradition describing *thalath ḥaqq ʿalá kulli muslim*, all of which deal with forms of ablution.

the kind of islām referred to by Ibn ᶜAbbās as the dīn of the Christians and the Jews before the coming of Muḥammad. In three instances (or four, as he mentions islām twice on one page) he specifically uses the phrase "at [or in] the beginning of islām". In one case the context is a discussion of temporary [mutᶜah] marriage (51^v-52^r), another it concerns the regulations of divorce (63^r), and in the third he is dealing with adultery (73^r). And on 14^r he talks about entering islām as involving the paying of alms. He specifically speaks of some as doing this unwillingly [dakhalū fī al-islām karhan]. Islām is used twice, then given in its verbal form so that "dakhala fī al-islām" and "aslama" are made equivalent.

It is possible, then, to "fit" Muqātil b. Sulaymān's treatment of islām into all of the categories we have set up. He sees it as external and internal, as individual and as a group phenomenon, and in several places certainly means the historical religious community established by Muḥammad. Yet one cannot help but be struck by the apparent artificiality of such divisions as we have made above. As has been observed before and will be again, the classifications of twentieth-century thinking do not lend themselves easily to the writings of earlier times. In discussing the question of whether or not the pre-Islamic Arabs were conscious of the distinction between religion as a personal act and as a set of ritual practices, Izutsu concludes that perhaps "such a distinction itself was something quite alien to [their] religious consciousness."[58] It seems clear that this is also true of the attempt to say that in one place islām to an early writer meant this, in another place that.

Here, then, is the most important conclusion to be reached in this short survey: Muqātil b. Sulaymān, and presumably such is the case with others of the early Muslim writers, seems to have made little conscious distinction between what we see as "types" of islām, between the sense of self-submission and the sense of a reified group islām. In fact he was much less concerned with a definition of islām as such than he was in making the points he had in mind and using the term islām freely and unselfconsciously, knowing that it would be understood by his readers. We will find in the tafsīr of succeeding centuries a much greater concern with interpreting and defining islām specifically and consciously, and correspondingly less of the usage of islām to mean at once the act of submission and the community of which, by this act, one becomes a member.

---

[58] God and Man, p. 227.

III

We come now to the third century hijrī, the era of the great historian and commentator Abū Ja^c^far Muḥammad b. Jarīr al-Ṭabarī. In this modern age when men often seem to react to the overwhelming accumulation of knowledge by specializing to the point of paralysis, it is almost beyond comprehension that one man could have extended his scientific and literary scope as far as did al-Ṭabarī. After spending only a brief time in the company of his writings one feels that the commendations sometimes heaped rather indiscriminately by Arab biographers on their subjects are in the case of this man, for the most part, genuinely merited.[59] This is not to say that al-Ṭabarī is without his critics, particularly among Western writers.[60] What must be respected, whatever criticisms one might make of his pure scholarship, is the breadth of his knowledge and the sheer magnitude of his labor and output.

Born in 224 or 225/839 at Āmul in Ṭabaristān, al-Ṭabarī is credited with an early interest in learning and is said to have committed the entire Qur'ān to memory at the age of seven.[61] Having begun his studies at Āmul,he left to work under Aḥmad b. Ḥanbal in Rayy, but arrived just after the death of the famous jurist and thinker. He then travelled through Egypt,[62] Syria

---

[59]". . . al-ḥibr al-baḥr al-imām Abū Ja^c^far M. b. Jarīr al-Ṭabarī, master of tafsīr and history and many literary works. One of the imāms Ibn Khazīmah said: 'There is no one on earth more knowledgeable than M. b. Jarīr'." (Ibn al-^c^Imād, Shadharāt, II, 260) "Abū Ja^c^far al-Ṭabarī the student of ḥadīth [al-muḥaddith], the jurisprudent [al-faqīh], reciter of the Qur'an [al-muqri'], the known [al-ma^c^rūf], the celebrated [al-mashshūr]." (Yāqūt, Irshād, IV, pt. 6, 423) Ibn al-Nadīm (Fihrist, pp. 326-7) called him sign of his time [^c^alāmat waqtihi], imām of his age and faqīh of his period, citing him as versatile in all the sciences: ^c^ilm al-Qur'ān, grammar, poetry, linguistics, and many varieties of fiqh.

[60]E.g. Carra de Vaux, Les Penseurs, III, 381: ". . . non pas qu'il soit ce que nous appelons aujourd'hui un très grand penseur; il n'a pas l'animation intellectuelle ni la curiosité ardente que nous avons recontrées chez d'autres historiens ou savants; et l'originalité assez limitée qu'on lui reconnaît porte surtout sur des détails techniques de la science du Coran et du droit, ou sur des questions théologiques dout l'intérêt n'est pas de premier ordre."

[61]Yāqūt (Irshād, VI [pt. 6], 423-4) describes the precociousness of the young Ṭabarī, quoting him as saying that at age seven he knew the Qur'ān by heart, at eight he prayed with the men in public and at nine began to write ḥadīth.

[62]In Cairo the dominant legal doctrines, to all of which al-Ṭabarī probably was exposed, were those of al-Shāfi^c^ī, Mālik,

and ᶜIrāq, settling in Baghdād as a teacher of *ḥadīth* and *fiqh*. Here he remained, with the exception of several brief trips, until he died in 310/923. He had been offered the position of *qāḍī*, but declined it in favor of research and composition.[63] He is reputed to have written forty pages a day, a figure which may not be too exaggerated in consideration of the prodigious amount of his output.

Having become acquainted in Egypt with the teachings of the legist al-Shāfiᶜī through one of the latter's students, al-Ṭabarī for some ten years adhered closely to these teachings. Unwilling, however, to accept without his own critical analysis the legal dogma prescribed by others, he determined personally to judge the sources of law, for which later historians have credited him with being an independent *mujtahid*. He later chose to begin his own legal school, the Jarīrīyah, a move that earned him the severe criticism of the Ḥanbalī partisans in Baghdād. They were particularly angry because in writing about the various extant legal views he failed to include Aḥmad ibn Ḥanbal, maintaining that he was not a teacher of law but a traditionist.[64] (Apparently the followers of Ibn Ḥanbal were not the only ones with whom al-Ṭabarī had difficulties. The Rāfidīyah, a group of more extreme Shīᶜah, had been prominent in Ṭabaristān and were attracted by al-Ṭabarī's early appreciation of ᶜAlī. When he also praised Abū Bakr they became antagonized and al-Ṭabarī had to flee. It is actually reported, however, that al-Ṭabarī's funeral had to be held at night for fear of the anger of the crowd at his suspected Shīᶜī leanings.[65]) Al-Ṭabarī's own school of law, which apparently differed only slightly from that of al-Shāfiᶜī, while frequently referred to and recognized by contemporaries, faded away quite soon after his death. Most of his early works on *fiqh* have disappeared.

It was not law and the direct application of law, however, that were the most immediate concerns of al-Ṭabarī. For him, it appears, the revelation of God was primary and it is this with which he deals in a kind of two-pronged approach in his two major life works. The Qur'ān *tafsīr* is concerned with the written (spoken) word of God and his great world history is concerned

---

and Ibn Wahb. (Carra de Vaux, *Les Penseurs*, III, 383).

[63]Wüstenfeld, *Geschichtschreiber*, p. 32.

[64]*Ibid.*, pp. 31-2.

[65]Yāqūt, *Irshād*, VI, pt. 6, 425.

with the manifestation of God's will in time.[66] The latter chronicle, Ta'rīkh al-rusūl wa'l-mulūk, is considered by many to be his outstanding achievement.[67] The work is reputed to have been ten times the length (in original form) of the text we now have. His main source for this world history, oral tradition, also forms the basis of his great Qur'ān commentary Jāmiᶜ al-bayān ᶜan ta'wīl āyāt al-Qur'ān,[68] which until recently was considered lost. In this work al-Ṭabarī, like Ibn ᶜAbbās, utilized ḥadith as the basis of commentary. He far exceeded his predecessor, however, both in the scope of his collection and in the degree of his critical analysis of these traditions. Heribert Horst[69] has computed that al-Ṭabarī's commentary contains some 13,026 different isnāds occurring in more than 35,400 places. The oldest traditionists to which the isnāds lead are Ibn ᶜAbbās and his students Mujāhid and al-Daḥḥāk. Horst concludes that al-Ṭabarī probably used only a few complete books of older authors,[70] others coming to him in abstracted or abbreviated form. Observing that tafsīr never really was subject to the same exacting rules of isnād classification as was legal ḥadīth, Harris Birkeland[71] comments on the fact that most of the isnāds in al-Ṭabarī's tafsīr do not go back to the Companions or the Prophet but stop about 100 hijrī.[72]

---

[66]See O. Loth ("Ṭabarī's Korankommentar" in ZDMG, XXXV [1881], 589) for a general comparison of these works.

[67]Loth (Ibid., 590), however, considers it weaker and faultier than the commentary, becoming influential more quickly because it had no competition as the Shīᶜah were practically the only ones who concerned themselves with history.

[68]Maḥmūd Muḥammad Shākir and Aḥmad Muḥammad Shākir, edd. (Cairo: Dār al-Maᶜārif, 1374- [1954-], several voll.) As what is currently available of this edition goes only through Q 12:18, for verses 39:22, 49:17 and 61:7 we shall use the following earlier edition: Jamiᶜ al-bayan fī tafsīr al-Qur'an (Cairo: al-Maṭbaᶜah al-Kubrá al-Amīrīyah, 1323-1329 [1900-1911]).

[69]"Zur Überlieferung" in ZDMG, CII (1953), 290-307.

[70]He hypothesizes that the following complete works may well have been available to al-Ṭabarī: the tafsīr of ᶜAlī b. a. Talḥa, the commentary of Mujāhid, the tafsīr of ᶜAbd al-Raḥmān b. Zayd b. Aslam, the Kitāb al-maghāzī of Ibn Isḥāq and perhaps a work from Ibn Saᶜd.

[71]"The Lord Guideth" in Skrifter, (1956), pt. 2, p. 9.

[72]He explains this in "Old Muslim Opposition" (in Avhandlinger, [1955], p. 2, p. 11) as another manifestation of the objection to tafsīr which existed even in al-Ṭabarī's time. He says that exegetes "were not generally believed by circles rejecting tafsīr when they tried to trace a tradition of exegetical

Although Jāmi^c al-bayān has been called tafsīr bi'l-ma'thūr, the very fact of his having made his own judgments on the material passed down somewhat invalidates this categorization.[73] Nonetheless it is certainly recognized that al-Ṭabarī's tafsīr marks the high point of traditional exegesis as well as constituting the basic work on which the majority of the exegesis of the succeeding centuries most obviously is based.[74] Presenting on the one hand the sum and substance of earlier tafsīr material, he expands this by use of lexical explanation, additional legends, grammatical and philological opinion, explanation of variant readings, poetic allusions, commentary on abrogation, and reference to points of law and dogma.

Best known as a traditionist, al-Ṭabarī has also been recognized as an outstanding philologist. Philological analysis occupies a large part of his tafsīr, as well as grammatical discussion based on the linguistic schools of Baṣrá and Kūfah.[75] While such analysis at times can become somewhat tedious for the reader, it is another instance of the persevering thoroughness of this diligent exegete. Always in these excursuses he adheres closely to the traditionalist viewpoints.

It is interesting to note that while al-Ṭabarī includes in his commentary much contradictory material, attempting by various means to determine the most accurate, he does not include the interpretations of such exegetes as are considered unreliable, such as the second century Muqātil b. Sulaymān. The primary criterion for exegetical authority for him is, not surprisingly, the ḥadīths transmitted by an uninterrupted chain of

---

contents back to the Prophet or a Companion. So they had to function as their own authorities, when they were not able to demonstrate their direct transmission from Ibn ^cAbbās."

[73]Yāqūt (Irshād, IV, pt. 6, 453-4) even alludes to his having been called a Mu^ctazilī because of certain elements in his tafsīr. It is reported, however, that at al-Ṭabarī's death his son affirmed his orthodoxy, indicating that he disagreed with the Mu^ctazilah in all areas in which they were in contradiction with the ijmā^c of the community.

[74]Ḥājjī Khalīfah (Kashf, II, 346) quotes al-Suyūṭī as saying that al-Ṭabarī's book is the most splendid [ajall] of the tafsīr works and the greatest [a^cẓam] of them because he looks critically at the orientation [tawjīh] of the sayings, giving predominance to some of them over others. One of the most often quoted sayings concerning al-Ṭabarī is that of Abū Ḥāmid al-Isfarā'īnī: If a man were to travel to China in order to obtain the tafsīr of M. b. Jarīr that would not be too great an effort. (Yāqūt, Irshād, VI, pt. 6, 424; Ibn al-^cImād, Shadharāt, II, 260; Ḥājjī Khalīfah, Kashf, II, 346.

[75]Goldziher, Richtungen, pp. 92-3.

authority. When, however, such witnessing does not seem reliable, he is free to claim the authority of the consensus of the community and ultimately, as we have noted, intervenes with some degree of personal judgment.[76]

Al-Ṭabarī classifies his principles in the tafsīr itself. Beginning, after a khutbah, with a chapter on the science of tafsīr, he discusses the various ways in which the Qur'ān can be interpreted, the lawful and the unlawful. He is open to a variety of ways of reading, excepting only those that he feels substantially alter the apparent meaning of the text or that are not supported by imāms whom he considers reliable. All of the various "methods" of exegesis employed by al-Ṭabarī are, however, secondary to what he feels to be the clear and obvious external [ẓāhir] meaning of the word or words under consideration based on their common usage in Arabic. Like Ibn ᶜAbbās he also uses legends from Jewish sources, a practice which, as we have seen, was not always sanctioned.

Where, then, can we place Muḥammad b. Jarīr in relation to the atmosphere of emerging dogmatic tendencies? Traditionalist though he seems to have been in intent, and for the most part in deed, he nevertheless occasionally seems to have departed somewhat from this approach. We have noted that he was harshly censured by the followers of Ibn Ḥanbal, not only for his slight of their imām but because he seemed to be moving toward the kind of speculative dogmatics which was so objectionable to the traditionalists, although he himself claimed to be the opponent of such tendencies. Especially in questions of man's will and choice he sometimes implied solutions that had much in common with the bilā kayf of al-Ashᶜarī. Al-Ṭabarī's work is of immeasurable value to us not only because he gathered together and preserved a tremendous amount of material from the past at a time when things were very much in flux, but because he was the first to organize and formulate this material, classifying it in terms of its subject matter and relationship to the structure of the Qur'ān verses. While his tafsīr is seen as the prototype of later traditional commentaries, he did allow either implicitly or explicitly for a certain breadth of interpretation. Yet despite the fact that al-Ṭabarī was associated on occasion with the Shīᶜah, with the Muᶜtazilah and with the new schools of mutakallimūn, one must not be tempted to forget that the basic

---

[76]Al-Ṭabarī's own understanding of the passages of the Qur'ān is usually prefaced with: "qāla Abū Jaᶜfar . . ."

orientation of his interpretation was a traditionist one. He was at all times arguing against any metaphorical or figurative interpretation. If he sometimes evidenced a certain flexibility, he was still in direct line with those who practiced tafsīr bi'l-ma'thūr, and it is in this capacity that he has been cherished by centuries of Muslims and serves as such an incomparable source of information for scholars of Islam.

* * *

Al-Ṭabarī follows a general pattern of giving a fairly brief and clear explanation of a section of verse based on general Arabic usage of words, occasional reference to poetry, and what he considers to be the obvious meaning of a phrase or sentence. He follows this with any number of clearly cited ḥadīths and often concludes these with his own opinion of their relative merit. In the discussion of his understanding of islām we will consider those sections that seem most relevant; the reader is asked to understand that the large amount of material offered by al-Ṭabarī precludes consideration of all of what he has to say. Whenever possible this material will be summarized rather than given in direct translation.

In his treatment of 3:19 ❴Truly al-dīn with God is al-islām❵, Abu Ja^cfar devotes himself to an understanding of al-dīn. In this case, he says, it means obedience [al-ṭā^cah] and submissiveness [al-dhillah]. (VI, 273) Citing a line from the poet al-A^cshá Maymūn b. Qays he interprets the usage of dāna specifically to mean to subject [dhallala] and al-dīn in the phrase "they despise al-dīn" to be al-ṭā^cah. (VI, 274)

> And similarly "al-islām"; it is being led [al-inqiyād] by humbling oneself [tadhallul] and surrender [al-khuḍū^c], and the verb from it: "aslama" meaning to enter into al-silm, as one says "aqhaṭa al-qawm" when they enter into drought and "arba^cu" when they enter into springtime. Like that "aslamu" when they enter into al-silm, and it is al-inqiyād by al-khuḍū^c and ceasing resistance. (VI, 274-5)

The editors of this edition of the tafsīr invite the reader to consider earlier comments of al-Ṭabarī on the meaning of islām in cases in which the word was not used specifically in the Qur'ān text. Thus in looking at the commentary of 2:111-12 we read:

> As for His saying: "Whoever submits his face to God", He means "islām of the face": submissiveness [al-tadhallul] to obedience of Him, and idh^cān to His command. And the source of "al-islām" is al-istislām, because it is from "istaslamtu li-amrihi", and it is al-khuḍū^c to

> His command. And "al-muslim" is called a muslim by the khuduᶜ of his limbs to obedience of his Lord . . . (II, 510-11)

In attempting to convey in an English translation the richness of meaning expressed by the many Arabic words which we can scarcely render by any term other than "submission", one appreciates again the difficulties of translation. Ṭāᶜah, dhillah, inqiyād, khuḍūᶜ and istislām express to the native speaker of Arabic a variety of subtle distinctions, an understanding of which the Western reader can only hope to approximate. What we can see, however, is that the several ways in which al-Ṭabarī has chosen to express the idea of humble submission illustrate his understanding of the totality of this act.

In the passages above, islām is seen as an action rather than as a condition. The dīn that is al-islām is man's response to God by humbling himself and entering into a state whereby he is in complete readiness to accept and fulfill the commands and desires of his Lord. This is beautifully illustrated by the comparison of the entering into islām being like entering into drought or springtime. The condition is al-silm, the act is al-islām, and when one thus engages himself he is expressing to God that he is in full obedience and complete openness to that will.

We have in this understanding of islām as personal submission the clear implication that it is not merely an outward obedience of the limbs, but is very much a matter of the will and inner acceptance of the individual. Looking again at the references to earlier definitions given by al-Ṭabarī to islām (as indicated in the footnotes to the present edition) we see that this is strongly supported. He concludes a discussion of 2:128 by saying: "We have indicated in what preceded that the meaning of al-islām is al-khuḍūᶜ to God through obedience." (III, 74) Then in explaining in 2:131 ❬When his Lord said to him 'submit', he said, I have submitted to the Lord of the worlds❭, Abū Jaᶜfar says that the words of God mean "devote yourself wholly [akhliṣ] to me, and submit [ikhḍaᶜ] to me in obedience." (III, 92) Here the obedient submission about which al-Ṭabarī has consistently been talking is expressly related to the sincere devotion [ikhlāṣ] of the individual. Akhlaṣa and its derivatives are in themselves a fascinating study; it is interesting to note here that as Helmer Ringgren has illustrated,[77] there are strong indications from early poetical usage that

---

[77] "The pure religion" in Oriens, XV (1962), 93-96.

ikhlāṣ (the Lisān has also defined it in this way) is often understood to be synonymous with tawḥīd. Discussing its occurrence in the Qur'ān, Ringgren concludes: "The purity, or sincerity of religion in most cases seems to imply the exclusive worship of God as the opposite of širk or polytheism."[78] We shall find in several of the later commentators, particularly al-Zamakhsharī, great stress on the fact that the dīn al-islām which al-Ṭabarī is defining as submission and obedience is precisely that recognition of God's unity which recognition is termed tawḥīd, drawing a full circle of relationship around the terms ikhlāṣ-dīn-islām-tawḥīd.

Returning to al-Ṭabarī's tafsīr of 3:19, we find continued and explicit indication that islām is the sincere and heartfelt response to God.

> If this is the case [the foregoing], then the ta'wīl of His saying "Truly al-dīn with God is al-islām" is that the obedience with which He is concerned is obedience to Him, and affirmation [iqrār] of the tongues and the hearts to Him through worship and submissiveness [al-dhillah], and the inqiyād of them [the tongues and the hearts] to Him by obedience in what He commands and forbids, and humble submissiveness [tadhallul] of them to Him in that without feeling arrogance toward Him, and not deviating from Him, and without associating any of His creation with Him in worship and deification. (VI, 274)

While ikhlāṣ is not used specifically in this instance, there is the clear implication that this activity means the recognition of God's oneness, tawḥīd, and supports the relationship outlined above between God's being and man's recognition of and response to that being. We translated ᶜubūdīyah as worship; this word deserves specific attention, however, as it is intimately related to the whole process of submission of which al-Ṭabarī has been speaking. Izutsu[79] has pointed out that because God is the one absolute Lord, man's response must be complete submission, ᶜibādah, serving Him in the only possible way a servant can relate to his master. (This has later, he says, come to mean "worship".) Once again we see the inescapable tie between the oneness of God and man's recognition of it, his tawḥīd, his ᶜibādah or ᶜubūdīyah, his dīn which is al-islām.

There can be no question from these very clear and detailed statements that islām for al-Ṭabarī is an individual act, involving both the tongue and the heart, the primary concern of which is not man but God. Islām and dīn are not defined as

---

[78] Ibid., 96.

[79] Izutsu, God and Man, p. 198.

historical or group phenomena, but as the personal relationship between man and his Lord. Those who would criticize al-Ṭabarī for pedantry or *tafsīr* for sterility must look far before finding a more direct and sensitive description of the way in which man acknowledges his bond to God.

Reading farther into the *tafsīr* of this and the following verses it becomes clear that while he does not mention *al-islām* specifically in connection with the Jews and Christians as does Ibn ʿAbbās, Abū Jaʿfar defines their relationship to God in precisely the same terms as he used in the above definitions of *islām*. Distinguishing the Jews and Christians from the *ummīyūn*, the *mushrik* Arabs who have no book, he says that when the Qur'ān says ❬and if they surrender [*aslamū*]❭ it means "if they have submitted to ascribing oneness to God alone [*li-ifrādi'l-waḥdānīyah li'l'llāh*] and to purifying towards Him servanthood and lordship [*wa-ikhlāṣ al-ʿibādah wa'l-ulūhīyah*]". (VI, 281) Here again, however, he refrains from using *islām* in its group sense, speaking of it only as an individual act. Concluding his comments on 3:19 ❬If they turn away then it is your duty only to convey the message❭ al-Ṭabarī says that God is giving instruction to Muḥammad about those who resist that to which the Prophet has called them in the way of *al-islām* and pure devotion to the unity of God. (VI, 282) (In this phrase "*ikhlāṣ al-tawḥīd lil-'llāh*" we find explicit support for Ringgren's contention cited above.) Even here it is apparent that the Prophet is the transmitter of a message from God concerning how man should relate to Him, rather than the spokesman for a religious system or group phenomenon.

Considering 3:83 ❬Do they seek other than [the] *dīn* of God, when to Him has submitted whosoever is in the heavens and the earth, willingly [*ṭawʿan*] or unwillingly [*karhan*], and to Him they will be made to return?❭, al-Ṭabarī supplies the *maṣdar islām* in his *tafsīr* of what it means to "*aslama*" and offers a brief discussion of the implications of individual submission.

> ❬Seek they other than [the] *dīn* of God❭ that is to say: If they request and seek other than obedience [*al-ṭāʿah*] to God ❬when to Him submits whoever is in the heavens and the earth❭ i.e. toward Him is humble [*khashaʿa*] whoever is in the heavens and the earth, and yields [*khaḍaʿa*] to Him in servitude [*bi'l-ʿubūdah*], and acknowledges lordship to Him uniquely; and submission [*inqād*] to Him is by sincere acknowledgement of [His] oneness and divinity [*bi-ikhlāṣ al-tawḥīd wa'l-ulūhīyah*] -- "willingly or unwillingly", i.e. any one of them whose *islām* to God is voluntary is said to have submitted to God freely, and that is like the angels and the Prophets and Messengers, for they submit to God obediently -- "Or unwillingly", whoever among them is unwilling. (VI, 564-65)

While on this occasion he unfortunately does not offer his own opinion, al-Ṭabarī does provide a variety of interpretations, with supporting ḥadīths, as to the meaning and description of the islām of the one who submits unwillingly. These include the islām of the one who affirms that God is his creator and Lord even though he associates others with Him in his service [fī'l-ᶜibādah], of the one who enters the agreement or covenant [al-mīthāq] and affirms it with his tongue but not by conviction (or the opposite: some feel that this verse includes the one whose islām is of the heart and who follows the command of God even if he denies His Lordship with his tongue), and of those who are seeking protection.

It is clear from these ḥadīths, and this conclusion is anticipated by the Qur'ān verse itself, that submission [islām] can be of an external (not by the heart) nature. It is interesting that al-Ṭabarī has not given any comment of his own here. In most of the tafsīr material under consideration in this study one gets the inescapable impression that while the writers are forced to admit, in the light of such verses as 3:83, 49:14 and others, that the term islām can be applied to an act that is purely external, it is really only when that act is performed with the full inner acceptance and affirmation of the one who submits that it can be considered islām in the full sense of the word.

Ibn ᶜAbbās expressed quite clearly his understanding that islām was the true dīn of the Christians and Jews and had been since the time of Ibrāhīm. We find a somewhat different emphasis in al-Ṭabarī when he says:

> And as for His saying ﴾and to Him you will be returned﴿, He means: "to Him", O assembly of those who seek other than al-islām as dīn from among the Jews and the Christians and the rest of the people -- "you return", i.e. to Him you will proceed after your deaths, and your recompense will be according to your deeds, he who has done good among you for his good deeds and he who has done evil for his evil deeds. And this is a warning from God to His creation that there returns to Him and reaches Him after death one who is from other than the millah of islām. (VI, 568)

While it is certain that al-Ṭabarī is saying that the Jews and Christians and others will receive recompense in terms of whether or not they accept islām as their way of responding to God, it is less clear that he is saying this has always been true (or at least from the time of Ibrāhīm on, as Ibn ᶜAbbās would maintain). One could interpret these words to mean that from among these Jews and Christians are some who seek other than islām as dīn and others who do accept islām. It seems much more likely, however, that he is warning all who are not from the millah of islām in its collective sense, saying that they will receive the judgment of God. Commenting on the last phrase of 3:84 ⸢and we are submitters unto Him⸣ al-Ṭabarī says that this means:

> We submit [nadīnu] to God in al-islām and do not submit to other than Him, but we dissociate ourselves from every dīn except it and from every millah other than it. (VI, 570)

It appears that while for al-Ṭabarī islām generally is seen as dīn as approved by God, the only acceptable way in which man can respond to Him, on occasion there is a certain ambiguity of reference, with the possibility that he may intend by it a millah or group among several such groups. This is implicit rather than explicit, however, and he does not use the plural milal as do some later commentators. We must certainly not lose sight of the fact that in the context of accepting the revelation made to all the Prophets, not distinguishing between any of them, al-Ṭabarī has used islām to refer to the ideal relationship which all the People of the Book have been privileged to share with God.

It is in this context that Abū Jaᶜfar understood the specific usage of islām in the Qur'ān text 3:85 ⸢If anyone seeks other than al-islām as [a] dīn, it will not be accepted from him⸣.

> He means by that, that whoever seeks as a dīn other than dīn al-islam in order to submit [yadīnu] by it, God will not accept it from him. (VI, 570)

We have argued from the above usage of dīn and millah, of which that of islām is apparently one among many, that al-Ṭabarī is bordering on an understanding of islām in the historical group sense. It is also worth considering whether or not this might be the case in his discussion immediately following the above-quoted tafsīr of 3:85:

> It is mentioned that the people of every millah claimed that it was they that were the muslimūn when this āyah descended, so God commanded them to the ḥajj if they were sincere, because one of the practices of al-islām is the ḥajj, and they refrained. So God at that refuted their argument. (VI, 570)

Al-Ṭabarī gives three traditions to support this, all of which quote sūrah 3:97 which cites the ḥajj al-bayt as one of the duties incumbant upon man. (VI, 571) In two of these it is specifically the Jews who say "We are the muslimūn", and in one it is simply the milal who make that claim. There is a sense, of course, in which specific religious groups are intended because of the use of milal (although it is interesting that the ḥadith says "fa-qālat al-milal" and not "so the other milal said"). Too, the ḥajj, unlike the rest of the arkān was really the only duty enjoined by God which the other Peoples of the Book would not accept.[80] In this sense when one speaks of one of the "practices of islām", in actuality islām can refer only to the specific group of the followers of the Prophet. It is nonetheless true, however, that God did prescribe the duty for man as such [li'llāh ᶜalá al-nās ḥajj al-bayt] and in this sense it is a requirement for islām in its most individual and personal meaning. It is precisely this point which the Jews seem to be arguing when they say that they are muslimūn -- there is no question that what they claim is not membership in the sect of islām but that they have personally submitted to God. This question can be and has been discussed from many sides, and we shall leave it with the observation that the point at which a Jew, or even a Christian, can be considered to be muslim is one which has engaged Muslim scholars for many centuries.

We observed earlier that verse 5:3 of the Qur'ān is generally seen in terms of the requirements and duties incumbent on the one who accepts islām as dīn. Al-Ṭabarī presents a lengthy and detailed exposition on this theme, and his tafsīr has obviously served as the basis of much of the commentary of the succeeding centuries. Beginning with the first section concerning the completion of dīn, al-Ṭabarī follows his usual pattern of suggesting that the people of ta'wīl have offered different interpretations.

> Some of them say: "Today I have completed for you your dīn" means today I have fulfilled for you, O mu'minun, the duties [farā'id] and limits [ḥudūd] I have set for you, and My command [amrī] and prohibition [nahī] for you, and those things permitted and forbidden by Me, and My revealing [tanzīlī] of those [moral injunctions] that I have revealed in My Book, and My explanation of what I explained to you of it through My revelation by the tongue of My Prophet, and the proofs that I set up for you concerning all that is necessary for you in the way of the command of your dīn; I have completed for you all of that, and there will be no increase in it after this day. (IX, 517-18)

As we saw before in the section on ḥadīth,[81] the early traditions were very much concerned with detail. Here, too, the ḥadīths supplied by al-Ṭabarī and his own comments on the verse center on the particularizing of specific information. The

---

[80]Discounting the second element of the shahādah, the Jews and even the Christians could and did affirm the oneness of God, did pray, did give alms and did fast.

[81]See above, pp. 13-27.

general consensus was that the "yawm" about which the verse speaks was "Yawm ᶜArafāt", the year of the Prophet's ḥajj al-wadāᶜ. It is also believed that the Prophet did not live after the revelation of that āyah more than eighty-one days.[82]

Other people of ta'wīl, says al-Ṭabarī, feel that this verse refers specifically to the perfecting by God of the place of pilgrimage for the muslims, so that no mu'min has to associate in his ḥajj with a mushrik. This, he feels, is a correct interpretation, saying that this perfection was the setting aside for them of "al-balad al-ḥarām" and keeping away the mushrikūn. In all of this discussion the emphasis has been on the appointed duties of islām, the external rather than -- although certainly not necessarily exclusive of -- the internal aspects of man's response, and to the extent to which the completion of duties implies a new set of prescriptions one might even say it borders on a somewhat reified islām. It is interesting to note, however, that the implicit understanding of everything presented here is that there is a continuity in what God prescribed earlier and is now prescribing. We will see that this is made more explicit by some of the commentators of the succeeding centuries.

Another point seems worthy of mention here. In one ḥadīth cited by al-Ṭabarī the narrator says: "'Today I have completed for you your dīn', and it is al-islām. He said, God announced to His Prophet and to the mu'minūn that He had completed for them al-īmān . . ." (IX, 518) Here we have the only instance in al-Ṭabarī's whole discussion of this verse of the equation of islām with īmān. The interesting thing is that Abū Jaᶜfar includes this in a group of ḥadīths that interpret islām in terms of external prescriptions without making any particular note of it. Here is another instance in which it appears that al-Ṭabarī, like other early commentators, was not particularly concerned with a distinction between islām and īmān. More important, it would seem to indicate that he also was not making a conscious distinction between islām in the reified group sense, toward which some of the exegesis of this verse seems to point, and

---

[82]One of the traditions cited by al-Ṭabarī and appearing in several other commentaries is that of ᶜUmar weeping. While some indicate that the tears were for the impending death of the Prophet, that cited by al-Ṭabarī says that when the Prophet asked ᶜUmar why he was weeping, he replied: I am weeping because we are at a peak of our piety. For if it has been completed, nothing is completed except it decrease." And the Prophet said: "You are correct." (IX, 519)

islām as the personal relationship between man and God.

The second clause of 5:3 ‹and I have fulfilled for you my blessing› is dealt with briefly by al-Ṭabarī who, with the support of several traditions, continues to interpret it as the purification of the ḥajj and the destruction of the manār[83] and places of sacrifice of the mushrikūn. It is in the interpretation of the third clause ‹and I have chosen for you al-islām as [a] dīn› that he makes his most clear statement of islām as the individual act of submission:

> By this He means: I have chosen for you surrender [al-istislām] to My command, and submission [al-inqiyād] to obedience of Me, according to what I have made incumbent upon you in the way of limits [ḥudūd] and duties [farā'iḍ] and formalities [maᶜālim] of it [the command] -- "as dīn", meaning by that: obedience from you to Me. (IX, 522)

Then al-Ṭabarī gives a most lucid explanation of the development of islām as the acceptance of a specific set of revelations from God when he says:

> And if someone says: Was God only accepting [rāḍiyan][84] al-islām from His servant on the day He revealed this āyah? the answer would be: God did not cease accepting for His creation al-islām as dīn, but He -- praise and exaltation to Him -- continued to entrust to His Prophet Muḥammad -- blessings and peace be upon him -- and his Companions the various successive levels [darajāt] and degrees [marātib] of islām level by level and degree by degree and condition by condition, until He perfected for them its ways [sharā'iᶜ] and its formalities [maᶜālim], leading them to the highest of its stages and degrees, then He said when this verse was revealed to them: "And I have chosen for you al-islām" in the shape that it has today and the condition of it that you have today -- "as dīn", so persevere in it and do not diverge from it. (IX, 523)

One can scarcely imagine a clearer statement of the fact that the requirements of submission have been progressively revealed by God, culminating in the final completion of all of its regulations and formalities. At no time did God not make acceptance of His will the proper behavior for man, but the levels and forms and conditions of that will changed as the Prophets made accumulative man's knowledge of the specifics that he must accept. The islām acceptable to God at any time is coordinate with His revelation made known at that time, and "today" the approved dīn is that which includes those specific duties

---

[83] The modern editors of this edition say that "manār", signpost, here means the customs of the people of the Jāhilīyah. (IX, 522)

[84] This difficult-to-translate verb implies that God fully accepts, approves and chooses, and anything other than the object of His choice is unquestionably unacceptable.

revealed through the Prophet Muḥammad, at which point the dīn for mankind -- the acceptance of and response to God's commandments -- is completed.

We cannot leave al-Ṭabarī's discussion of 5:3 without noting a ḥadīth that he gives from Qatādah in which both islām and īmān are discussed:

> It has been told to us that on the day of resurrection the people of every dīn will be represented by their dīn. And as for al-īmān, it will give good tidings to its companions and its people and will promise them well, until al-islām comes and says, "Lord, you are the salām and I the islām." Then He will say, "Today I accept you and by you this day I will give recompense." (IX, 523)

In the earlier consideration of ḥadīths on islām,[85] we noted several instances of the phrase "anta al-salām wa-anā al-islām". The possibilities of interpretation of this tradition are less important here than Abū Jaᶜfar's own comments on it, in which he gives probably the clearest statement thus far in the tafsīr we have considered of his understanding of īmān and islām:

> I think that Qatādah intended the meaning of "al-īmān" in this khabar to be the meaning of al-taṣdīq as well as al-iqrār by the tongue, because that is the meaning of īmān among the Arabs -- and he intended the meaning of "al-islām" to be istislām of the heart and khuḍūᶜ of it to God in tawḥīd, and inqiyād of the body to Him in obedience to what He commands and forbids, and for that reason it is said of al-islām: "Today I accept you and by you this day I will give recompense." (IX, 523-4)

While īmān is comprised of taṣdīq and the verbal acknowledgement of taṣdīq, islām includes both the internal submission of the heart and the expression of that submission by carrying out God's commandments. Thus īmān is acceptance and confirmation of that to which the total response is submission of the inner and the outer man. This leads us directly to his discussion of those verses in which he deals specifically with the relationship between islām and īmān.

For the most part the Qur'ān verses with which we have thus far been concerned in the tafsīr of al-Ṭabarī have been dealing with an understanding of islām in relation to dīn and, as al-Ṭabarī has interpreted them, with a definition of islām in terms of specific individual duties and prescriptions (although as we have seen, he has clearly implied that man's dīn is based on an inner as well as an outer or external response). The next several verses to be considered, on the other hand, do not lend themselves to this kind of definition of islām and as we might

---

[85] See above, p. 16.

therefore expect, al-Ṭabarī interprets islām as a condition of the heart, an internal response in direct relation to īmān. Thus in 6:125 ❬and whomever God wills to guide, He lays open his breast to al-islām❭ we read:

> God -- may the mention of Whom be exalted -- says: And whomever God wills to guide to īmān in Him and His Prophet and what he brought from his Lord, He adapts him to it -- "He expands his breast to al-islām", i.e. he widens his breast to that and facilitates it [submission] for him and makes it easy for him through His benevolence and assistance so that al-islām is illuminated in his heart . . . (XII, 98)

Here we have not the exact equation of islām and īmān (and from al-Ṭabarī's comments on the tradition from Qatādah above we know that he probably does not understand them as identical), but the idea that he whose breast is made wide for islām is prepared for īmān. Correspondingly, of course, as the Qur'ān implies, al-Ṭabarī tells us that when God wishes to lead someone astray He fills him with kufr of Him and turning away from His path [yashghuluhu bi-kufrihi wa-ṣaddihi ᶜan sabīlihi]. (XII, 103) It is noteworthy that while Abū Jaᶜfar says that the one whose breast is expanded is filled with the illumination of al-islām, he describes the breast of the one led astray as that "into which the light of al-īmān does not enter, because shirk has overcome him". (XII, 103) It seems that he intends islām and īmān here to express the same general concept, but he does not make this any more explicit.

We find in al-Ṭabarī no explanation of islām in 9:74 ❬. . . they said the word of kufr and rejected [Him] after their islām❭. Apparently he, like the other commentators, felt that the meaning here is obvious. Having submitted to God, they actively rejected and renounced Him to Whom they had surrendered. In discussing the conditions prevailing when this āyah descended, al-Ṭabarī cites several ḥadīths. One, which we shall find repeated by later commentators, relates that Jallās, after his islām, said: "If what Muḥammad brought is right [ḥaqq], then we are worse than asses", after which he denied having made such a statement. (XIV, 361-3) We are not told if Jallās submitted sincerely and then changed his mind, or if his islām was not based on a firm conviction of all that the Prophet brought. If the latter was true, then we have another instance of an act of islām which does not necessarily involve inner taṣdīq or confirmation. In any case, however, the point seems to be that if islām is done in terms of the message brought by

Muḥammad, and that is defined as reality [*ḥaqq*],[86] then one's personal submission is a response to reality itself.

As the structure of 39:22 ⸢Is he [the one] whose breast God has expanded for *al-islām* so that he follows a light from his Lord?⸣ is very similar to that of 6:125, so al-Ṭabarī continues with an interpretation of *islām* focused on its relationship to inner acceptance. Giving a rather more specific statement than earlier, he says:

> He -- may mention of Whom be exalted -- is saying: Is he whose heart God has made wide for knowledge [*ma^{c}rifah*] of Him and affirmation [*iqrār*] of His oneness and submission [*idh^{c}ān*] to His divinity and surrender [*khudū^{c}*] to obedience to Him? "And he has a light from his Lord" -- He says, he is understanding [*^{c}alá baṣīrah*] of what is upon him and he is secure because of the illumination of truth in his heart. (XXIII, 134)

It is obvious that the intention here is an understanding of *islām* as individual and heartfelt, involving knowledge, affirmation, submission and the obedience which is the corollary of this acceptance. Perhaps in all of al-Ṭabarī's *tafsīr* no clearer statement is to be found than the above of the intensely personal quality of this response of man to that which is so specifically and reassuringly instituted by God. The reward of a careful perusal of the many pages of research and analysis in the early commentaries lies in the discovery of a passage such as this, in which the living faith of the writer and his understanding of God's initiative are so warmly expressed.

There can be no question but that for al-Ṭabarī *islām* in its fullest personal sense does involve the internal acceptance of the heart. How, then, does he deal with the 49:14 verse in which it is apparently expressed that *islām* is external as opposed to internal *īmān*? Al-Ṭabarī divides the traditions concerning this verse into three general categories. In the first the understanding is that those who claimed sincerity were speaking (the truth) only with their tongues and did not corroborate this with their actions. (XXVI, 89) The second group of *ḥadīths* indicate that the Prophet has commanded that ⸢Say: You do not have faith⸣ be said to these particular Arabs, of Bani Asad, because they wanted to be called by the names of the emigrators before they emigrated (XXVI, 90), while God knew that they had the names of pagan Arabs, not *muslim muhājirūn*. In the third category are traditions that stress that these people make their *islām* a favor to the Prophet out of fear of capture and

---

[86] See W. C. Smith, *Orientalism and Truth*, pp. 8-9 for a discussion of the implications of the term *ḥaqq*.

being killed. (XXVI, 90)

While not discounting any of these interpretations, al-Ṭabarī returns to the first, saying:

> God has said previously, concerning those Arabs who entered al-millah affirming their good will by speech [iqrāran mannahum bi'l-qawl] and not authenticating their words by their deed, that they said "we have faith" [āmanna] absolutely, without further restriction, namely, [without] saying "we have faith in God and His Messenger". Therefore He commands them to say something unambiguous to its hearers and that can be verified [or whose speaker can be called true or sincere]; namely, they should say "we submit" [aslamnā] in the sense of joining the millah and [participating in] the property arrangements and witnessing to the truth. And His saying "al-īmān has not yet entered your hearts" means -- may mention of Him be exalted -- knowledge of the ways [sharā'iᶜ] of al-īmān and the reality of its meaning [ḥaqā'iq maᶜānīhi] has not entered into your hearts. (XXVI, 90)

If we look at this statement in light of what Abū Jaᶜfar has had to say previously about islām and īmān, it appears that he had a kind of dual understanding of islām. (Again we must stress that to force a structured and precise definition from his comments is unfair; the best we can do is infer an understanding which may or may not have been explicit in his own mind.) That is, while we saw earlier that islām as well as īmān includes sincere acceptance and affirmation, here we have the opposite, an islām involving not the heart but the tongue only. Yet following the outline of the Qur'ān verse, al-Ṭabarī does not deny that these Arabs have participated in islām; he denies only that what they profess is really īmān. Since the act of submission in this case is the entering into al-millah, may we not posit the following as a plausible interpretation of al-Ṭabarī's understanding of islām?

The purely verbal (necessarily external) submission by which one enters al-millah is not of the same depth as is īmān, which involves knowledge [al-ᶜilm] and affirmation [taṣdīq] within the heart. But this īmān is coordinate with the deeper islām which includes the total surrender of the heart, mind and body, the emotional response which leads to the physical acts of obedience. Since the submission of the Arabs of Bani Asad is specifically equated with entering into al-millah, it seems that islām in the external sense means both the act of joining the group of muslims and the name of this group. As an act of submission, however, this external act is really only incidental to the deeper, personal surrender of the heart, islām in the fullest meaning of its expression. Except where islām is associated with millah, and we have seen little instance of this usage in al-Ṭabarī's tafsīr, it is to be seen as verbal or active, either the act of joining the group of muslims or, and here is al-Ṭabarī's emphasis, the total response of man to God which is the dīn acceptable to Him, in the fullest sense of which it is understood as īmān.

Reiterating this verbal quality in the exposition of 61:7 ❛and who does greater wrong than he who invents a lie against God when he is called to al-islām?❜, al-Ṭabarī says, "when he is called to entering [al-dukhūl fī] al-islām. (XXVIII, 57) He obviously intends by this the internal rather than the external act, for in explaining the following verse ❛they wish to extinguish the light of God with their mouths❜ he equates the light of God with al-islām:

> They wanted to nullify the truth with which God sent Muḥammad by their mouths, by their saying that he was a sorcerer and that what he brought was sorcery. (And God is the completer of His light [mutimmu nūrahu], i.e. God is the announcer of truth [muᶜlinu'l-ḥaqq] and the manifester of His dīn [muẓhiru dīnahu] and the helper of Muḥammad against whoever opposed him. And that is the perfection of His light. And by light in this instance is meant al-islām. (XXVIII, 57)

By announcing the truth God has perfected His light in the breast of man (see the tafsīr of 6:125 and 39:22 above) and clarified to him what his dīn should be. Those who are trying to extinguish the light, by which is meant the understanding of what is involved in this perfect dīn, islām, are attempting in vain to call this truth a lie. The real import of these words is brought out even more clearly as al-Ṭabarī continues with the tafsīr of 61:9. Let us temporarily render the key phrases without translation:

> God is the one who sent His Messenger Muḥammad with (the) guidance [al-hudá] and dīn al-ḥaqq, meaning with bayān al-ḥaqq and dīn al-ḥaqq, meaning [He sent him] with the dīn Allah, and it is al-islām. And His saying (to make it prevail over all dīn) means to make prevail the serving [dīn] of Him, al-ḥaqq with which He sent His Messenger, over all dīn [ᶜalá kulli dīn] other than it. And that will be at the descent of ᶜĪsá b. Maryam when al-millah will become one and there will be no dīn other than al-islām. (XXVIII, 58)

In his tafsīr of 3:19 al-Ṭabarī told us that dīn involves obedience and submissiveness, action on the part of man in response to the expressed will of God. It is this response that may well be the key to an understanding of the above passage. Al-Ṭabarī seems to indicate here that Muḥammad brought both guidance, by which he means bayān al-ḥaqq (the elucidating of truth), and dīn al-ḥaqq (the way in which truth is served). That is, he came on the one hand with that which God is transmitting to man in the way of His assistance toward the understanding of reality, and on the other hand with the means whereby man *can* respond to that reality, which is God. *Dīn al-ḥaqq* thus means not "the true *dīn*", which would have to be *al-dīn al-ḥaqq*, but obedience, submissiveness, service to truth in terms of that which God has made known in His *hudá* and *bayān*. This, then is the *dīn* Allāh (not "the religion of God" but "the service of God"), the total response to God Himself, and we have seen frequently in the foregoing that this *dīn*, the only kind acceptable to God, is *al-islām*.

In the next clause he says that "to make [*islām*] prevail over all *dīn*" means to proclaim that the service of Him or response to Him, that is, the truth of God's explanation of how man should respond, which He transmitted through Muḥammad, is above and beyond any other way in which man can serve God. When ᶜĪsá comes to earth all of the different sects and groups will become one because it will be made known to them all that there can be no real or true response other than *islām*, a fact already clarified to those who have heard the message of God spoken by His Prophet.

This brief and lovely passage actually summarizes what we outlined above as the essence of al-Ṭabarī's understanding of *islām*. There is a sense in which *islām* is expressed by one among other *milal*, and on the final day all of these *milal* will be joined. Yet that in which they will be unified is the common recognition that man's real relationship to God is through the submission, *islām*, of the whole being as revealed and clarified by the guidance of Him Who is Lord of all creation.

IV

In giving due credit to the achievement of al-Ṭabarī in the third Islamic century, and often by limiting their scope of understanding to the better-known Sunnī works of *tafsīr*, many historians of Muslim writing have stated that with the completion of *Jāmiᶜ al-bayān* came the end of the great traditionist period of Qur'ān commentary. Certainly it is true that the outstanding Sunnī works of the succeeding centuries were either specifically non-traditionist in their orientation or were very heavily dependent on the compilation of *ḥadīth* materials made by al-Ṭabarī. To another branch of Islam, however, the fourth century was a period in which traditionist writing really came into its own, and it is on this group that we now focus our attention.

As is well-known to any student of Islamic history, the third and fourth centuries *hijrī* gave rise to very serious political disruptions and ended in the virtual disappearance of the political power of the Sunnī *khalīfah*. In 334 Mu^{c}izz al-Dawlah, the Daylamī Buwayhī prince, became *amīr al-umarā'*, and the Sunnī *khalīfah*, while still titular head of state, had to submit to the authority and control of the Shī^{c}ī rulers. Thus protected by Buwayhī power, Shī^{c}ī influence in matters of religious interpretation came to be more strongly solidified. This took the form of a keen interest in traditional Shī^{c}ī material. Before this time the collectors of tradition had been generally under the surveillance of the dominant Sunnī authorities and thus had found their works heavily censured. With the ascendancy of Shī^{c}ī political power, however, traditions extolling the family of ^{c}Alī and denying the validity of the regimes of the houses of Umayyah and ^{c}Abbās came to the fore,[87] and it is to the fourth and fifth centuries that we credit the four major works of Shī^{c}ī traditionism:[88] *al-Kāfī fī ^{c}ilm al-dīn* by Muḥammad ibn Ya^{c}qūb al-Kulaynī (d. 329), *Kitāb man lā yaḥḍuruhu'l-faqīh* by Ibn Bābawayhī, al-Qummī[89] (d. 381), and *al-Istibsār fī-ma 'khtulifa fīhi min al-akhbār* and *Tahdhīb al-aḥkām*, both by Abū Ja^{c}far Muḥammad ibn Ḥasan al-Ṭūsī (d. 460). These are known to the Shī^{c}ah as the "Four Books".

The last two of these writers each composed a *tafsīr* of the Qur'ān at which we shall look in more detail. While al-Ṭūsī actually lived into the fifth century, we shall view the two together in this section as being representative of the particular movement just described. (In the next section we shall consider the fifth century *tafsīr* of the Mu^{c}tazilī al-Zamakhsharī.) Especially important in this context is al-Qummī, whose *tafsīr* has been quite popular despite the assessment of Nöldeke that it

---

[87] Donaldson, *The Shi'ite Religion*, pp. 283-4. We must not assume, however, that there was little or no common ground between Sunnī and Shī^{c}ī traditionists. In many cases one group included transmitters of *ḥadīths* of the other school in its *isnāds* and often the best known of the Shī^{c}ī authorities were scarcely distinguishable from their Sunnī counterparts. Cf. Hodgson, "Dja^{c}far al-Ṣādiḳ" in *EI*$_2$, II, 374-5.

[88] See Donaldson, *The Shi'ite Religion*, pp. 284-89; Strothmann, "Shī^{c}a" in *EI*, IV, 354; and Browne, *Literary History*, IV, 358.

[89] Strothmann gives Ibn Bābūya.

"ist ein elendes Gewebe von Lügen und Dummheiten."[90]

Abū'l-Ḥasan ᶜAlī b. Ibrāhīm b. Hāshim ibn Mūsá ibn Bābawayhī is known as al-Ṣadūq (an interesting appelation in the light of Nöldeke's accusation), or more commonly as al-Qummī. Born in Khurāsān, he came in the year 355 to Baghdād, ten years after the Buwayhī ascendancy. He is most commonly mentioned in the Arabic chronicles as a compiler of ḥadīth, not always favorably,[91] although the specifically Shīᶜī sources understandably give him more credit.[92] The story is told that after the imām of the age (who was, of course, hidden) had been notified that al-Qummī's father desired a son, the father was endowed with not one but two sons. This gave al-Qummī the enviable advantage of being able to claim that he was born through the prayers of the imām of the age.[93] In any case, he certainly was blessed with the capacity for prodigious literary output; the sources offer impressive listings of his works, which are said to have numbered around three hundred. Al-Qummī died in 391/991.

It seems clear that any assessment of his works and authority must be seen in relation to one's appreciation of the Shīᶜah point of view. That to those of his own school he has been exceptionally important is shown by the inclusion of the above-mentioned Kitāb man lā yaḥḍuruhu'l-faqīh in the four canonical books of Shīᶜī law and tradition. The importance of his commentary on the Qur'ān has been noted by several Western scholars. Blachère contrasts him with the earlier-discussed Muqātil b. Sulaymān, indicating that while the latter represented a much more moderate position, both al-Qummī and Fayḍ al-Kāshānī (whose tafsīr we shall view in the section on the eleventh century) are representative of the "extreme" approach, i.e. that which clearly embodies Shīᶜī principles.[94] Goldziher points to the importance of al-Qummī's tafsīr by saying: "Seither ist die Tafsīrerzeugung ein fruchtbares Betätigungsgebiet der schīᶜitischen

---

[90]Geschichte, II, 180. Cf. Brockelmann, GAL, I, 192.

[91]"All of the tafsīr is ḥadīth except a few words and a few expressions. However in some of the sections [maqāmāt] there is no connection between that which precedes and that which follows . . . . the tafsīr of ᶜAlī b. Ibrāhīm . . . lacks cohesion." (al-Kantūrī, Kashf, p. 131.)

[92]"He is an authority in ḥadīth, reliable and truthful." (al-Najāshī, Rijāl, p. 197) ". . . a reliable authority in ḥadīth, established, accredited, sound of doctrine." (al-Ṭūsī, Fihrist, p. 209).

[93]Donaldson, The Shi'ite Religion, pp. 285-86.

[94]Blachère, Introduction, pp. 215-16.

Theologie geblieben."[95] As to the merit of the work, we have seen conflicting, and of course partisan, opinions in the sources and have noted the extremity of Nöldeke's comments. R. Strothmann, who through the depth of his study of Shīʿī materials seems to have reached a more appreciative understanding of this approach, replies to Nöldeke, saying that even if the commentary is not uncontradictory, it is still much used and valued today. He then adds:

> Nun sind gewiss in diesem Kommentar die shīʿitischen, den Qorān erklärenden oder vielmehr vergewaltigenden Tradition stark zusammengedrängt massiert, und rein literarkritisch betrachtet, hat jenes Urteil Berechtigung, übrigens nur eine relativ grössere als für die sonstige islamische Exegese.[96]

What are the real points at issue in the more extreme ʿAlawī works such as that of al-Qummī? A primary aim of the Shīʿah was to promote the house of ʿAlī and the legitimacy of his caliphate and line. This was done, of course, at the expense of the Umawī and ʿAbbāsī caliphates, and by the fourth century the political situation made condemnation of the latter dynasties possible. Along with this was the deep distrust of the ʿUthmānī redaction of the Qur'ān and the belief both that it contained material that rightfully should not be present and that certain passages, particularly those relating to ʿAlī, had been deleted.[97] We have seen that in the Sunnī tradition the most acceptable chain of authority goes back to a Companion of the Prophet (and, of course, to the Prophet himself). For the Shīʿah, however, the chain of a valid tradition goes through ʿAlawī authorities directly to one of the members of the house of ʿAlī, for only they were reliable, indeed infallible, interpreters of truth.

The most common criticism that has been made of al-Qummī is that his tafsīr lacks continuity, that it is often disjointed and fragmented. Goldziher notes that if he was particularly guilty of this it was because of the Shīʿī view that the Qur'ān as they had it was not in its true order and that properly to comment on it one must try to piece together the fragmented

---

[95] Richtungen, p. 279.

[96] Die Zwölfer-Schīʿa, p. 153.

[97] Great effort was made to reconstruct the original [in Shīʿī terms] Qur'ān, but with little success; in general this "true" version is thought probably to be more extensive than the extant ʿUthmānī Qur'ān. The true Qur'ān, they feel, will come in the fullness of time at the arrival of the expected Mahdī.

verses in their natural continuity.[98]

As an aid to the understanding not only of this tafsīr but of ᶜAlawī commentary in general, it seems appropriate to give in some detail a few of the introductory comments made by the editor of the most recent edition[99] of the tafsīr, Ṭayyib al-Musawī al-Jazā'irī. He says that for six reasons this tafsīr deserves special notice: (1) It is the original of many other tafsīrs, i.e. they are highly dependent on it. (2) The ḥadīths are related from the truthful ones (i.e. the members of the ahl al-bayt or house of ᶜAlī) with few intermediaries. (3) The author lived in the time of the Imām al-ᶜAskarī and (4) his father was one of the associates of the Imām al-Riḍā. (5) It contains much information about the deeds of the ahl al-bayt which their enemies tried to delete from the Qur'ān. (6) It is guaranteed to explain many of the Qur'ān verses which have been difficult to understand without the guidance of the ahl al-bayt. (I, 15-16)

Particularly interesting is al-Jazā'irī's understanding of that which it is necessary to know in order to understand this tafsīr. He quotes the Prophet as having said, "ᶜAlī and I are of one light", and stresses that God made Muḥammad the greatest of the Messengers and ᶜAlī the next. He discusses the wilāyah[100] of Muḥammad and ᶜAlī and says that God created them both of one light and after them the angels and the creatures. According to al-Jazā'irī they were actually pre-existent: their holy essence was there before the creation. (I, 18)

It is necessary to recognize the likelihood that some part of the tafsīr of Ibn ᶜAbbās was not actually his. The same is true, although to a much lesser degree, of the tafsīr of al-Qummī. Al-Jazā'irī says that there were several editions of this work extant before the present copy, but that they were rare and full of error. This copy in his judgment was superior to the others when he found it, although it contained many errors and many words were missing. (I, 7, 14-15, 17) In his attempt to restore the tafsīr to its original form, it is likely that the editor may have manipulated the material to some extent to fit his own interpretation. Recognizing this possibility we

---

[98] Richtungen, p. 286. It is interesting to compare this with the procedures of modern Western scholarship in studying the Qur'ān.

[99] Tafsīr al-Qummī, al-Najaf, 1386-87 [1967].

[100] The meaning of this term is difficult to render in English, especially by a single word. It can best be understood, perhaps, as meaning saintliness or nearness to God. See below, p. 152.

must nevertheless accept the copy at hand as the closest approximation to the original intentions of al-Qummī that we have available, and hope that its material contains some clue to his understanding of the nature and meaning of *islām*.

We said earlier that both al-Qummī and Muḥammad ibn Ḥasan al-Ṭūsī were representative of the fourth-fifth century Shīʿī literature which appeared in such profusion. This is true, but the contrast in their approaches is immediately clear when one sets in juxtaposition their *tafsīrs* of the Qur'ān. Al-Qummī has just been described as representative of the more extreme ʿAlawī position and his commentary, in several places, will indicate him to be such. ("Extreme" here does not mean, of course, that he was one of the *ghulāt al-Shīʿah*, but rather that he was strict in adherence to the tenets of the Ithnā ʿAsharīyah, of which he was a member.) Al-Ṭūsī, though an Imāmī, seems to have been much more in line with the kind of interpretation that we have seen from Sunnī traditionists; in many places his commentary is direct quotation from the *Jāmiʿ al-bayān* of al-Ṭabarī.

Abū Jaʿfar Muḥammad b. al-Ḥasan b. ʿAlī, often called Shaykh al-Ṭā'ifah, was born in Ṭūs in 385/995. In 408 he journeyed to Baghdād where he studied under the Shāfiʿī al-Shaykh al-Mufīd and later under the famous al-Sayyid al-Murtaḍá, with whom he was associated some twenty-odd years.[101] The sources are unqualified in their praise of him[102] and Hidāyat Ḥusayn describes him as "the greatest doctor of the Shīʿa sect."[103] Inoffensive to Sunnīs as his commentary may appear, he was nonetheless a controversial figure and suffered from the serious reactions of his opponents. Accused, perhaps unjustly, of having cursed the Companions of the Prophet, his books and house were burned and he was forced to leave the city of Baghdād.[104] He died in Najaf in 460/1067 (or 458/1065).

That for which al-Ṭūsī probably is best known in the West is his list of Shīʿah books, *Fihrist kutub al-Shīʿah*.[105] He is

---

[101] Subkī, *Ṭabaqāt*, III, 51-2; al-Baḥrānī, *Lu'lu'at*, p. 295.

[102] "He was the head of his sect. He was truthful and knew the reports, the men, law, theology, literature, and all good things were given to him. He wrote on all aspects of *islām*." (al-Astarābādī, *Manhaj*, 292).

[103] "Al-Ṭūsī" in *EI*, IV, 982.

[104] al-Astarābādī, *Manhaj*, p. 292; al-Baḥrānī, *Lu'lu'at*, pp. 293-94.

[105] Edited by A. Sprenger (Caluctta: Baptist Mission Press, 1855).

also the author of many works highly valued by the Shīᶜah. His Qur'ān commentary, al-Tibyān fī tafsīr al-Qur'ān,[106] is a large twenty-volume work whose value is attested by al-Baḥrānī in the succinct tribute, "lam yuᶜmal mithluhu [there has been produced nothing like it]".[107]

Orientalists in general have not been overly appreciative of Shīᶜah commentary;[108] these writings, however, afford as with Sunnī exegesis an opportunity to observe the application of characteristic dogmatic affirmations. One must be careful of such a statement, of course, for the implication is that both Sunnī and Shīᶜī commentators have read into the holy text their own principles, whereas in fact both have felt strongly that these principles were inherent in the Qur'ān itself.) It will be interesting to discover if, and how, the tafsīrs of al-Qummī and al-Ṭūsī differ in the understanding of islām from the exegesis we have already considered.

* * *

Al-Qummī's tafsīr, as can be expected from the above, consists of very little other than a stringing together of traditions. Occasionally he begins the treatment of a particular verse with a comment that seems to be his own, as happily is the case with 3:19:

> ❴Truly al-dīn with God is al-islām❵ He said, [by al-islām is meant] submission [al-taslīm] to God and to His saints [awliyā'ihi] and that is confirmation [al-taṣdīq], and God has called al-īmān tasdīq. (I, 99)

Immediately we are introduced to a dimension of islām not seen before. It is submission [taslīm] through internal affirmation and self-dedication not only to God but also to the saints, by which he means the ᶜAlawī line of imāms.

---

[106] Najaf: al-Maṭbaᶜah al-ᶜIlmīyah, 1377-82 [1957-63].

[107] al-Baḥrānī, Lu'lu'at, p. 296. Indicative of the high esteem in which the tafsīr was held by many, this statement is nonetheless open to some question as al-Ṭūsī not only echoed many of the phrases of al-Ṭabarī but in several places apparently copied whole sections.

[108] E.g. Nöldeke, Geschichte, II, 180: "Angesichts ihrer ausschweifenden, den Zusammenhang der Texte völlig ignorierenden Allegoristik (ta'wīl) könnte man veilleicht geneigt sein, die Frage aufzuwerfen, ob die Dreistigkeit der Lüge einen grösseren Anteil daran habe als die Dummheit." And in Goldziher, Richtungen, p. 270: "Es ist auf keinem Gebiete der tendentiösen Koranauslegung in so unersättlicher Weise und mit solch übertreibenden Resultaten gearbeitet worden als eben in diesem Kreise."

He follows this statement with a reference to a ḥadīth attributed to Abū Jaᶜfar, in which it is related that God gave preference to al-īmān over al-islām by a degree [bi-darajah]. 'Abū Jaᶜfar' in this case does not refer to al-Ṭabarī, probably, but to Muḥammad al-Bāqir, great-grandson of ᶜAlī's son Ḥasan and fifth Shīᶜī imām.[109] After this tradition al-Qummī gives a very interesting statement, which he ascribes to amīr al-mu'minīn (by which he designates ᶜAlī, the fourth khalīfah and progenitor of the ᶜAlawī line):

> I explain al-islām by way of a nisbah [relationship]. No one has done this before me and no one will do it after me. Al-islām is al-taslīm [total submission] and al-taslīm is al-yaqīn [certainty] and al-yaqīn is al-taṣdīq [confirmation] and al-taṣdīq is al-iqrār [affirmation] and al-iqrār is al-adā' [rendering (of a service)] and al-adā' is al-ᶜamal [performance]. The mu'min is the one who takes his dīn from his Lord; truly the mu'min makes known his īmān in his activity. O people! Your dīn is your dīn. And truly that which is good in it is better than the good in other than it, and the evil in it will be forgiven, and the good in other than it will not be accepted. (I, 99-100)

In these brief statements quite a bit is revealed about the nature of islām. The last sentence may or may not represent a group idea of dīn. In any case, however, it does not appear to be reified, since the evil in their dīn presumably means the evil in their behavior, their personal religious life, rather than an idealized or reified islām (which one expects to be understood as free of evil). Thus basically islām is presented as an individual matter. Secondly, it is an internal assurance and affirmation. The import of these statements is that while there is a difference between islām and īmān, they are related in terms of degree and both involve inner submission. Thirdly, islām is manifested through activity, as is evidenced by the fact that the chain of relationship leads through the steps of acceptance and concludes with al-adā' and al-ᶜamal. Al-adā' conveys the meaning not only of activity as such but of carrying something out, fulfilling it and bringing about a result. Unfortunately because we know the text has been heavily edited[110] and because for the most part we are dealing with a series of traditions rather than a carefully developed thesis we must be aware of the limitations of the attempt to present an accurate picture of the

---

[109] Born in 57 or 58/676-8, Muḥammad al-Bāqir is said to have been poisoned by the Banū Umayyah in 104 or 107/722 or 726-7. (Browne, Literary History, IV, 393).

[110] We will discover, however, that in those several cases in which the later Fayḍ al-Kāshānī quotes al-Qummī, the material given is exactly what we have in the tafsīr of al-Qummī here at hand.

thought of al-Qummī. What we can say, however, and in the long run it is perhaps more important to the development of our historical perspective, is that through the traditional material we probably are getting in general what the early Shīʿī community, or members of it, interpreted this verse to mean.

The style of al-Ṭūsī's *tafsīr* is quite different from that of the present edition of al-Qummī. While he includes many *ḥadīths*, al-Ṭūsī amplifies and interprets these with a good deal of material which we would suppose to be his own. He sets the scene immediately in the explication of 3:19 by stating that "the meaning of *al-dīn* here is obedience [*al-ṭāʿah*] and the meaning of that is that obedience to God -- great and glorified is He -- is *al-islām*." (II, 418) This is expanded with a discussion of *dīn* as recompense [*al-jazā'*] as when God is described as king of the day of recompense [*mālik yawm al-dīn*]. Here is an interesting continuum in the concept of *dīn* (*islām*); on the one hand it involves the obedience of man in performing those things which it is necessary to do [*wujūb al-qaḍā'*] and on the other hand the requital by God in terms of man's obedience.[111]

It is not surprising, then, to see that al-Ṭūsī's ensuing discussion of *islām* focuses on the active response of man to God. After describing *aslama* as meaning the entering into *al-silm* as one enters a drought period or springtime,[112] he says that the source of *silm* is *al-salāmah* [soundness], and that the source of that is *al-taslīm* [surrender] because it is surrender to the command of God. This *taslīm* is that which leads from corruption [*al-fasād*] and want [*al-nuqṣān*] to soundness or wholeness [*al-salāmah*], and *al-islām* is the transformation from defects [*al-adghāl*] to soundness through doing those things the execution of which constitutes obedience to God. (II, 418)

That this *islām* is very much an internal matter for al-Ṭūsī is apparent from his discussion of the acts of the limbs as part of *īmān*. *Īmān* and *islām* for him and for the Muʿtazilah, he says, mean the same. But while for the latter the external acts of the body [*afʿāl al-jawāriḥ*] constitute a part of *īmān*, for al-Ṭūsī they are incumbent upon the individual but are not *īmān*. (II, 418-19) In a kind of concluding statement to what has gone before, he says:

---

[111] See Izutsu, *God and Man*, pp. 219-29.

[112] This discussion is almost word for word that presented by Abū Jaʿfar al-Ṭabarī (*Jāmiʿ al-bayān*, VI, 274-5). See pp. 88-89 above.

> Al-islām conveys the meaning of being led [al-inqiyād] by all of what the Prophet brought in the way of ordained acts of devotion [al-ʿibādāt al-sharʿīyah][113] and forsaking that which has been rejected, submitting [al-istislām] to it. And if we say that the dīn of the mu'min is al-īmān and it is al-islām, then al-islām is al-īmān. This is the same as our saying man, and man is an animal in human form, and the animal in that form is a human being. (II, 419)

We shall find the parallel of man and animal used several centuries later by Fakhr al-Dīn Rāzī as an example of the relationship between īmān and islām when he says that "the general and the specific are different in generality, one in being."[114] Here in al-Ṭūsī we have the same idea expressed when he indicates that islām, though one with īmān, is nevertheless distinguished from it with regard to the performance of duties. He defines islām as an orientation, a willingness to take on certain duties and a self-dedication to carrying them out. This is also īmān. But he is not willing to say, as do the Muʿtazilah, that the actual carrying out of these duties is also a part of faith. Islām as īmān plus the performance of the specific requirements as outlined by the Prophet constitutes the dīn in terms of which man receives his ultimate reward from God.

Thus for both al-Qummī and al-Ṭūsī islām is seen as individual, internal and active, although as has been indicated the ways in which this is developed differ considerably. So far in al-Tibyān we have seen nothing that would show the author to be a Shīʿī, while al-Qummī immediately removed his tafsīr from that acceptable to Sunnī Muslims by the inclusion of the awliyā' in that to which one surrenders.

Al-Qummī quotes the whole of 3:85 without giving any comment. Al-Ṭūsī, however, uses this verse as an opportunity to reiterate his insistence that islām consists basically of the performance of those things which God has commanded:

> Al-islām: it is submission [al-istislām] to the command of God through obedience to Him [bi-ṭāʿatihi] in that to which He calls; all of that is [an] islām even when the prescribed obligations [al-sharā'iʿ] in it differ and the interpretations [al-madhāhib] diverge, since whoever seeks it as [a] dīn is saved and whoever seeks other than it as [a] dīn is destroyed. (II, 520)

This passage not only supports his previous interpretation but underlines by the use of islām without the article the fact

---

[113] See above, p. 64, for a discussion of the implications of ʿibādah. The phrase here refers to those things enjoined to man because of his creaturehood, his role as a servant of God.

[114] Mafātīḥ al-ghayb, VII, 608-9. See below, pp. 166-67.

that the term primarily indicates a personal act rather than a reified group. He who posits *islām* as his religious goal, and only he, is saved.

He devotes a section to reiterating that *islām* and *īmān* are one, and then cites the tradition from cIkrimah in which the Jews claimed to be the *muslimūn*, or the ones who are *muslim*, whereupon God commanded them to make the *ḥajj* "which is a part of the duty of submission [*al-islām*]."[115] But they refrained from it, as a result of which their not being *muslim* (not being submitters to God's will) was made clear [*bāna insilākhuhum min al-islām*], because of their opposition to Him. Thereupon God revealed this verse: ‹If anyone seeks other than *al-islām* as [a] *dīn*, it will not be accepted from him . . .›

Here again we see al-Ṭūsī emphasizing very strongly that *al-islām* involves doing, or here the intention of doing [*yabtaghi*], the command of God. That this is not merely an external act is implicit in his frequent reminders that *islām* and *īmān* are really the same.

Both al-Qummī and al-Ṭūsī, like many of the other commentators, discuss 5:3 ‹Today I have completed for you your *dīn* and fulfilled for you My blessing, and have chosen for you *al-islām* as [a] *dīn*› in terms of the divine revelation of injunctions incumbent upon man. Al-Qummī is brief, quoting again from Abū jacfar who said, "The last duty [*farīḍah*] God revealed is *al-wilāyah*[116] and he did not reveal after that [any other] duty." (I, 162) Al-Ṭūsī, however, devotes some space to the three clauses of this verse, a great deal of which is obviously taken directly from al-Ṭabarī. But before we examine this, we might also note several of the comments that he makes about the preceeding verse, ‹Today despair those who disavow [*kafarū min*] your *dīn*›. Indicating that one interpretation is that they despair of [proving] the invalidity [*buṭlān*] of *al-islām*, he says: "*al-dīn* is a name for all of that by which God's creation worships [serves] Him, and with which He has commanded them to busy themselves [*al-dīn ismun li-jamīci mā tacabbada'llāh bihi khalquhu wa-amarahum bi'l-qiyāmah bihi*]." (III, 434) Then he quotes from Ibn cAbbās[117] and Suddī cAṭā that this was the day of the Ḥajj al-Wadāc after the entry of all the Arabs into *al-islām*.

---

[115] See the discussion of al-Ṭabarī (*Jāmic al-bayān*, VI, 570-71) above, pp. 67-68.

[116] From the context of his earlier statements we can assume that he means here specifically the *wilāyah* of *amīr al-mu'minīn*.

[117] This was not contained in our edition of the *tafsīr* of Ibn cAbbās.

Here we have one of those instances where it seems hard to imagine that the author was making a distinction between the act of submission and the community of the Prophet. The Meccan Arabs, realizing that they could not defeat Muḥammad, decided to enter islām as a whole. This suggests the group sense of the term. Yet al-Ṭūsī is not willing to say that these Arabs were not submitting themselves to God and choosing to obey Him, regardless of whether or not this islām could be defined in the same terms he used in the discussion of 3:19. His use of buṭlān indicates that they had given up hope of proving that islām was an invalid response to God (particularly when followed by such a poignant expression of the meaning of dīn) as much as discouragement over the possibility of conquering the followers of the Prophet.

The rest of al-Ṭūsī's discussion of 5:2-3 is, for the most part, either a paraphrase or a direct word-for-word copy of the material we have already seen in al-Ṭabarī. The stress on islām as istislām to God's command and submission [inqiyād] to obedience to God (III, 436) is very much in line with what he has said above on the previous verses.

In treating the next three verses in which islām is mentioned, 6:125, 9:74 and 39:22, al-Qummī is as usual brief, but unfortunately not to the point insofar as any concrete references to islām are concerned. Al-Ṭūsī is more expansive, but gives few new insights into his understanding of the term.

In 6:125 ❴whomever God wills to guide, He expands his breast for al-islām . . .❵ the stress is on the meaning of guidance. Here al-Ṭūsī says that two things can be said. The first is that "by guidance He intends facilitation [tashīl] of the way to al-islām by signs [dalā'il] through which the breast is opened . . ." (IV, 288) Here clearly God is the agent. But in keeping with his usual emphasis on man's activity, al-Ṭūsī adds that "it is merely an incitement to effort [ḥaḍḍ ᶜalá'l-ijtihād] in seeking the truth so that the breast opens because of the signs . . ." (IV, 288) God provides the signs, but man must do his part by striving to recognize them.

The second thing that can be said about guidance is that it is guidance to recompense [al-thawāb]:

> The assumption is, whomever God wills to guide towards recompense in the hereafter [fi'l-ākhirah] He opens his breast to al-islām in this world [fi'l-dunyā] by giving him grace [luṭf] at the time of which he chooses al-islām. (IV, 289)

These two interpretations are really facets of the one understanding which al-Ṭūsī has given of islām, especially in his tafsīr of 3:19. Through a combination of man's effort and God's guidance one performs those acts of obedience which constitute islām in this world and on account of which one is rewarded in the next. Skipping 9:74, in terms of which al-Ṭūsī discusses mainly the conditions of its revelation, we find that his tafsīr of 39:22 also includes the use of laṭafa, to be kind, as a description of God's role in the expanding of the breast. Here man's role is seen in terms that assure al-Ṭūsī's recognition of the internal nature of islām:

> ❴Is he whose breast God has expanded to al-islām❵ i.e. the one to whom God was kind so that he had faith and knew God and proclaimed His oneness and confirmed His Prophet . . . (IX,20)

The āyah preceding 49:14 says ❴The noblest of you in God's sight is he who fears Him most❵. The relationship between Arab and non-Arab Muslims has been a problematic one from the days of the earliest expansion of Muḥammad's community. Al-Qummī directly admonishes those who would overly prize their Arab birthright when he stresses that while the arrogance of the jāhilīyah (the "period of ignorance") permitted boasting about one's lineage, Arabic is not a father or mother and whoever speaks it is an Arab. By saying that God has taken man away from this arrogance by al-islām al-Qummī clearly intends that anyone, Arab or non-Arab, can participate in islām.

Neither al-Qummī nor al-Ṭūsī uses 49:14 specifically to elaborate on the relationship between īmān and islām, as do so many commentators. The latter contrasts ṣaddaqa and qarrara, which the Arabs described in the verse illegitimately claimed to have done, with istaslama, which they actually did and which is only outward submission out of fear of captivity or being killed. He does not use islām as a maṣdar here and we know that even if he did allow for an islām which is only external it would have little meaning for him in comparison with the internal islām that he has so often described.

We find, then, that aside from a few points made by al-Qummī, particularly that of islām as submission to the saints as well as to God, there is nothing in these two Shīʿī tafsīrs to distinguish them from comparable Sunnī works. Obviously al-Ṭūsī finds himself in general agreement with al-Ṭabarī as so much of his material is a direct parallel. On the whole, we are left with the same conclusions reached after examining their comments on 3:19, that islām excepting its apparent group usage in connection with 5:3 is individual, that it is a sincere affirmation, and that it involves an active response and obedience on the part of man to the guidance and directives of God.

V

After the laborious collection of traditional material that characterized the first centuries after the Prophet, rationalism swept across the face of Muslim scholarship like a fresh, if sometimes gusty, breeze. Exercise of the mind came to be valued by many over the recollections of the memory, and reason played a new and creative role in the development of kalām[118] and tafsīr. Many commentators began to feel that dependence on the traditions was insufficient for a true understanding of the Book. These preferred to exercise what has been termed tafsīr bi'l-ra'y or exposition by means of independent opinion.

Most notable among the proponents of this kind of exegesis were the Muᶜtazilah. First appearing about a century after Muḥammad, this school did not really make its influence felt until the next century. For them reason was a primary source of knowledge and could never be ignored. Al-Zamakhsharī, one of the most eloquent and qualified proponents of iᶜtizāl, is quoted as having said in opposition to the traditionists: "A man with proof is more honorable than a lion in its lair. An imitator is more despicable than a mangy goat."[119] Reason is a gift of God and is to be used in His service.

It would be far too simplistic to see the development of the Muᶜtazilah merely as a reaction against the traditionists. The emergence of the different schools of theology was a complicated process and one about which there are still many unanswered questions. It is apparent, however, that the basic elements of rationalism were present very early in Islam. As Goldziher points out,[120] in the early ᶜAbbāsī times there was a merging of the radical rationalist with the pious ponderer in a broadening of the circle of those who favored greater freedom of thought. This movement, in addition to direct confrontation with the opposing traditionists, sought to ground its ideas in the text of the Qur'ān.

---

[118] I will use kalām with the general meaning of "scholastic theology" as given by D.B. MacDonald in the SEI (p. 210), keeping in mind such objections to the equation of kalām with theology in the Christian understanding as were raised by Gardet and Anawati in Introduction à la Théologie Musulmane, 210-19.

[119] Quoted by Rashīd Ahmad ("Qur'ānic exegesis" in IQ, XII [1968], 150) from Yāqūt, Irshād, VII, 150.

[120] Richtungen, pp. 99-102.

Having its earliest stirrings in the second century hijrī and coming into its own in the third century, by the late fifth and early sixth centuries (the era of al-Zamakhsharī) the Muᶜtazilī school had ceased to be the influential movement it once was. Failing to achieve the official sanction that in religious circles so proudly is termed orthodoxy, the Muᶜtazilah gradually faded into small pockets of the Islamic world, of which one was the region where Abū'l-Qāsim Maḥmūd b. ᶜUmar al-Zamakhsharī was raised.

Born in Khwārizm in 467/1075, al-Zamakhsharī is generally considered by Muslims of all persuasions to have been one of the outstanding thinkers and leaders of his, or indeed any, age. As a young man he did considerable travelling in the course of his studies, including a trip to Mecca where he remained for some time, for which he has frequently been called "Jār Allāh", the neighbor of God.[121] Among the anecdotes often related by the chroniclers about al-Zamakhsharī are those that offer explanations for the loss of his foot.[122] This affliction does not seem to have hampered his activities; he was master of a great many fields and wrote a number of highly respected works. Some have counted as many as thirty separate disciplines or categories of learning in which al-Zamakhsharī is considered to have been proficient.[123] Al-Anbārī tells us that Abū'l-Qāsim, never noted for diffidence, used to maintain that in all of his writings there was no subject left uncovered, though many tried to disclaim this.[124]

Of these many accomplishments, his contributions to the science of tafsīr and to grammatical analysis and advancement of the understanding and appreciation of the Arabic language are probably, in retrospect, the most valuable. Unlike his predecessors in tafsīr (and indeed most of those to follow), al-Zamakhsharī was not particularly devoted to the study of ḥadīth

---

[121] al-Yāfiᶜī, Mi'rāt al-janān, p. 269; Yāqūt, Irshād, VI, pt. 8, 147.

[122] The most common understanding is that the loss occurred after frostbite incurred during a heavy snowstorm in Khwārizm. Al-Zamakhsharī himself is supposed to have said that his mother, having seen her young son pull the leg off a sparrow, wished the same fate for him. (Ibn Khallikān, Wafayāt, III, 322-23; Yāqūt, Irshād, VI, pt. 7, 147).

[123] Cf. al-Yāfiᶜī, Mi'rāt, p. 269; Yāqūt, Irshād, VI, pt. 7, 147; al-Suyūṭī, Bughyat, p. 288.

[124] al-Anbārī, Nuzhāt, p. 231.

and wrote only two works on this subject. Aside from his tafsīr, he is probably best known for the grammatical work al-Mufaṣṣal (written 513-515 hijrī) in which he expressed his esteem for the Arabic language by disavowing any Shu^cubīyah influence on it.[125]

That al-Zamakhsharī considered himself to be of Mu^ctazilī persuasion we know through his own insistence as well as through his writings.[126] He made public profession of such opinions, and tradition has it that on paying a social call he liked to have himself announced as Abū'l Qāsim the Mu^ctazilī.[127] He originally began his commentary on the Qur'ān with the words: "al-ḥamdu li'llāh 'lladhī khalaqa'l-Qur'ān". Upon being assured, however, that this would earn public disapproval, he modified the phrase to: ". . . 'lladhī ja^cala [or: anzala] al-Qur'ān."[128] Al-Zamakhsharī died at the age of seventy-one in 538/1144 at al-Jurjānīyah in Khwārizm.[129]

Al-Kashshāf (completed in 528 hijrī) can be described, particularly in comparison with some of the preceding works of tafsīr, as a rational commentary, one in which the author is specifically concerned with philological and philosophical analysis. The text, not lengthy, is written very concisely and carefully and contains a great deal of material in a relatively few pages. It is most definitely not light reading, especially for one to whom Arabic is not native. The commentary gives immediate evidence of this Persian writer's thorough familiarity with and unusually clear understanding of the Arabic language. While al-Ṭabarī's style was to present various understandings of the text based on traditional interpretations, and Fakhr al-Dīn Rāzī's, as we shall see, is to offer lengthy philosophical discourse, al-Zamakhsharī generally gives the sense of the passage as it appears most obvious, notes the progression of ideas and then suggests possible interpretations based on grammatical and

---

125 Brockelmann, "Al-Zamakhsharī" in EI, IV, 1207.

126 Ibn al-^cImād, Shadharāt, IV, 120.

127 Ibid., IV, 120; Ibn Khallikān, Wafayāt, III, 323.

128 al-Yāfi^cī, Mi'rāt, p. 270; Ibn al-^cImād, Shadharāt, IV, 120. According to Ibn Khallikān (Wafayāt, III, 323) al-Zamakhsharī himself substituted "ja^cala" [to make or establish], a verb which could imply either that God was the agent (to please the orthodox) or the creator (to please the Mu^ctazilah), but "anzala" has been substituted by later editors. Our edition (al-Kashshāf ^can ḥaqā'iq ghawāmiḍ al-tanzīl; Beirut: Dār al-Kitāb al-^cArabī, 1386 [1966] gives "al-ḥamdu li'llāh 'lladhī anzala'l-Qur'ān". (I, n.p.)

129 Brockelmann in EI, IV, 1205.

philological analyses. His constant tributes to the rhetorical beauty of the text give life to the technical structure of his work.

A primary concern of the Muᶜtazilah was the inimitability [iᶜjāz] of the Qur'ān, to which they pointed by extensive use of metaphor and rhetoric. Al-Zamakhsharī himself went to great lengths to indicate the rhetorical loftiness of the style and diction of the Qur'ān. This approach, along with his tendency to reconcile apparently contradictory verses in the light of the rational interpretations of the Muᶜtazilah, earned him both commendation and severe criticism. In his very extensive consideration of the work of al-Zamakhsharī, Goldziher says that while his opponents respected and even used his work, they harshly opposed the dogmatic deductions which they felt were often strained to fit the rationalist formula.[130] The fact remains, however, that despite the claims of the author and the obvious intention of the text itself to interpret in the light of Muᶜtazilī viewpoints, al-Kashshāf has been recognized by those of all theological persuasions to be one of the classical bases of tafsīr and has become extremely popular in the Muslim world.[131]

On the question of free-will/predestination the Muᶜtazilah, of course, had very specific ideas. In the following consideration of selected passages from the Kashshāf we shall have several occasions to see the support that al-Zamakhsharī gives in his interpretations to the general Muᶜtazilī view that man determines his own actions, and thus his own fate. Rashīd Aḥmad expresses the opinion that "Zamakhsharī sometimes appears in his commentary more as a rigid Muᶜtazili than as a commentator."[132] We will see here, I think, that he was most definitely both, his interpretation of and commentary on the Qur'ān strongly

---

[130] Richtungen, pp. 117-19. Ibn Khaldūn says that the kind of Qur'ān interpretation that operates through linguistic knowledge and philology is best represented in al-Zamakhsharī's Kashshāf. Yet because the author is a Muᶜtazilī in dogmatic views, "Competent orthodox scholars have . . . come to disregard his work and to warn everyone against its pitfalls. However they admit that he is on firm ground in everything relating to language and style (balāghah)." (Muqaddimah, II, 447).

[131] It was one of the tafsīr texts studied in the advanced courses at the Azhar in the eighteenth century, along with the tafsīrs of al-Suyūṭī and al-Maḥallī, al-Bayḍāwī, al-Shirbīnī and Abū'l-Suᶜūd. (Heyworth-Dunne, An Introduction to the History of Education in Modern Egypt, pp. 45-46).

[132] "Qur'anic exegesis" in IQ, XII (1968), 95.

influenced by his theological viewpoints.

We will consider in later sections the relationship of succeeding commentary, specifically that of al-Bayḍāwī and Fakhr al-Dīn Rāzī, to the tafsīr of al-Zamakhsharī.

* * *

We do not have to read very far into the portions of al-Kashshāf relevant to our topic to discover certain emphases particularly characteristic of the Muᶜtazilī outlook. The attribution to God of unity [tawḥīd] and of justice [taᶜdīl] are central to the concerns of this school. It is therefore appropriate that these two concepts are the foci of al-Zamakhsharī's tafsīr of 3:18-19, which verses he sees as a continuing thought. One cannot understand what is meant by ❴Truly al-dīn with God is al-islām❵ until he grasps the import of the preceding verse which states: ❴God has borne witness that there is no God but He, likewise the angels and the people of knowledge; [It is He who] maintains justice [qā'iman bi'l-qisṭ] . . .❵. He begins his commentary on 3:19 by saying that this phrase confirms what immediately preceded. And, he says, if it were asked what is the use of such confirmation, he would reply:

> The use of it is that His saying (there is no God but He) is tawḥīd, and His saying (maintaining justice) is taᶜdīl, and if it is followed by His saying (truly al-dīn with God is al-islām) then He is announcing that al-islām is justice [al-ᶜadl] and the attribution of unity, and it is al-dīn with God, and anything other than that has nothing to do with religion. (I, 345)

He continues in a strikingly Muᶜtazilī vein by stressing that anthropomorphism [tashbīh] or such things as seeing God [al-ru'yah] or fatalism [al-jabr] are pure outrage and have no connection with the dīn of God, al-islām. This is followed by a very detailed grammatical analysis designed to demonstrate that verse 19 recapitulates verse 18, supporting his main point that ". . . dīna'llāhi huwa al-tawḥīd wa'l-ᶜadl." (I, 345)

As is often the case, it is in the attempt to understand the meaning of words which usually are given a too simple one-word translation, or are deemed "untranslatable" and thus left in transliteration, that one begins to grasp the deeper sense of the material at hand. In this case the terms of interest are, as indicated above, tawḥīd and taᶜdīl (or simply ᶜadl). Therefore the Western reader may ask himself whether taᶜdīl means justice in the abstract, acting in a just manner, or attributing justice to God. Looking at al-Zamakhsharī's tafsīr of 3:18, we find that he gives the following explanation of "qā'iman bi'l-qisṭ":

> . . . maintaining justice [al-ᶜadl] in His distribution of [man's] means of livelihood [al-arzāq] and of the time of [each man's] death [al-ājāl], and in His meting out of rewards and punishments, and in what He commands His servants in the way of acting justly [inṣaf] one to another and acting equitably toward each other. (I, 343)

Here we find that all three of the possible interpretations of justice are involved. God Himself acts justly; since for the Muᶜtazilah there is no existence of divine attributes apart from God's essence, this means that He is justice or just-ness, yet at the same time He has commanded man to act in a just manner toward his fellows. Man acts justly because God acts justly and his very act of justice is his dīn, his islām, his recognition of the justice of God. Thus we see that far from choosing one of the above possible translations of taᶜdīl or ᶜadl, one must see them all as dimensions of the whole.

The same is true of the word tawḥīd. The following interpretation has been offered of this term which is so basic to the understanding of the faith of the Muslim: "Tawḥīd is something that man does: It is the recognition of God's unity, at the lowest level, and in a series of ascending levels, it is the appropriation to one's self, also the proclamation, also the implementation of that unity: the living of a life that has integrity, because oneness is divine. . ."[133]

When we consider again, then, that for al-Zamakhsharī al-islām is al-ᶜadl and al-tawḥīd, we begin to see the depth and breadth of his understanding of man's dīn, man's way of responding to God: man acts because God acts, and because God is. That for this author the islām here described was in no sense a concept or response newly revealed through Muḥammad is made clear in his interpretation of 3:20:

> ❨Say: I submit [aslamtu] my face to God❩ i.e. I dedicate my being [nafsī] and my totality [jumlatī] to God alone, not associating in my being and my totality any other with Him by serving [another] or calling upon [another] as a god; this means that my dīn is al-tawḥīd and it is the eternal religion [al-dīn al-qadīm] the authenticity of which was established with you as with me, and I do not come with anything inventive concerning which you might quarrel with me. (I, 346-47)

Personal submission to God means an acceptance of the eternal dīn, i.e. that which has always been the response of man acceptable to God, which is again defined specifically as

---

[133]From an unpublished personal communication from W.C. Smith, Harvard University, May 1969.

al-tawḥīd. When one submits, when he accepts the perfect unity of God, then the recognition of this unity is his dīn. The Qur'ān verse ❬Say: I submit my face to God❭ is concerned specifically with man's act of submission; al-Zamakhsharī's tafsīr centers again on the dominant fact of God's oneness.

In none of the succeeding passages of al-Kashshāf in which al-Zamakhsharī deals with the Qur'ān verses mentioning islām does he present such an unequivocal understanding of its meaning as in the tafsīr of 3:19. Having made his point he apparently does not find any need to elaborate further. Thus concerning 3:85 ❬If anyone seeks other than al-islām❭ he says only: ". . . meaning al-tawḥīd and submission (islām) of the face to God." (I, 381) In discussing 3:20 he did not specifically use the maṣdar islām in speaking of the individual submission. Here with 3:85, however, he leaves no question whatsoever that as we saw before, islām involves the open-ended relationship between the attitude and deed of the individual person and the being of God; to submit one's face is to profess God's unity with all of the many ramifications of the term tawḥīd.

When we turn to al-Zamakhsharī's interpretation of 5:3 we find he takes what might be seen as a new direction in his interpretation of islām as dīn. After viewing what he has to say we shall consider whether or not this is really the case.

The more traditional exegetes usually concern themselves with describing the exact day on which 5:3 was revealed, and quote several ḥadīths to illustrate this. Al-Zamakhsharī, however, definitely states that by "al-yawm" is meant not a particular day, but "the present":

> ❬Today❭. He did not mean by it an exact day, but He meant the present time [al-zamān al-ḥādir] and the past and future times related to it and near it, just as one says: Yesterday I was a youth and I am older today, not meaning by yesterday the day which preceded this day, nor by today this [exact] day . . . (I, 604)

We saw earlier that there is a certain timeless quality about islām in al-Zamakhsharī's understanding, as when he called it the eternal religion [al-dīn al-qadīm]. This is supported here; the present, the time in which the particulars of al-dīn are revealed, seems to be unrelated to any specific date in time.

In examining 5:3, which he views in terms of its natural three-fold division, al-Zamakhsharī offers two general interpretations, the first of which is more specifically historical or time-based, the second more general and not necessarily related to a particular period or event. From his understanding of al-yawm, and in the light of his preceding understanding of dīn and islām, it seems obvious that the second explanation is the one that al-Zamakhsharī himself prefers.

Thus he indicates that by saying ⁅I have completed for you your dīn⁆ God may have been saying, "I have protected you against the authority of your enemies and have given you the upper hand [over them] . . ."[134] (I, 605) This is paralleled in the first possible interpretation he gives of the second phrase of the verse, ⁅and I have fulfilled for you My blessing⁆, which is that God has provided for the conquest of Mecca and the entry [of the faithful] into it in safety and triumph". (I, 605) The second understanding he offers of these phrases is that what God was intending was the perfection of that which man is commanded in terms of what is permissible and forbidden, and the apprehension of laws [sharā'i^c] and the rules of analogy [qanūn al-qiyās] and the sources of independent judgment [al-ijtihād]. (The mention of the permissible and the forbidden and the laws is similar to what was found in al-Ṭabarī and Ibn ^{c}Abbās, but with the introduction of qiyās and ijtihād we see not only al-Zamakhsharī's rationalist leanings but the fact that by the fifth century legal elaboration had reached a more developed stage.) And again he says, I have completed for you My blessing, which means "by the perfection of the command of al-dīn and al-sharā'i^c . . . because there is no blessing more complete than the blessing of al-islām." (I, 605) All this is not only in keeping with what al-Zamakhsharī said earlier about islām, but follows in a kind of natural succession. The dīn al-islām is professing God's oneness and recognizing His justice, thereby acting justly oneself by observing the regulations of the sharī^{c}ah. In this verse 5:3, then, comes a more specific understanding of what acting in a just manner -- i.e. according to the commands of God -- involves.

It is when we get to the last phrase of this verse, ⁅and I have chosen for you al-islām as [a] dīn]⁆ that we see an element which appears to be different from the author's earlier emphasis. Heretofore in the passages that we have considered, dīn has been used only in the singular, meaning the dīn acceptable to God and thus the only true dīn. Now, for the first time in our reading since the passage on 61:7 in Ibn ^{c}Abbās (which, as was discussed,

---

[134]Izutsu (God and Man, pp. 221-3) discusses the two aspects of dīn which he sees expressed in the Qur'ān. ". . . the word dīn has two opposite faces, one positive and the other negative. On its positive side, it means 'to subdue, oppress, govern by power', and on its negative side it means 'to submit, yield, to be obedient and submissive'."

may well have come from a later hand) we again find the use of the plural. This verse, says al-Zamakhsharī, means:

> I have selected it [al-islām] for you from among the religions [al-adyān] and made it known to you that it is the chosen religion alone. (I, 605)

One could understand al-Zamakhsharī's interpretation to be that of the various ways in which man might possibly respond to God, He has specified this particular way with all of the regulations discussed immediately above. This would not necessarily imply a comparison between a reified islām and the other organized religious systems. Let us look, however, at the tafsīr of the following verse which deals with eating forbidden food. Here al-Zamakhsharī says:

> The forbidding of these abominations is part of complete dīn [al-dīn al-kāmil] and the fulfilled blessing [al-niᶜmah al-tāmmah] and al-islām which, unlike any of the [other] milal, is characterized by [divine] approval. (I, 605)

Now if we could oppose the dīn al-kāmil and niᶜmah al-tāmmah and al-islām, the response of man which has been outlined and approved by God, to the milal, omitting the "other" from the translations and seeing islām in a different category from the milal or organized religions, we would be able to avoid the conclusion that al-Zamakhsharī intended a reified islām. It seems, however, that this stretches the Arabic too far. What he apparently is saying is that the dīn of islām is one of several milal, albeit the only one with divine approval. This is not to invalidate the uniqueness of islām, nor is it inconsistent with what al-Zamakhsharī has said previously. It does seem to indicate, however, that despite his continuing emphasis on the timeless and non-historical aspects of [the] true dīn, he did of course recognize that it was one among several organized religious systems and was anxious to clarify its absolute difference from those systems.

It will be useful to consider the rest of the passages in which al-Zamakhsharī treats the Qur'ān verses dealing with islām together rather than one by one, as the ideas that they contain are interrelated, even if on occasion seemingly inconsistent. The interpretation of 9:74 ❬and they rejected [Him] after their islām❭ provides little interest as the author gives only a brief paraphrase: "They evidenced their kufr after their evidencing of al-islām." (II, 291) In 6:125 and 39:22, however, we find some interesting commentary on God's luṭf in relation to man's islām. For the first we read:

❛And whomever God wills to guide❜ to be kind to him [an yalṭufa bihi], and He does not wish to be kind to anyone to whom He has not given His grace [luṭf], ❛He expands his breast for al-islām❜ He is kind to him so that he craves al-islām and his soul is calm in it and he loves entering into it. ❛And whoever He wills to lead astray❜ to abandon him [yakhdhulahu] and forsake him [yukhallīhi] and his condition, he is the one who does not have grace [lā luṭf lahu] ❛He makes his breast narrow and tight❜ forbidding him His grace, so that his heart is hardened and he is far from acceptance of the truth and obstructed, and there does not enter into him al-īmān. (II, 64)

And in discussing 39:22 ❛Is he [the one] whose breast God has expanded for al-islām❜ he says:

God knew that he was among the people of grace [those to whom God has given luṭf] and so He was kind to him so that his breast was expanded to al-islām and he desired it and accepted it . . . (IV, 122)

Here al-Zamakhsharī makes it clear that it is only when God bestows His grace or kindness [luṭf] on one that he can be in a position to accept and enter into al-islām. On the positive side, concerning God's guidance toward islām, there is really little to indicate that al-Zamakhsharī does not hold a position of predestination. The basic question, which at least in these passages he leaves unanswered, is how one becomes one of the ahl al-luṭf. That is, if God knew that one was among the people of grace, did he also foreordain that inclusion? As the editor of this edition of the text points out (II, 64), however, it is on the negative side of the passage, concerning those whom God wills to lead astray, that he betrays some Mu^{c}tazilī leanings. Rather than making God the agent of man's undoing, actively leading him into delusion, he draws it as a more neutral situation whereby God abandons and forsakes man rather than specifically misguiding him, as the more orthodox ahl al-sunnah might have indicated. In all of this there is no indication that the islām that man craves, to which his heart is opened and in which he is calm, is other than that islām towards God that he so clearly has defined before as tawḥīd.

Continuing with his tafsīr of 39:22, he says:

And it was said: O Messenger of God, how is the expanding of the breast? He said: When the light enters the heart it is expanded and widened. And it was said: O Messenger of God, what is the sign of that? He said: Inclination toward the house of eternity [al-inābah 'ilá dār al-khulūd] and shunning the house of deception [al-tajāfī ^{c}an dār al-ghurūr] and preparation for death before its arrival. (IV, 122)

Again with the strong moral emphasis of the Mu^{c}tazilah he seems to be saying that that man has received God's favor who evidences that favor by spending his time in the realm [*dār*] of good deeds and shunning the realm of evil. Now if we apply the understanding of justice [*^{c}adl* or *ta^{c}dīl*] from the commentary on 3:19 to these verses dealing with *luṭf*, we can conclude that in one sense God's grace bestowed on man results in a receptivity on the part of man to that grace, involving ethical responsibilities. Because God grants grace or kindness, man therefore responds in kindliness, congeniality in the sense of "being in harmony with". That is, man expresses *^{c}adl* or *tawḥīd* or *islām* because of what God is and does, because of His *luṭf*, and *islām* is both the response to God's command and the reward for that response. Thus in 61:7 we read that

> God calls [one] by the *tongue* of His Prophet to *al-islām* in which is the joy [*sa^{c}adah*] of this world and *the hereafter* [*al-dārayn*]. (IV, 525)

When one's heart is expanded, he experiences personal happiness and joy which is both in this life and for all eternity. This verse suits al-Zamakhsharī's purposes well, for it is clear even in the Qur'ān that the one called to *al-islām* is free to reject it by giving the lie to the word of God. Continuing in the *tafsīr* of 61:8-9 he says that by saying that they wish to extinguish the light of God with their mouths, the Qur'ān means that they desire the negation [*ibṭāl*] of *al-islām* by calling God's word sorcery. One can refuse to heed the call to *islām* if one chooses, but to attempt to invalidate the response of him in whose heart the light of God has come is as vain as the efforts of the one described in al-Zamakhsharī's metaphor who hopes to extinguish the light of the sun by blowing it out with his mouth!

There is more to be examined in al-Zamakhsharī's *tafsīr* of this verse as he continues on to 61:9, but let us break in here to note how the continuing thought of 6:125, 39:22 and 61:7 seems to be in some contradiction to his commentary on 49:14-17. This verse about the Arabs of Bani Asad, to whom God said the term *muslim* rather than *mu'min* should be applied, has been a continual thorn in the flesh of those who would attempt to reconcile it with the verses in which *islām* and *īmān* appear to be equated. Many commentators, particularly al-Ṭabarī (see above), seem to have harmonized what might appear to be a contradiction and have presented a clear and consistent picture. We shall see that the sixth-century Fakhr al-Dīn Rāzī relies on the particulars of semantics to coordinate this verse with his contention that *islām* and *īmān* are one. Al-Zamakhsharī, however, does not seem to give a very satisfactory explanation of how this verse can be reconciled with the rest of his analysis of the meaning of *islām*.

Interestingly enough, he never tries specifically to equate islām and īmān, and it is perhaps for this reason that he does not feel a necessity to attempt to modify the impact of 49:14-17. One senses, however, a certain inconsistency in his explanations. For example, we saw that in the tafsīr of 6:125 he said that God's expanding one's breast to al-islām means "He is kind to him so that he craves al-islām and his soul is peaceful in it [wa-taskunu ilayhi nafsuhu] . . ." (II, 64) In contrast to this he says about 49:14:

> al-īmān: It is al-taṣdīq with trust [al-thiqah] and peacefulness of the soul [ṭuma'nīnatu'l-nafs]. And al-islām: entering into peace [al-silm] and cessation of fighting with the mu'minīn by witnessing the two shahadahs. Do you not see His saying (and al-īmān has not yet entered their hearts)? Know, therefore, that what is by affirmation [al-iqrār] with the tongue without agreement of the heart is islām and what the heart and the tongue agree on is īmān. (IV, 376)

In the one verse it is islām which gives peace to the soul, in the other it is īmān particularly distinguished from islām. It is difficult to see how islām, which he says does not involve agreement of the heart, can be the same as that described as the dedication of one's being and totality to God (I, 346-7 and Q 3:20).

The most plausible explanation seems to be that al-Zamakhsharī, like al-Ṭabarī and others, apparently understood that the islām of the individual could be both external and internal, could in some cases involve inner acceptance of the heart and in other cases meant purely the verbal acknowledgement of the oneness of God and the apostleship of His Prophet. This would not be inconsistent with his unusual and noteworthy use of islām without the article -- ". . . what is by affirmation with the tongue without agreement of the heart is islām [fa-huwa islām]" -- which one might even translate as "an islām", one kind of islām. It is interesting that this most clearly non-reified usage of islām is found in the context of a verse that al-Zamakhsharī obviously sees as referring to the specific requirements by which one joined the community of the followers of the Prophet. For the name of these followers, however, he does not use muslimūn, but rather mu'minūn, and while the "externality" of the individual act of islām is related to the group, this group is never in this section of tafsīr called by the name islām or muslimūn. That this was not always the case for him, however, we have seen before and shall see again as we pick up his commentary on 61:7-9.

We noted in al-Zamakhsharī's tafsīr of 5:3, particularly the last phrase, that despite his stress on the more personal piety-oriented conception of islām, he is certainly aware that in another sense islām was one of several milal and does refer to it in that way. Continuing with 61:9 we find another reference to such a reified understanding when he says:

> ⟨And dīn al-ḥaqq⟩ al-millah al-ḥanifīyah ⟨to make it victorious⟩ to elevate it ⟨over all dīn⟩ over all the adyān differing from it. And upon my life, it was done! And there does not remain one dīn from among the adyān not vanquished and overcome by dīn al-islām. (IV, 526)

Here he clearly changes the Qur'ānic "ᶜalá'l-dīn kullihi" to "ᶜalá jamīᶜi'l-adyān", indicating both that dīn can be applied to more than one kind of response (or: group of responders) and that islām is one among many of these adyān. For a muslim sitting in the center of the Islamic world in the fifth century all other communities must have appeared negligible. The Jews and Christians were a tiny minority and others such as the Manichees, or even the Arabs as a group of pagans, had virtually disappeared. Small wonder that it was easy for him to see the victory of islām as the triumph of the group of muslims over all the rest of these peoples.

Looking at the whole of al-Zamakhsharī's tafsīr as it has been outlined here, however, it is clear that one dīn among many adyān, one specific group of followers, was not the primary reference for his understanding of islām. Running through all of the commentary in which a personal individual submission is intended, and this includes all but the last portions of 5:3 and 61:7-9, is the very strong stress on islām as tawḥīd and doing justly as God does justly. Even in the controversial statements on 49:14 it is clearly stated that islām consists of saying the two testimonies [al-shahādatayn], the first of which is, of course, the confession of God's oneness. In all of this al-Zamakhsharī is true to the basic tenets of the Muᶜtazilah. It will be interesting to see how the conclusions of Fakhr al-Dīn Rāzī, who at many points devoted himself to a refutation of the Muᶜtazilī dogma, compare with those of al-Zamakhsharī. It is to this great thinker as the representative of the theological development of the sixth century that we now turn.

VI

There is a sense in which the sixth Islamic century could be called the "post-" era. The Muᶜtazilah had left their mark but had long since faded from the popularity they had earlier enjoyed. Kalām, or scholastic theology, having come into its own in the lively disputation between the rationalists and the traditionalists, had become arid and tendentious. The incomparable al-Ghazālī had come and gone, leaving his successors to cope with the problem of living out his syntheses of the rational and emotional, the legal, philosophical and theological. The age, beginning with what seems to us to be a long period of semi-darkness, or at least a period about which we know far less than about the preceding centuries, was in need of a bright light. That such a light was indeed present in the figure of Fakhr al-Dīn (Glory of Religion) al-Rāzī[135] is only slowly coming to be appreciated in the West.[136]

Al-Rāzī, whose brilliance has long been recognized by Muslims,[137] combined a rare ability of philosophical speculation with the genuine pietism of a man of faith as well as the convictions of the orthodox generally understood as the school of al-Ashᶜarī. In his article on "The 'Controversies' of Fakhr al-Dīn Rāzī",[138] Paul Kraus describes him as "A subtle dialectician, possessor of a vast philosophical and theological culture as well as of an intellectual courage rare in his time, . . . among the leading representatives of Sunnite Islām." In his writings one finds the consistent understanding and application of philosophical speculation as the basis of theology.

Abū ᶜAbd Allāh Muḥammad b. ᶜUmar b. al-Ḥusayn al-Rāzī was born at Rayy in Ṭabaristān in 543/1149. Known most commonly as Fakhr al-Dīn, he is also called Ibn al-Khaṭīb (son of the

---

[135]Each Islamic century is said to have one outstanding figure considered to be the "mujaddid" or reviver of Islam. As al-Ghazālī carried this title for the fifth century hijrī, so al-Rāzī did for the sixth. Cf. Nasr, "Fakhr al-Dīn Rāzī" in A History of Muslim Philosophy, I, 642-43.

[136]Recent scholars have decried the absence of any treatment of al-Rāzī in the Encyclopaedia of Islam, an omission which has been corrected in the SEI and hopefully will be in the new edition of the former.

[137]"He was one of the outstanding men of his age in law [fiqh], fundamentals of religion [uṣūl], theology [kalām] and wisdom [maᶜrifah]. (Ibn al-Qiftī, Akhbār al-ḥukamā', p. 191) "He was the incomparable one [farīd] of his age and a theologian [mutakallim] of his time . . ." (Ibn al-ᶜImād, Shadharāt, V, 21) "Fakhr al-Dīn was the pearl of the age, a man without a peer; he surpassed all his contemporaries in scholastic theology, metaphysics, and philosophy." (Ibn Khallikān, Wafayāt, II, 652).

[138]IC, XII (1938), 131-153.

preacher);[139] his father Ḍiyā' al-Dīn ᶜUmar, well-known as a preacher in Rayy, was also a Shāfiᶜī jurist and educated his son in that discipline. We know little more of al-Rāzī's early years except that he continued his education as a Shāfiᶜī and Ashᶜarī scholar.[140] Among others, he studied under the well-known Muḥammad al-Baghawī[141] and according to Horten,[142] after the death of his father turned his attentions to the attainment of spiritual perfection. One of the first endeavors about which we are informed is his journey from Rayy to Khwārizm where he attempted to dispute with the Muᶜtazilah still prevalent there.[143]

Al-Rāzī began to gain real stature in Hirāt, where he received the protection of the Ghūr sulṭāns Shihāb al-Dīn and Ghiyāth al-Dīn. However he soon ran into opposition there, too,[144] and so moved on to Ghaznah where he gained the patronage of the Khwārizm-Shāh ᶜAlā' al-Dīn.[145] He gained there a great number of disciples and even enjoyed the honor of being eponym of a madrasah. Ibn al-ᶜImād gives a wonderful description of him walking and discussing, always with some three hundred people directing questions to him about tafsīr, law, theology and other concerns.[146] He preached in both Arabic and Persian and also wrote poetry in both languages, although the latter is not generally recognized as among his more notable achievements.[147]

Al-Rāzī remained at Hirāt until he died in 606/1209, but despite his respected position his life was not free from difficulty. He ran into considerable opposition from the sect of the Karrāmīyah, who accused him of apostasy in following the philosophical directions of Aristotle, Ibn Sīna and al-Fārābī. His

---

[139] Ibn Khallikān, Wafayāt, II, 652.

[140] According to Ibn Khallikān (Ibid., II, 653) he concentrated his studies on scholastic theology and philosophy, learning by heart Imām al-Ḥaramayn's al-Shāmil. (Cf. al-Ṣafadī, al-Wāfī bi'l-wafayāt, p. 249)

[141] al-Ṣafadī, Ibid., p. 248.

[142] Die philosophischen Ansichten von Rāzi und Tusi, p. i.

[143] Kraus, "Controversies", p. 132.

[144] Ibn Khallikān, Wafayāt, II, 653.

[145] Nasr, "Fakhr al-Dīn Rāzī, p. 642; Kraus, "Controversies", p. 132.

[146] Ibn al-ᶜImād, Shadharāt, V, 21. (Cf. al-Safadī, al-Wāfī, p. 248.) Ibn al-ᶜImād describes Fakhr al-Dīn as being of medium height with a plump body, a great long beard and a loud voice, carrying himself with dignity and decorum.

[147] al-Ṣafadī, al-Wāfī, p. 249.

attacks on that sect were equally harsh.[148] When he died he was buried in his house for fear that his enemies would mutilate his dead body. It is even rumored that his death was through poisoning by the Karrāmīyah.[149]

The variety and extent of Fakhr al-Dīn Rāzī's interests and endeavors has been adequately attested to by Sayyid Ḥusayn Nasr[150] in his consideration of al-Rāzī's thought under the categories of theology, philosophy, science, Qur'ān commentary, law, dialectic, rhetoric and poetry, and mysticism. In a brief introduction such as this one can scarcely do more than acknowledge his proficiency in these areas and point to the variety of influences apparently at play in the development of his thought.

We know that al-Rāzī was well-versed in the thought world of Greek philosophy -- his commentary on Ibn Sīna is famous -- but was not bound by it.[151] Exercising his own capacity for reason he accepted certain elements of it and rejected others. The same is true of his occupation with theology. Trained in the school of al-Ash^c^arī he remained of that persuasion, but felt free to contradict those elements with which he could not agree.[152] Like al-Ghazālī he was very seriously concerned with reconciling philosophy with theology, but throughout his life he continued to be far more dedicated to the former than did his predecessor. While al-Ghazālī became increasingly involved in a mystical understanding of the divine, al-Rāzī devoted his attentions in the main to articulating the relationship between the Qur'ānic worldview and the primary tenets of contemporary philosophical understanding.[153]

Despite this continuing devotion to the philosophical approach, however, al-Rāzī insofar as it was necessary to choose

---

[148] Kraus, "Controversies", p. 132; al-Ṣafadī, al-Wāfī, p. 249.

[149] Ibn al-Qiftī, Akhbār al-ḥukamā', pp. 190-91.

[150] Nasr, "Fakhr al-Dīn Rāzī", pp. 642-56.

[151] Nasr (Ibid., p. 649) summarizes al-Rāzī's contribution by saying: ". . . his greatest philosophical importance lies in the criticisms and doubts cast upon the principles of Peripatetic philosophy, which not only left an indelible mark upon that school but opened the horizon for the other modes of knowledge like ishrāqi philosophy and gnosis, which were more intimately bound with the spirit of Islam."

[152] Kraus ("Controversies", p. 132) gives the example of al-Rāzī's rejection of atomism in his earlier writings, noting that later in Mafātīḥ al-ghayb he changed his mind and accepted it.

[153] Horten (Ansichten, p. iii) feels that al-Rāzī, along with his student Naṣīr al-Dīn Ṭūsī, signified an even greater influence of Greece on Islam than did al-Ghazālī.

sides in the controversy between Sunnī orthodoxy and rationalist philosophy, aligned himself with the former. Kalām, which had begun as a rationalist response to the dominant traditionalism, had developed by al-Rāzī's time into a philosophical theology which found its greatest spokesman in Fakhr al-Dīn. His theological treatise Kitāb al-muḥaṣṣal combines the basic principles of Ashᶜarīyah theology with a rare depth of philosophical understanding. It exerted a great influence on the seventh/thirteenth century and became a primary reference work on kalām.

The work with which we are here primarily concerned is al-Rāzī's enormous commentary on the Qur'ān, Mafātīḥ al-ghayb.[154] Georges Anawati summarizes its importance when he says that it contains ". . . pour la première fois dans l'Islam, un traitement systématique et philosophique des données coraniques, où sont groupés, sous formes de Quaestiones (masā'il), les différents points que soulève l'examen du texte sacré."[155] The Mafātīḥ, which is only one of a number of al-Rāzī's works on the Qur'ān, though by far the largest and most important, is considered by many to be the most comprehensive and inclusive commentary on this holy book ever composed. Here again he combines his interests in the philosophical and theological by discussing the basic problems of rationalistic philosophy at the same time that he expounds the primary elements of God's revelation.

Although it is an oversimplification to claim that the main thesis of al-Rāzī's commentary is to refute certain doctrines of the Muᶜtazilah, it is unquestionably true that he did devote himself to this task whenever possible in his interpretations. The frequency and length of these refutations have caused some to speculate, suspicious as with the lady who protested too much, that perhaps al-Rāzī was influenced more than he cared to admit by the Muᶜtazilī school of thought. Certainly it continued to be wide-spread in the area in which al-Rāzī was educated and in his Ashᶜarī upbringing he came constantly into contact with it.[156]

---

[154] Mafātīḥ al-ghayb al-mushtahar bi'l-tafsīr al-kabīr. Istanbul: al-Maṭbaᶜah al-ᶜĀmirah, 1307 [1891], 8 voll.

[155] "Un traité des noms divins de Fakhr al-Dīn al-Rāzī", p. 36. Daud Rahbar ("Reflections on the tradition of Qur'anic exegesis" in MW, LII [1962], 303) calls it "an ocean of various waters, having as ingredients reports of later sectarian developments."

[156] Goldziher examines this problem in his very interesting essay, "Aus der theologie des Fachr al-dīn al-Rāzī" in Isl., III (1912), 213-247.

Gardet[157] suggests that both in the Muḥaṣṣal and the Mafātīḥ al-Rāzī deals primarily with the response to the theses of the Muᶜtazilah in which they insist on man's free will, based on the proposition that God would not desire infidelity on the part of man. Al-Rāzī counters repeatedly in his commentary with the insistence that God can command that which he does not desire, and prohibit that which he does desire. We shall see several examples of this response in our consideration of specific passages in the Mafātīḥ. The commentary is replete with an insistence on determinism; God is the supreme will and it is by His command that everything takes place. While the Muᶜtazilah would say that this unfairly puts the blame on God for the sinfulness of man, al-Rāzī insists that as God is the supreme ruler, what He does is not to be held to man's judgment. In this as in other areas, al-Rāzī expresses the ijmāᶜ of his time and gives us along with his philosophical interpretations a good understanding of orthodox interpretation in the fifth-sixth centuries.

As was mentioned above in the quotation from Anawati, al-Rāzī has arranged his commentary in the form of a very extensive and detailed outline, in which he replies to questions posed by developing a series of points and sub-points. It is perhaps more difficult to select isolated verses and sections to consider (to dip down into the middle as it were) from this work than from any other of the commentaries considered in this essay. An entire thesis devoted to the Mafātīḥ could only begin to penetrate its depth; in this endeavor I shall attempt to summarize passages relevant to our theme and express the hope that not too great a disservice is done to the continuity of his arguments by presenting only a small portion of them. It goes without saying that a translation of all eight of the massive volumes of this commentary, enormous task that it would be, would be an inestimable service to Western study of the Qur'ān and Muslim theology.

Any attempt to categorize al-Rāzī as a thinker and writer is doomed to frustration. He was at once a philosopher and an opponent of rationalistic Greek philosophy, a man of deep faith and an ardent exponent of the intellectual processes. Overshadowed in the eyes of most Westerners by his famous predecessor al-Ghazālī, he is still coming to be recognized as one of the most deeply pious as well as intellectually creative of Muslim thinkers. It is reported that the mystic Muḥyi'l-Dīn Ibn ᶜArabī once sent a letter to Fakhr al-Dīn in which he pointed

---

[157] Dieu, p. 115.

out the futility of seeking after formal knowledge.[158] It may well be that al-Rāzī took this advice to heart and realized its merit, for we are told that at the end of his life he several times expressed this thought:

> If only I had not occupied myself with ᶜilm al-kalām . . . . . I have searched the paths of theology [al-ṭuruq al-kalāmiyah] and the ways of philosophy [al-minhāj al-falsafīyah] (sic) and I have not found that which quenches the ardent desire or heals the sick. I see now that the best [aṣaḥḥ] of ways is the way of reading the Qur'ān in al-tanzīh [deanthropomorphism].[159]

* * *

As has generally proved to be the case with the foregoing commentators, al-Rāzī gives his most illuminating definition of islām in the exegesis of the first verse (according to the ordering of the Qur'ān) in which islām is mentioned, 3:19 ❴Truly al-dīn with God is al-islām❵. Here we are immediately struck by the fact that al-Rāzī strongly emphasizes the verbal or active nature of submission.

He begins his discussion of 3:19 in his usual style by saying that there are several issues to be considered. The first two concern the correct reading of the phrase and the grammatical implications of saying "inna" or "anna". (Unlike al-Kasā'ī, whose position he discusses in some detail, al-Rāzī chooses the reading "inna".) It is in consideration of the third issue that we come to the first real understanding of al-Rāzī's interpretation of islām. He discusses the term linguistically, and again sees three ways in which it can be viewed:

---

[158] Goldziher, Vorlesungen, p. 347.

[159] Ibn al-ᶜImād, Shadharāt, V, 21-22. See Makdisi, Ashᶜarī and the Ashᶜarites, who sees the dual aspect of al-Rāzī's thought as an extension of the whole question of whether al-Ashᶜarī, as well as his followers, was a traditionalist, a rationalist, or both. "Bāqillānī, Juwainī, Shahrastānī and Rāzī, all had death-bed repentence for having used kalām, if we are to believe their biographers . . . . Whatever be the facts concerning the works attributed to Ashᶜarī, the image of Ashᶜarī as presented by the Ashᶜarite propagandists is one which admits of opposites. So also that of the great Ashᶜarites just mentioned. On the one hand they are presented as partisans of metaphorical interpretation (ta'wīl); and on the other, as partisans of the way of the Ancestors (Salaf), namely, the acknowledgment of all the scriptural and traditional data concerning God's attributes without attempting to interpret them for fear of falling into anthropomorphism, or of explaining them completely away and thus denuding God of His attributes, or of using tanzīh which is an attenuation of the doctrine of denudation. These two views are diametrically opposed." (II, 31-32).

> The first is that it is an expression for entering into al-islām, i.e. into submission [al-inqiyād] and following [al-mutāba^c^ah] . . . . The second is that whoever "aslama", i.e. enters into al-silm, is like their saying he entered into a state of sunshine or drought. And the basic meaning of al-silm is al-salāmah [wholeness, peace, security]. And the third is that al-Anbarī said the meaning of al-muslim is al-mukhlis [the one sincerely devoted] to God in his servanthood [^c^ibādah] from their saying sallama meaning to someone, i.e. entrust it to him. And the meaning of al-islām is making sincere (or pure) to God one's dīn and one's belief [ikhlāṣu'l-dīn wa'l-^c^aqīdah li'llāh]. (II, 628)

This, he says, is what can be understood by the tafsīr of islām linguistically. The noun may indicate, first, becoming muslim (the act of becoming muslim, or a muslim), secondly, in its more original sense, it signifies the act of becoming peaceful or secure; his third meaning seems to designate that which it is necessary to do once one has accepted the state of being muslim. The three possibilities of interpretation, islām as submitting, as entering into wholeness, and as expressing sincerity of devotion, all imply an active approach on the part of the individual, a verbal understanding of the maṣdar islām. If this is the linguistic understanding of the term, al-Rāzī also views it next in its religious sense [fī ^c^urf al-shar^c^]. Here we move into the area of the relationship of islām and īmān, and find some very interesting statements concerning their connection.

Al-Rāzī's position is made immediately clear when he begins his discussion by the unequivocal assertion that islām IS īmān [fa'l-islām huwa'l-īmān]. He offers two pieces of evidence for this. The first is the verse under consideration. If the dīn acceptable to God is islām, then īmān must be islām. For if īmān were other than islām, by definition it would be necessary that it not be a dīn acceptable to God, and there is no doubt that such an idea is false. (II, 628) In like manner he cites a portion of 3:83 ❴If anyone seeks other than al-islām as [a] dīn, it will not be accepted from him❵, saying again that if al-īmān were other than al-islām it would necessitate al-īmān's not being a dīn acceptable to God. (II, 628)

Al-Rāzī then gives us a preview of how he will deal with 49:14, a verse that would seem to contradict his above interpretation; he naturally develops his arguments much more fully when he comes to that verse in his tafsīr. Here he says that if someone quoted 49:14 as a clear indication that islām is different from īmān, he (al-Rāzī) would say that as has already been explained, islām is linguistically an expression of submission [inqiyād]. Then he says that this submission as it applies to the munāfiqūn is external submission done out of fear of the sword. But, he maintains, īmān can also be external as was found in God's saying (2:221) "Do not wed idolatresses until they have faith." This īmān, or faith, really means verbal affirmation [iqrār]. Thus both īmān and islām can sometimes be external [fī'l-ẓāhir] and sometimes internal or real [fī'l-ḥaqīqah]. "And as for the munāfiq," says al-Rāzī, "external islām [al-islām al-ẓāhir] obtains in his case and internal islām [al-islām al-bāṭin] does not obtain because his inner being is not submissive [munqād] to the service of God." (II, 628) He goes on to elaborate by saying that the meaning of the verse (49:14) is: "You have not submitted at heart and internally; say, rather, 'we have submitted externally'." The addition of the almost standard "wa-Allāhu aʿlam [God knows best]" perhaps indicates that he recognizes that his opinion is but an opinion, that his interpretation is to some degree tentative.

Here, then, we see al-Rāzī making two specific points which will be repeated in other areas of his tafsīr. One is that islām is īmān (we shall find later that he makes a subtle distinction between them although does not disavow this statement) and the other is that both islām and īmān on some occasions are external and on others are internal.

The afore-mentioned emphasis in al-Rāzī's tafsīr on the active or verbal element of islām is again brought out when in discussing 3:20 ❴And if they argue with you, say: I have surrendered my face to God, likewise whoever follows me❵ he refers to the 3:19 verse that al-dīn with God is al-islām and no other:

> Then He said "and if they argue with you", meaning if they dispute with you concerning your saying that religion with God is al-islām, then say the proof of it is "that I submit my face to God", and that is because what is intended by [the term] al-dīn is nothing other than the discharging of requirements of divinity and servanthood [al-wafā' bi-lawāzimi'l-rubūbīyah wa'l-ʿubūdīyah]. And when I submit my face to God I serve none other than Him and I do not anticipate good except from Him and I have no fear except of His overwhelmingness and His overpowering strength and I do not associate with Him anything other than Him. And if this be the completion of the fulfilling of the requirements of divinity and servanthood, then it is true that the perfect dīn is al-islām. (II, 630)

It is often too easy to get caught up in al-Rāzī's elaborate systemization of argument and tend to see him exclusively as a theoretician and master of the forensic. In the above passage we see Fakhr al-Dīn the man of faith, illustrating while arguing his point his concept of man's total surrender to the might and authority of God. Along with the emphasis on the acceptable dīn, islām, as performance of the specific requirements, he injects this wonderfully personal element of what those demands really are: not formal legalism but a vivid sense of awe and majesty, and of what such submission really means to the individual. Here there is no question but that he is describing islām in its deepest, most subjective and internal sense.

In a later portion of his discussion of this same verse (II, 631), al-Rāzī again brings out this subjective element when he talks about what is meant by submitting the face. Primarily, he says, it involves dedicating one's activity to God. "And the meaning is, all of what proceeds from me in the way of works." (Note again the activist element.) The turning of the face is accomplished through worship of God and submission [al-inqiyād] to His divinity and rule. Finally, he says, "'I submit my face to God' equals 'I submit my soul [nafs] to God' and there is not in worship any station higher than the islām of the nafs to God." We saw earlier that for al-Rāzī islām, as well as īmān, can be external or internal. Here is another poignant expression of the latter and a clear indication that for Fakhr al-Dīn Rāzī this islām of the soul takes the highest priority.

In his tafsīr of 3:19 he has given us a considerable amount of material and in general has outlined his position on the nature of islām. The explication of the succeeding verses tends to give a less complete picture and more of an elaboration of the specific points brought out in this initial discussion. Let us turn now to his comments on 3:85 ❴If anyone seeks other than al-islām as [a] dīn it will not be accepted from him . . . ❵

We noted above that for al-Rāzī the maṣdar islām is certainly seen in its verbal sense. In this next discussion he again brings out the idea of activity. Having spent a good deal of time in discussing what is involved in being muslimūn (the end of 3:84 says "and we are submitters unto Him"), he says that God followed that statement with the explanation that

> . . . al-dīn is nothing but al-islām and that all dīn other than al-islām is unacceptable to God because the acceptance is of action [al-qabūl li'l-ᶜamal] -- that God approves of that action and is pleased with its doer and rewards him for it. (II, 735-36)

Again we find that al-Rāzī stresses the individual and particularly activist interpretation. Thus far he has used the word ᶜamal for this action, though we will see later that he also designates fiᶜl as the expression of islām.

Continuing with his tafsīr of 3:85 we see that after briefly describing the nature of the loss in the hereafter experienced by the one who chooses other than islām as dīn, al-Rāzī goes back to a discussion of the relationship of islām and īmān. "And know that the obvious meaning of this verse points to the fact that al-īmān is al-islām." (II, 736) Giving the same argument as he expressed earlier, he says that if īmān were other than islām it would necessitate īmān's being unacceptable by the terms of the verse under consideration. Again he refers to 49:14, but now we are given a hint of how īmān and islām may differ yet be the same.

> Al-īmān is al-islām . . . except that the apparent meaning [ẓāhir] of His saying "The Arabs say: We have faith. Say: You do not have faith, but rather say 'We submit'" necessitates that al-islām be different from al-īmān. And the way of reconciliation between the two is that the first āyah [3:85] relates to religious usage and the second [49:14] relates to linguistic denotation. (II, 736)

We shall find this elucidated more fully in al-Rāzī's discussion of 49:14 per se.

As we have seen to be the case for several of the foregoing writers of tafsīr, particularly al-Ṭabarī, in discussing 5:3 ❬Today I have completed for you your dīn and fulfilled to you my blessing, and have chosen for you al-islām as [a] dīn❭ al-Rāzī takes the opportunity to introduce a wide variety of possible interpretations. The phrase ❬completed . . . your dīn❭ particularly lends itself to several interpretations. Among those mentioned in this tafsīr (III, 527-28) (to some of which he himself objects) are the following: (a) the elimination of fear and demonstration to them of (His) power over their enemies, (b) perfection of the command to know what is permissible and what is forbidden, and (c) the contention that dīn is never imperfect although it can be incomplete, meaning that the laws of God are sufficient for the individual ages in which they are extant but may be supplemented for another age. "As for the final time of sending, God revealed a perfect sharīᶜah and regulated its continuation to the day of resurrection. The sharᶜ is always perfect, except that the first perfection is up to a particular time and the second perfection is up to the day of resurrection." (III, 528)[160] Al-Rāzī also mentions the tradition that the Messenger of God did not live over eighty-one days after the revelation of this verse and that ᶜUmar wept for fear of the

---

[160] See W. C. Smith, "The concept of shariᶜa among some mutakallimun", in which he reports preliminary findings that sharīᶜah is used quite infrequently in classical Muslim writing, and that its usage is much more particularized than is that of sharᶜ, which is generally viewed as absolute.

extinction of his dīn.[161]

It is clear in reading these comments, however, that while they are of interest they are not his main concern. Already in earlier parts of his tafsīr having devoted himself to an understanding of dīn and islām, he now uses this verse as occasion to press the insistence that the dīn (and the islām) are by God's initiative rather than man's.

> This āyah points to the fact that al-dīn does not occur except by the creation of God and His production of it. And the proof of it is that He attributes the perfection of al-dīn to Himself [in this āyah] . . . . The perfecting of dīn would not be from Him were it not that the emergence of it is also from Him. And know that whether we say [that the term] al-dīn is an expression for activity [al-ᶜamal] or we say that it is an expression for knowledge [al-maᶜrifah] or we say that it is an expression for the concurrence of conviction and verbal confession and activity [majmūᶜ al-iᶜtiqād wa'l-iqrār wa'l-ᶜamal] the conclusion is evident. (III, 529)

The conclusion, of course, is that God alone is the creator of dīn in men's hearts. Here is another indication that for al-Rāzī dīn, like islām, is an inner existential orientation or activity. Never missing a chance to jibe the Muᶜtazilah, al-Rāzī says that they relate this to the perfecting of the expounding of dīn and the disclosing of (its) particulars, and that there is no doubt that what they mention is a departure from the truth. Then after saying that the completing of God's favor means the completion of the command (or matter) of al-dīn and the sharīᶜah, he again equates the dīn with al-islām by stressing that "there is no favor more complete than the favor of al-islām." (II, 529) Then comes these very interesting words: "And know that this āyah also points to the fact that the creator of al-īmān is God. And that is because we said al-dīn which is al-islām is a favor and every favor is a handiwork [fann] of God." Two things are revealed here. First we see again the implication that islām is īmān, and secondly the pointedly anti-Muᶜtazilī assertion that man's individual faith is not of his own doing but is God's creation. Taking all of Fakhr al-Dīn's comments in summary, then, we can say that for him dīn = islām = īmān = man's activity by the creation of God. We shall see how this formula stands up in the light of his continued commentary.

The two elements predominant in the exegesis of 5:3 are also immediately apparent in al-Rāzī's treatment of 6:125 ❴And whomever God wishes to guide He opens his breast for al-islām . . .❵ That is, islām is īmān, and God is responsible for its creation.

---

[161] See above, p. 69.

It is clear that for him these two terms are interchangeable, for in interpreting a verse dealing with islām he spends several pages discussing īmān with scarcely any specific mention of the former maṣdar. Here is a sample of what al-Rāzī has to say about this verse:

> The explanation of it is that the servant [^{c}abd] is capable of al-īmān and is capable of al-kufr, in such a way that his capability in regard to these matters is the same. The emergence of faith in a man, rather that kufr, is impossible except when there occurs in the heart an impulse towards it . . . . And that call has no meaning other than his knowing [^{c}ilmihi] or his being convinced [i^{c}tiqādihi] or his thinking [ẓannihi] that that is the deed [fi^{c}l] which includes greater benefit and preponderant advantage. (IV, 208)

Again we find that al-Rāzī specifically designates īmān (or islām) as an action, a deed (here he uses fi^{c}l where earlier he used ^{c}amal). We find a kind of modification of the theory of acquisition [kasb] propounded by al-Ash^{c}arī in al-Rāzī's contention that the call is less meaningful if the recipient is not convinced of the value of the deed. While far from the traditional Mu^{c}tazilī position, he still seems to want to leave room for a measure of individual freedom. Nevertheless that the origin is always with God he reiterates again and again, as is stated so clearly in the following:

> We have explained with proof that the occurrence of these motivations must inevitably be from God Most High, and that the whole of the capability to act along with the motivation necessitates the action. If this is established, we say īmān cannot possibly proceed from a creature unless God creates in his heart conviction that īmān has more benefit [than the opposite] and that it serves more [his] best interests. If this conviction occurs in the heart, the heart is widened [toward īmān] and there occurs in the soul [nafs] a strong desire for its acquisition [taḥṣīl]. And this is the opening of the breast to īmān. But if the conviction occurs in the heart that faith [īmān] in Muḥammad, for example, is the cause of a great corruption [mafsadah] in spiritual and world affairs [fī'l-dīn wa'l-dunyah] and necessitates many harmful things, then the attainment of this conviction results in a great repulsion against faith in Muḥammad. And this is what is meant by God's making his breast tight and narrow. So the interpretation of the verse is that in whomever God wills īmān He strengthens the motivations toward īmān, and in whomever God wills kufr He strengthens the factors of aversion away from īmān and strengthens the motivations toward kufr. (IV, 208-9)

The remainder of the tafsīr of this verse continues in a defense of the power and ultimate justice of God, expressing the conviction that although God leads to and away from islām whomever He wills, He is benevolent and not arbitrary. In particular he uses this occasion to elaborate and renounce in great detail the theories of the Mu^{c}tazilah. For our purposes al-Rāzī has already made his point, and that is that islām is īmān, that it is personal and internal, and that it originates with God.

It has generally proved to be the case that the least fruitful of these eight verses, at least in terms of our investigation, is 9:74 ﴿They swear by God that they said nothing, yet they said the word of kufr and rejected [Him] after their islām﴾. Like most of the other writers, al-Rāzī devotes himself mainly to a discussion of the conditions of descent of the verse and offers no interpretation to amplify what is already given in the āyah about islām. (The maṣdar as used in the verse, as a parallel to kafara [and kufr], does display an obvious verbal quality.) Rather than examining this in greater detail, let us turn to his understanding of 39:22 ﴿Is he [the one] whose breast God has expanded for al-islām so that he follows a light from his Lord?﴾ which, we shall discover, provides a kind of elaboration of the comments on 6:125.

Perhaps the first thing to be noted is that aside from occasionally quoting the verse in question, and also 6:125, al-Rāzī never uses the term islām. He makes it clear that the general point has already been expressed earlier, and attempts to elucidate further how it can be that the breasts of some are expanded. Here we see al-Rāzī the philosopher saying that

> God created the essential natures [jawāhir] of the souls differing in kind, in such a way that some of them are good, brilliant, noble, inclining toward the divine, greatly desiring to be connected with spiritual things and some of them are depraved, impure, base, inclined toward corporeality. . . And we say the intention of His opening of the breasts is that strong readiness [al-isti^c-dād al-shadīd] existent in the natural disposition of the soul [fiṭrat al-nafs]. And when that strong readiness occurs it is sufficient for the emergence of this condition out of potentiality [al-quwwah] to actuality [al-fi^cl] by the nearness of the cause, like the sulphur which burns at the closeness of the fire. (VII, 250-51)

This clear stance on predestination, i.e. God's absolute determination of who shall share in al-islām and who shall be among the kāfirūn, is particularly interesting in the light of al-Zamakhsharī's comments on God's luṭf.[162] There it was by God's active guidance that one's breast is expanded to al-islām, but his going astray is because God forsakes rather than actively misleads him. For al-Rāzī the responsibility is completely on God in both instances. He continues by saying that the light that enters the heart is an expression for guidance [al-hidāyah] and knowledge [al-ma^crifah], this light occurring only after the

---

[162] See above, pp. 97-9.

breast is expanded. When this happens it is because of the potentiality of the soul; the ability to take advantage of this does not at all take place through the hearing of proofs, which indeed may even serve to increase hardness and antipathy.

We have made note of the fact several times that al-Rāzī has referred to 49:14 in his tafsīr of earlier verses. Thus far we know that both islām and īmān can be external or internal, and that while islām is īmān, nevertheless they have a certain point of differentiation. This subtle distinction he finally elucidates in some detail in the interpretation of 49:14 itself:

> We say that between the general [al-ᶜāmm] and the specific [al-khāṣṣ] there is a difference. For īmān does not occur except in the heart and it may occur on the tongue. And islām is more general. However the general is in the image of the specific, amalgamated with the specific and cannot be another matter apart from it. An example of this: The animal is more general than man, however the animal is in the image of man. It is not a matter that can be separated from man and it is not possible that the animal should be an animal and not be a human being. Therefore the general and the specific are different in generality, one in existence. Likewise are the mu'min and the muslim. (VII, 608-9)

Thus we can assume that likewise are īmān and islām. One of the most interesting sentences here is that which says that īmān does not occur except in the heart, though it may occur on the tongue. Here we find a qualification to the earlier understanding that īmān, like islām, can be both internal or external. Apparently what al-Rāzī really means is that while it can be both, it cannot be external without at the same time being internal. (This is particularly noteworthy in the light of his comments on 2:211 above.) Since he does not make this specific statement about islām, and taking it in the context of the above distinction between the general and the specific, it seems that islām can be external without being internal, thus justifying the intent of this 49:14 verse.

This seems to be substantiated in reading al-Rāzī's comments of the following passage 49:17 ❴Say: Do not deem your islām a favor . . .❵. The one having īmān, he says, frees his soul from the blemish of ignorance [al-jahl] and adorns it with truth and sincerity. (VII, 610) However those mentioned in the verse who deem their islām a favor "do not seek through their islām nearness to God and do not seek the nobility of their souls." (VII, 610) Here al-Rāzī seems clearly to distinguish between īmān as internal and islām as external. However in the succeeding sentences he apparently expresses the conviction that the islām of these Arabs in the verse, not sufficient to prove sincerity, may not even be islām. "He said, Say: Do not deem your islām a favor, that is, what you have as [an] islām." (VII, 610) He clarifies that God has not said, You have surrendered (or: You have become muslim), but rather He has said, Say: We have surrendered (or: We have become muslim) -- since the former would have confirmed their islām [taṣdīqan lahum fī al-islam]. God, al-Rāzī seems to be saying, may have ordered them to say that they had islām, but this does not mean they actually had it. Then he goes on to say that if one felt that the islām that is found in both speech and activity is sufficient to indicate sincerity, even when conviction and knowledge are not found, he would not be correct, since islām is submission. These Arabs lacked sincerity because they came to the Prophet out of necessity, seeking alms and protection.

We find al-Rāzī, then, apparently coming to a somewhat different conclusion about this 49:14-17 passage from others of the commentators. While most have seemed to feel that islām can be of two kinds (expressed particularly in al-Ṭabarī), al-Rāzī is unwilling really to say this. Although he admits a difference between islām and īmān in generality, he does insist that they are one in existence. He also says that īmān can be internal and external, but if it is external it must also (always) be internal, for it is always of the heart. It appears, then, that al-Rāzī really does mean to say that the islām predicated of those who are not sincere is not for him true islām, or even islām at all.

One verse dealing with islām remains to be examined, 61:7 ❴And who does greater wrong than he who invents a lie against God when he is called to al-islām?❵. His comments are brief, indicating that the meaning is, "They certainly knew that what they had received, of favor and bounty, they had received only from God Most High, and then they rejected it." (VIII, 197) Here the original meaning of kafara as ingratitude is nicely expressed, the implication again being a verbal islām parallel to the verbal act of rejection.

More interesting than this commentary, however, is that accompanying the following verse, 61:8 ❴They wish to extinguish the light of God with their mouths❵. Here al-Rāzī reveals some surprising tendencies in his attempt to define what is meant by this light. First he says that they are trying to put out the light, like men who try to put out the light of the sun by blowing at it, by saying about the Qur'ān that it is sorcery. If the Qur'ān were sorcery, then islām, the human response to what the Qur'ān,presents, would be invalidated.

Then for the first time in the sections of Mafātīḥ al-ghayb examined here (with the possible exception to the reference to knowledge in 6:125) we find al-Rāzī exhibiting a kind of mystical tendency. He says that

> The light of God is always radiant, ascending from a point of departure with no possibility of extinction at all. And it [this point] is the divine presence [al-hadarah al-qudsiᶜah]. The light is analogous to knowledge [ᶜilm] and darkness is analogous to ignorance [al-jahl]. Or, the light is al-īmān taking them out of darkness to the light. Or, al-islām is leading the intelligent ones to good things [al-khayrāt] by their choosing of that which is commendable. And that is the light . . . . And the Book is the light, or the Book is evidence of its being miraculous, or the evidence is the light. And the Book is like that. Or, it is said about the Messenger that he is the light or else he would not have been described by the adjective of his being a mercy to all the worlds. For the mercy lies in the making manifest of what is [has been] among the secrets; and that is by light. Or we may say that he is the light because through his instrumentality mankind is guided. Or, he is the light because of his being [the one who] makes clear to men what has been sent down to them -- and the one who makes clear is the light. (VIII, 198)

In this passage al-Rāzī places particular emphasis on the ability to see and comprehend. The various equations of nūr with islām, īmān, dīn and even the Prophet himself (whom he says is "radiant in all regions of the world") illustrate that the light is that by which one sees that what is divine, is divine. (He precludes the equation of various of these manifestations to each other [e.g. saying that because both islām and Muḥammad are the light, they are therefore equivalent] by saying later [VIII, 199] that "al-nūr is more general than al-dīn and al-rasūl".) Underlying all of this description is the basic element of God's guidance; the ability to see the light in any of its manifestations is a divine gift.

Alone of all the commentators considered in this essay, al-Rāzī presents no instance in which al-islām might have even a possible group reference. Concerned above all with the initiative of God in determining man's response, islām, he is devoted to an appreciation of those factors in his environment, chiefly or wholly divine, that enable him to make this response. We have seen in previous works that the external understanding of islām, both in its more reified usage and as the outward act of submission for the purpose of receiving alms or ceasing warfare, is seen in contrast to the internal response which is equated with īmān. For al-Rāzī it is only this latter understanding that seems to have validity, and he will not identify as [an] *islām* anything other than the spiritual vision and heartfelt confirmation of God's revelation.

THREE: THE SOLIDIFICATION OF TRADITIONALISM

The first six centuries of Qur'ānic exegesis, while dominated to a great degree by the kind of commentary exemplified by Ibn ᶜAbbās, al-Ṭabarī and al-Ṭūsī,[1] nonetheless still exhibited major variations on the theme of traditionalism. Thus the Muᶜtazilī tafsīr of al-Zamakhsharī remains one of the most popular and widely-read of the shorter works of exegesis, and the great commentary of al-Rāzī, while generally considered formidable by mere virtue of its size, is certainly accepted as one of the most important works ever written in the history of Islamic theology and philosophy. Both of these commentaries, as we have seen, are rich in the personal opinions, speculations and conclusions of their writers.

With the seventh century the situation becomes markedly different. Reading, as we are doing in the course of this study, representative material from fourteen centuries of exegesis one becomes aware of a kind of natural division between the writings that have been chosen as illustrative of the sixth and those of the seventh centuries, specifically those of al-Rāzī and al-Bayḍāwī. In the former it is still very clear that we are reading the thought and interpretation of al-Rāzī himself, and with it the variety of interpretation expressed by the ijmāᶜ of the community as al-Rāzī understood it. With al-Bayḍāwī we find much more summary of preceding exegesis as well as repetition of major passages from the works of earlier centuries than we have seen before.[2]

Since we are dealing in this essay with material representing both the Ahl al-Sunnah and the Shīᶜah, it is difficult to generalize as to what processes of solidification among the Muslim community as a whole led to this change in tafsīr.

---

[1]We have seen, of course, that the traditionalist approach of these writers, their inclination to consider the Qur'ān text primarily in terms of the dominant ijmāᶜ of the community expressed in ḥadīths and sayings, did not preclude a considerable amount of personal opinion and conclusion.

[2]There is a very definite sense in which al-Ṭūsī was more representative of the later centuries than the earlier ones in his tendency to quote long passages from al-Tabarī and others. It might well be that a more exacting and specific study of Shīᶜī tafsīr could illustrate that the kind of transition we are pointing to in al-Bayḍāwī took place somewhat earlier in the Shīᶜī community as such.

Obviously the period of ijtihād or individual interpretation had ended, and it is not surprising that the reflection of this in Qur'ān commentary resulted in an era, lasting some seven centuries, in which repetition was considered more valid than initiative. Harris Birkeland puts the case succinctly when he says that "In reality every earnest discussion had finished when al-Baiḍāwī wrote his commentary."[3] With the hope that the investigation will not prove to be as unrewarding as that forewarning would imply, let us consider the tafsīr of the seventh through the thirteenth centuries in the attempt to determine what effect this dwindling of individual interpretation had on the historical understanding of the term islām.

VII

It is interesting to consider why, in the light of the situation just described, ᶜAbd Allāh bin ᶜUmar al-Bayḍāwī is probably the best-known of all the Qur'ān commentators in the West and indeed the most widely read in the Muslim world. Born in Bayẓá near Shīrāz, he was the son of the chief judge of Fārs and himself became qāḍī first in Shīrāz,[4] then at Tabrīz. There he died sometime between 685 and 710.[5] He was well versed in fiqh and tafsīr and grammar, a good theoretician and a pious Shāfiᶜī.[6] Taking his first law studies at Āmūl he continued to Baghdād where he worked under a variety of celebrated Shāfiᶜī doctors. He produced a variety of writings, ranging from jurisprudence,[7] theology,[8] metaphysics, logic and grammar to a history of the

---

[3]"The Lord guideth" in Skifter (1956), pt. 2, p. 11.

[4]Ḥājjī Khalīfah (Kashf al-ẓunūn, I, 469-70) relates a delightful story in which al-Bayḍāwī's remarkable performance in feats of memory and problem analysis at a majlis session in Tabrīz secured for him the position of qāḍī there.

[5]The sources are divided and give a variety of possibilities for his death date.

[6]Al-Suyūṭī, Bughyat, p. 286. Al-Yāfiᶜī (Mir'āt al-janān, IV, 220) calls him the most learned of the eminent doctors [a'lam al-ᶜulamā' al-aᶜlām]; Ibn al-ᶜImād quotes al-Subkī as saying that he was an imām superior in his views, correct, accurate and pious, and Ibn Junayb as saying that all the community spoke of his works with great praise. (Shadharāt, V, 392).

[7]His major work on jurisprudence is entitled al-Ghāyah al-quswá. See Margoliouth, Chrestomathia, pp. vi-vii.

[8]Al-Bayḍāwī belonged to the school of al-Ashᶜarī.

world, entitled Niẓām al-tawārikh, dealing with the period from the time of Adam to 674 hijrī. Unlike most of his other writings, this last was in Persian so that, by his own words, it might be more generally useful.[9] He is also reported to have shown a distinct tendency toward mystical theology, a fact not surprising in consideration of his place of birth.

That for which al-Bayḍāwī is certainly best known, however, is his great commentary on the Qur'ān, Anwār al-tanzīl wa-asrār al-ta'wīl,[10] on which a great number of supercommentaries have been made. We noted above that it is representative of the trend to borrow heavily from preceding works. And Anwār is based primarily on the tafsīrs of al-Zamakhsharī,[11] al-Rāzī and al-Rāghib (c. 500 hijrī). Ḥājjī Khalīfah[12] calls it a work rich in grammatical explanation, saying that "in it he summarized from the Kashshāf [of al-Zamakhsharī] that relating to grammar, meanings and explanations and from the tafsīr al-kabīr [of al-Rāzī] that which deals with wisdom [al-ḥikmah] and theology [al-kalām] and from the tafsīr of al-Rāghib that concerned with derivations and hidden truths [ghawāmiḍ] and allusions." To these, says Ḥājjī Khalīfah, he added the sparks of his own intellect, wise sayings and acceptable propositions sufficient to alleviate any doubt or misinterpretation. He simplified the material but conditioned it in such a way that we can approach it with greater insight.

Here, then, seems to be the real explanation of al-Bayḍāwī's popularity among Muslims and corresponding fame among Western students of Islam. Despite Margoliouth's contention that "the interpretations given by B. are not ordinarily, if ever, original, but are traceable to earlier commentators of the Qur'ān, commencing with . . . Abdallah B. ᶜAbbās"[13] it seems to have been the particular virtue of al-Bayḍāwī to present in a nutshell, as it were, the conclusions of earlier commentators in such a way as to make the passages in question clear and comprehensible to the reader wishing a quick reference rather than a comprehensive analysis.

---

[9] Elliott, History of India, II, 252-53; Brockelmann, "al-Baiḍāwī" in EI, I, 591.

[10] Istanbūl, 1285 [1868], 2 voll.

[11] Margoliouth (Chrestomathia, p. vii) notes that al-Bayḍāwī "sometimes refutes, sometimes neglects and occasionally, by oversight, copies" those passages particularly Muᶜtazilī in character.

[12] Kashf, I, 471.

[13] Chrestomathia, p. viii.

By the seventh century the scholastic system was well established. It was general practice for a writer to accept material already judged by the community to be acceptable and to adopt it, in many cases, verbatim; in most areas of the Islamic sciences it was easy to identify a man's sources simply in terms of his geographical location and his group affiliation. The situation was somewhat different with tafsīr, however, which never became as clearly differentiated into types representing the various schools or madhāhib as did some of the other sciences. We have already seen, for example, that there is little to distinguish the commentaries of the Shīʿī al-Qummī and al-Ṭūsī from that of their Sunnī counterparts. It became the function of a mufassir like al-Bayḍāwī, then, to represent the "mainline" of Muslim commentary, to provide a concise statement of the issues involved in the tafsīr of the various verses as well as the generally acceptable resolutions of those issues. The Anwār al-tanzīl has been long used as a basic textbook for the student of tafsīr,[14] with the earlier and more voluminous commentaries such as those of al-Rāzī and al-Ṭabarī consulted when one wishes a more specific and detailed approach to the material.

We shall see in the succeeding sections that many commentators take whole sections of Anwār al-tanzīl and incorporate them into their own works without acknowledgement. With the understanding that academic activity always includes the dual aspects of repetition and originality, Muslim scholarship has accepted this practice insofar as one's sources are well known and do not need specific identification. The extent to which such use has been made of al-Bayḍāwī's work, like that of al-Ṭabarī, is a clear indication of the esteem in which it is held.

* * *

As did al-Zamakhsharī, al-Bayḍāwī begins his discussion of 3:19 by indicating that ❴Truly al-dīn with God is al-islām❵ confirms the preceding declaration that ❴there is no God but He❵. Thus, he says,

> . . . no dīn is acceptable to God other than al-islām, and it is the profession of God's oneness [al-tawḥīd] and arming oneself with the sacred law [sharʿ] which Muḥammad brought. (I, 197)

---

[14] In many cases it has been surpassed in this function only by the Tafsīr al-Jalālayn of al-Maḥallī and al-Suyūṭī (to be considered in a later section) which is even briefer.

In this brief and concise statement is expressed the two-sided nature of man's dīn: his affirmation of God's oneness, and his acceptance of the shar^c brought by the Prophet, through the recognition of which one expresses that affirmation. The word chosen here is not sharī^{c}ah, by which we might understand a specific set of regulations set up by the Prophet (implying perhaps the more reified meaning of the muslim community) but shar^c in the sense of that which has been established by God, the revelation of His guiding rule for mankind.[15] We shall find this idea taken up again in the section on 3:85.

In his discussion of the differing of those to whom the Book had already come (3:20), al-Zamakhsharī, as we saw above, indicated that they left or went away from [tarakū] al-islām which is tawḥīd and ^{c}adl (I, 346), the implication being that they had once participated in it. Al-Bayḍāwī says much the same thing when he indicates that the Jews and the Christians differed in regard to al-islām and in regard to al-tawḥīd. Some recognized al-islām as truth [ḥaqq] while others said it is peculiar to the Arabs and some denied it completely. The Christians deny God's unity by professing three [gods] and the Jews by saying ^{c}Uzayr is the son of God. (I, 198) Again the implication seems to be that that which some call "peculiar to the Arabs" is not a religion in the reified sense but rather the characterization of their practice as a group of individuals. This is supported by al-Bayḍāwī's commentary on the succeeding verse ❴Say: I submit my face to God❵ in which, much like al-Zamakhsharī, he says:

> I dedicate my individuality [nafsī] and my totality [jumlatī] to Him, not associating in my whole being any other with Him. And it is al-dīn al-qādim which the proofs [al-hujaj] established and to which the signs [al-āyāt] and the Prophets called. (I, 198)

The dīn al-qādim is the response of man to God which has been preordained and in which all of the Peoples of the Book have been called to participate.

Al-Bayḍāwī's initial definition of islām as tawḥīd and embracing the shar^c is repeated in slightly different terms in the commentary on 3:85:

> ❴And whoever chooses other than al-islām as dīn❵ i.e. other than the profession of God's oneness [al-tawḥīd] and submission [al-inqiyād] to God's dominion and rule [ḥukm] ❴it will not be accepted from him and he will be a loser in the hereafter❵ remaining in depravity. And the meaning is that he who turns away from al-islām and seeks other than it forsakes all advantage, falling

---

[15] See W. C. Smith, "The concept of sharī^{c}a" (above, p. 111, n. 160).

> into depravity by spoiling the sound disposition [al-fiṭrah al-salīmah] with which man is endowed. (I, 317)

In the first place we find support for the contention that by saying islām involves acceptance of God's sharᶜ, al-Bayḍāwī is referring to God's guiding rule rather than to the laws of Muḥammad's community. Instead of sharᶜ here he uses ḥukm, an inclusive term which comprehends God's ordinance, power, authority and judgment. Man's islām is his submission to that ḥukm, but as was so evident particularly in the tafsīr of al-Zamakhsharī, man's act can be described only in terms of what God is and does.

The second item of interest here is the reference to the sound disposition, the innate condition of men by which they naturally are inclined toward the recognition of a submission to God's oneness and dominion. In this al-Bayḍāwī touches on a theme which is to be taken up again in modern commentary. Later pre-modern writers, particularly Abū'l-Suᶜūd and al-Kāshānī, echo al-Bayḍāwī's words here, but it is in the tafsīr of the fourteenth/twentieth century that we find frequent references to the fiṭrah or natural disposition of man, particularly in relation to islām. Here the author says that if one forsakes his natural disposition to islām he is no longer the recipient of God's guidance and is utterly lost in sinfulness.

The remainder of al-Bayḍāwī's commentary on 3:85 is also interesting, especially in response to those who would equate islām and īmān:

> [This verse] points to the fact that al-īmān is al-islām, for if it were other than that, it would not be accepted. However the answer [to this argument] is that the text denies the acceptability of any dīn differing from it, not the acceptability of anything at all differing from it. And perhaps al-dīn also includes works. (I, 317-18)

It is easy to imagine that al-Bayḍāwī is speaking to the argument put forward several times by Fakhr al-Dīn Rāzī that it is precisely because anything other than islām is not acceptable to God, and of course faith must be acceptable, that faith [īmān] and submission [islām] are one and the same. Al-Bayḍāwī sees this as reading too much into the verse and argues that only another dīn, a way of responding to God other than by al-tawḥīd and submission to His rule, is unacceptable to Him. This leaves open the possibility that dīn, al-islām, may also involve works, implying that he does not consider that īmān can have such a reference.

This "works" aspect of islām comes to the fore in al-Bayḍāwī's discussion of 5:3. He obviously is dependent to a great degree on al-Zamakhsharī here, saying that the completion of dīn by God is either by making it victorious over all other religions [al-iẓhār ᶜalá'l-adyān kullihā] or by specifying the foundations of doctrines and establishing the theoretical analyses of the laws [al-sharā'iᶜ] and the rules that govern al-ijtihād." (I, 323) It is interesting to note that in discussing the specific regulations set up for members of the muslim community in terms of established laws he does not use sharᶜ, which of course has no plural, but sharā'iᶜ. Like al-Zamakhsharī he uses the plural of dīn in commenting on the final phrase of this verse ❬as [a] dīn❭, saying it means "from among the religions [min bayna'l-adyān]". (I, 323) We have just seen that al-Bayḍāwī also uses this plural in connection with God's completion of dīn.

Because al-Bayḍāwī's commentary here so closely parallels al-Zamakhsharī's although it is an abridgement of it, it is superfluous to attempt a reanalysis. The reader is thus referred to the discussion above (pp. 96-97). It appears that while the primary thrust of al-Bayḍāwī's understanding of islām has been set forth clearly as personal submission rather than reified communalism, there is here some suggestion of the latter. This is, however, certainly not the main emphasis of his commentary as a whole.

Skipping his tafsīr of 9:74, in which he does not discuss islām at all, we find in looking at 6:125 and 39:22 that al-Bayḍāwī is again dealing in the area of the relationship of īmān and islām. However he does not explicitly treat this relationship here, as for example did al-Rāzī, and we are thus left in some confusion as to how he really understood them in terms of each other. In 6:125 he says that God's guidance, His making one fit for al-īmān, is by His opening of one's breast to al-islām. By this God "makes the soul [nafs] accepting of the truth [al-ḥaqq] prepared for its conditions in it [i.e. the states in which truth is received in the nafs] and characterized by avoidance of what is forbidden and prohibited to it." (I, 401) This discussion of the nafs is elaborated in his commentary on 39:22 ❬Is he [the one] whose breast God has expanded for al-islām?❭:

> . . . so that it is made easy for him. By this He describes the one whose nafs He created in great readiness for acceptance of it [al-islām] with no rejection of it, so that the breast [al-sadr] is the locus of the heart [al-qalb], source of the spirit [al-rūḥ], connected to the soul [al-nafs] which accepts al-islām. (II, 357)

Attributed to the Māturīdīyah is an elaborate system by which knowledge of God is understood according to successive stages. Knowledge is correspondingly located in successive "levels", from the most external, the ṣadr which is the locus of islām, to the most internal, the sirr which is the locus of tawḥīd. Al-Bayḍāwī seems to have a similar understanding of stages and levels, yet is obviously not following the Māturīdī system strictly, because for him islām is tawḥīd. We are still unclear about his understanding of the precise relationship of islām and īmān, although it is apparent in these later verses that both are specifically involved with the most heartfelt of internal responses. One can scarcely imagine a more poignant expression of the personal and individual character of surrender [islām] to God.

If al-Bayḍāwī thus far has been less than explicit about īmān and islām -- and even about 3:85 he said only that the verse does not prove that they are the same -- he makes himself much more clear in his comments on 49:14-17. Again, however, he uses almost the exact words of al-Zamakhsharī when he characterizes al-īmān as "taṣdīq with trust [thiqah] and peacefulness [ṭuma'nīnah] of the soul" and al-islām as "being led [inqiyād] and entering into al-silm and witnessing the two shahādahs." (II, 454) He does use one highly interesting phrase which we have not seen before when, after giving the above definition of īmān, he says:

> And it will not befall you except when you bestow upon the Prophet the favor of al-islām [wa'lam yaḥsulu lakum wa-illā manantum ᶜalál-rasūl bi'l-islām] and cease fighting, as the previous sūrah indicated. (II, 454)

The phrase of note is, of course, that dealing with the bestowal of islām upon the Prophet. Obviously this cannot be taken to mean submitting to the Prophet according to al-Bayḍāwī's previous definition of islām as tawḥīd and inqiyād to God's ḥukm. What he intends, then, is that one indicates to the Prophet that he has submitted and ceased fighting those in the ummah of Muḥammad. Here is another instance where the act of joining the community is not distinguished from the act of personal submission to God. In either case, however, islām is clearly the name for what man does, not for that group with which he is associating himself. We also get a clearer insight into al-Bayḍāwī's understanding of islām and īmān here, for he says that it is not until one evidences his islām that he can be in such a state that al-īmān can occur in him. That islām is an act is again brought out in his commentary on 49:17 and following when he says that īmān was denied to these Arabs, even though they claimed it, and the name islām applied. (II, 455) Like al-Zamakhsharī, he uses both īmān and islām without the article in commenting on this verse, so that one can even imagine that the act could be "an islām, a kind of submitting, a personal and individual thing.

We have found only the slightest suggestion in the brief commentary of al-Bayḍāwī, that under 5:3, that islām for him indicated the name of a group rather than the act of an individual. This continues to hold true in his understanding of 61:7-9. Suggesting as he did on 49:14 that islām initially can be of an external nature, he says

> there is none more evil than the one whom God calls to al-islām al-ẓāhir, the reality of which [ḥaqīqatuhu] necessitates for him the excellence of the two domains of this world and the next [al-dārayn], and he gives as his answer calumny against God . . . (II, 518)

Then after indicating, as did al-Zamakhsharī, that the dīn al-ḥaqq is the millah in which have participated all of the faithful Peoples of the Book [al-ḥanīfah], he concludes that

> 'to make it victorious over all dīn' [means] to elevate it over all adyān 'even if the mushrikūn object' because it is pure tawḥīd and negation of shirk. (II, 518)

Thus even though he uses al-adyān, a plural which seems to have come into much more common usage after the time of al-Zamakhsharī, he clearly intends that the dīn al-ḥaqq, al-islām, is the genuine act of attributing unicity to God [maḥḍ al-tawḥīd] and the negation of anything that would deny His oneness [ibṭāl al-shirk]. This is consistent with his original definition of islām and with the general understanding of all of the commentary that we have viewed here. It is interesting that although he obviously is dependent to a fair degree on the Kashshāf of al-Zamakhsharī, we do not find in his tafsīr, as we did in the latter work, any real suggestion that he intends by islām the name of a particular religious group. His consistent and clear understanding is that islām is that act which, while it may entail membership in the group of muslims, means primarily the recognition of God's oneness and the acceptance of His guiding rule for man.

VIII

Turning now to the eighth century of Muslim history, we find that writing a commentary on the Qur'ān was not only a respected but a very conventional thing to do for one considered a master of the Islamic sciences. Among the most important of this period were the works of Abū'l-Barakāt al-Nasafī,[16] Abū Ḥayyān al-Gharnāṭī,[17] and Abū'l Fidā' Ismāᶜīl b. ᶜUmar Ibn Kathīr, the last of whom we shall consider in detail.

---

[16] Madārik al-tanzīl wa-ḥaqā'iq al-ta'wīl.

[17] Al-Baḥr al-muḥīṭ.

Celebrated as an historian as well as commentator on the Qur'ān, Ibn Kathīr is perhaps best known for his universal history al-Bidāyah wa'l-nihāyah, which covers the substantial scope of time from the creation to 738 hijrī.[18] Born in a village near Baṣrah in 701/1301, he moved early to Damascus and there enjoyed the instruction of several prominent men including Ibn Qāḍī Shuhbah, Ibn ᶜAsākir and the famous Taqī al-Dīn Ibn Taymīyah (d. 728).[19] He was prominent as a jurisconsult [faqīh] of the Shāfiᶜīyah and contributed to the chronicle of that group, the Ṭabaqāt al-Shāfiᶜīyah.[20] His legal training was considerable and although he never completed a large work begun on the aḥkām (the ordinances or injunctions)[21] he was considered an authority in this area and adhered closely to the principles of Ibn Taymīyah.[22]

We have noted that with al-Bayḍāwī we entered a period in which commentary on the Qur'ān became less flexible, less subject to individual interpretation and almost exclusively traditional in content. Ibn Kathīr fits into this pattern with comfortable ease.[23] His commentary, al-Qur'ān al-ᶜaẓīm,[24] is very largely devoted to ḥadīth and traditions related from the Companions, in addition to which he adds some explanatory comment of his own.[25] This commentary, which has attracted very little attention in the West, has been much appreciated by Muslims and is considered standard among the great works of tafsīr.

---

[18] Brockelmann, "Ibn Kathīr" in EI, II, 393.

[19] Al-Shawkānī, Badr, I, 153; Wüstenfeld, Geschichtschreiber, p. 184. Henri Laoust (Essai, p. 496) calls him "le disciple de beaucoup le plus fidèle et le plus actif d'ibn Taimīya."

[20] Ibn al-ᶜImād, Shadharāt, VI, 231.

[21] Ibn Ḥajar, al-Durar, I, 374.

[22] Laoust (Essai, p. 497) notes, however that he was not completely dependent on Ibn Taymīyah, studying the uṣūl al-fiqh and uṣūl al-dīn with a variety of other teachers.

[23] Tashköpruzade (Miftāḥ, p. 204) quotes the Shāfiᶜī traditionalist al-Dhahabī as saying in al-Muᶜjam al-mukhtaṣṣ that Ibn Kathīr was the traditionist leader [imām al-muḥaddith] and eloquent interpreter of law [al-muftī al-bāriᶜ]. Cf. Ibn Ḥajar (al-Durar, I, 374) who quotes "al-imam al-muftī" and "al-muḥaddith al-bāriᶜ".

[24] Beirut: Dār al-Andalus, 1386 [1966], 7 voll.

[25] Ḥājjī Khalīfah, Kashf, II, 349.

In 748 Ibn Kathīr became head instructor of tradition at the chapel Umm al-Ṣāliḥ in Damascus, after which for a short time he was professor at the Ashrafīyah.[26] He died in 774/1373 and was buried next to his beloved teacher and friend, Shaykh Ibn Taymīyah.

Now Ibn Taymīyah, according to the usual interpretation, has been seen as the epitome of traditionalism, a kind of bastion of conservatism in a time in which the more middle-of-the-road Ashᶜarī compromise between kalām and traditionalism had won the day as orthodoxy. That Ibn Taymīyah was a conservative Ḥanbalī cannot be questioned; he opposed innovations, allegorical interpretation of the Qur'ān, kalām, and all the sects which in any way advocated these. That the traditionalist approach that he represented was outnumbered and outdated, however, has been seriously questioned by George Makdisi,[27] who sees the traditionalist mode as the dominant and continuing attitude of the Shāfiᶜī school of law.

The relationship between the schools of law and the "theological" approaches, if one may use such a term, is most interesting. For example, one could be a Shāfiᶜī strongly advocating the use of kalām or a Shāfiᶜī who was absolutely opposed to such usage. What Makdisi convincingly maintains is that the Ashᶜarī advocates of kalām really failed in their efforts to infiltrate the schools of law, particularly the Shāfiᶜī school, and that the vast majority of Muslims always had been and continued through and past the fifth, sixth and seventh Islamic centuries predominantly traditionalist in approach.

If Makdisi's argument is accepted, it becomes easier to understand how Ibn Kathīr, a Shāfiᶜī, could have been so close to Ibn Taymīyah, a Ḥanbalī, to the extent of sharing the persecution received by his teacher at the hands of his enemies.[28] Makdisi maintains that while professors of law necessarily instructed those of the same school of law, a student from one legal persuasion interested in traditions could study under a professor of traditions from another school of law. "In this way, Ḥanbalite traditionalism was able to bolster and strengthen Shāfiᶜite traditionalism against the common enemy:

---

[26]Brockelmann, GAL, II, 49; Wüstenfeld, Geschichtschreiber, p. 184.

[27]Ashᶜari and the Ashᶜarites.

[28]Cf. Brockelmann, "Ibn Kathīr" in EI, II, 393.

rationalism."[29] Thus, he says, the Ḥanbalī traditionalist Ibn Taymīyah influenced a long line of Shāfiᶜīyah, including Ibn Kathīr.

The strength of Makdisi's position has been well illustrated in this study of tafsīr. In perhaps no area of the Islamic sciences can one see so clearly the final subduing of the forces of rationalism and the ensuing dominance of the traditional modes of understanding. It is not surprising to find the thirteenth/nineteenth century al-Shawkānī, for whom traditionalism is the sine qua non of Qur'ān commentary, praising Ibn Kathīr's work as one of the best of the tafsīrs, of which there is none better.[30]

One would expect to find, on the basis of the foregoing, nothing startlingly new or creative in the tafsīr of Ibn Kathīr, and for the most part such indeed seems to be the case. Yet to say that his commentary is merely a repetition of what has been handed down is also incorrect. Every man adds his own peculiar stamp to the material at hand and we will find several instances where he seems to be giving familiar matter a somewhat different interpretation. In reading this tafsīr one can understand something of the esteem in which the work has been held by Muslims. He expresses his understanding of the truth of the Qur'ān message in such a way that one senses immediately that he is not simply repeating what he has learned but is witnessing to his own faith in a direct and deeply sincere way.

* * *

Like many others before him, Ibn Kathīr immediately establishes verse 3:19 ❴Truly al-dīn with God is al-islām❵ as a continuation of the previous āyah which proclaims that "there is no God but He", saying:

> God witnesses, and He is sufficient as witness, and He is the most veracious of witnesses and the most just and most veracious of those who make this proclamation [al-qā'ilīn], that there is no God but He, i.e. the one who alone, over against all creatures, has divinity, and that all are His servants and His creation; they are poor in His sight [they stand in need of Him] and He is independent of all that is other than He [huwa al-ghanīy ᶜammā siwāhu]. (II, 233)

The focus is upon God Himself and it is only in the light of this understanding of God that one can see what is meant by

[29] Makdisi, Ashᶜari and the Ashᶜarites, p. 79.

[30] Badr, I, 153.

al-islām as the "dīn ᶜinda'llāhi". In the tafsīr of 61:7 ❴And who does greater evil than the one who forges a lie against God when he is called to al-islām❵ Ibn Kathīr says "when he is called to al-tawḥīd and al-ikhlāṣ".[31] (VI, 648) Recognition of the oneness of God and acting in terms of it through sincere devotion -- in this is the essence of Ibn Kathīr's understanding of islām, and with this he is a true representative of the traditionalist position. Now the way in which al-tawḥīd and al-ikhlāṣ are expressed, i.e. the content of the dīn acceptable to God, is [i.e. islām is]:

> . . . following the Prophets in that with which God sent them in every age, until they were sealed by Muhammad -- blessings and peace be upon him -- who closed off all ways to Him except [the way that leads] from [alladhī sadda jamīᶜ al-ṭuruq ilayhi illā min jihati] Muḥammad. And whoever encounters God after the mission [baᶜthah] of Muhammad with a dīn based on other than his sharīᶜah, will not be able to find acceptance [fa-laysa bi-mutaqabbal]. (II, 233)

One might be reminded here of the controversial words of Jesus that "no one comes to the Father, but by me". (John 14:6) The difference, and it is of course a crucial difference, is that Jesus' words were preceded by "I am the way, and the truth, and the life", a statement that Muḥammad would never have uttered. (He might rather, one supposes, have said, "I point to the way, the truth, and the life.") In any case, we have here a very specific emphasis on Muḥammad and the clear understanding that the dīn which he has made incumbent [sharaᶜa] is the only acceptable one. Now this raises the interesting question of whether it was Muḥammad or God who enjoined this dīn. In commenting on 3:20, Ibn Kathīr says that God commanded His servant and His Messenger Muḥammad

> to call -- to his [His?] way [ṭarīqatihi] and his [His?] dīn and entrance into his [His?] sharᶜ and that with which God sent him -- the Peoples of the Book from the two millahs and those without scripture from among the mushrikūn. (II, 234)

Now if one decides that a capital H is appropriate for the possessive pronouns, it means that the way and the dīn and the sharᶜ are specifically God's and are the content of that with which He sent Muḥammad. Even if one decides that a small h is correct, this understanding is not negated but is certainly de-emphasized and the stress is again placed on the idea of Muḥammad's dīn. This latter understanding would seem to be correct because the succession of four hu's in a row indicates that they

---

[31]See above, pp. 63-64.

all have the same referent (i.e. because the last hu obviously refers to Muḥammad it would appear that all the others do too). One cannot build a strong case on this, but at least it may be said that a dīn described as Muḥammad's carries overtones of reification that are not present if one sees it as the dīn of God. Or in other words, if one uses a capital H it becomes the dīn of God meaning man's way of relating to God. On the other hand, we could not understand the dīn of Muḥammad to be man's relationship to him, therefore it would carry the implication of a specific dīn practiced (or established?) by the Prophet.

Lest we are tempted to make too much of this, however, it is well to balance these possibilities against Ibn Kathīr's first words about 3:85 ❛and whoever chooses other than al-islām as dīn . . . ❜

> God says [it] disavowing whoever wants as dīn other than the dīn of God which He revealed in His Books and with which He sent His Messengers. (II, 272)

Here, clearly, when the author days dīn Allāh he is speaking of the way in which man is enjoined to respond to God concerning which Muḥammad was only one of several Messengers (albeit the last) and the Qur'ān only one among other Books. This may indicate that grammatical construction notwithstanding, Ibn Kathīr intended that God be the referent of the first three hu's, but it seems more likely that it is another instance whereby the writer does not consciously attempt to distinguish between the different kinds of dīn, or islām, here specifically between reified and non-reified group islām. Later in the tafsīr of the same verse we see him moving as easily into an understanding of islām as a personal act when he likens choosing other than islām as dīn (which, he says, means "treading a path other than what God has enjoined") to the saying of the Prophet, "Whoever does a deed that We have not commanded [will have] it denied." (II, 273)

When we come to Ibn Kathīr's tafsīr of 5:3 we immediately encounter another of the succession of hu's which seem so important to the understanding of the writer's intent. This time we will give the passage using all small h's:

> "Today I have completed for you your dīn and fulfilled for you My blessing and have chosen for you al-islām as dīn." This is the greatest of God's blessings on this community, in that God completed for them their dīn, for they have need of no dīn other than it and of no prophet other than their Prophet, may the blessings and peace of God be upon him. Therefore God made him the seal of the Prophets, and sent him to mankind and the jinn. And nothing is permitted [ḥalāl] except what he declared to be permitted nor forbidden [ḥarām] except what he declared to be forbidden. And there is no dīn except when he enjoined

> [sharaᶜa] and every thing he has told about is reality [ḥaqq] and truth [ṣidq] and there is no lie in it and no disparity.

Here again it seems most probable that Ibn Kathīr was intending Muḥammad rather than God to be the immediate referent of the pronoun hu and the subject of the verbs in each case. It is the Prophet who was sent and the Prophet who told about the ḥaqq and ṣidq and thus also the Prophet who clarified what is permitted and forbidden, doing all of this, of course, as the transmitter of God's message for mankind. This seems, then, to support our understanding of his interpretation of 3:20, and we shall let the above comments on that section apply to this passage also.

Continuing with his discussion of 5:3 Ibn Kathīr quotes Ibn ᶜAbbās' saying that the perfection of al-dīn, which is al-islām, means that God has perfected for them al-īmān, and it will never increase or decrease, for God is content with it as it is. It is unusual in the tafsīr we have examined to find islām equated with īmān in this context, a verse and a situation which seem to allude more to group islām than the individual and internal response which one understands by īmān. (We should also note that an equation of islām and īmān in the context of this verse was not found in the tafsīr that we have in the name of Ibn ᶜAbbās.)

This leads easily into Ibn Kathīr's tafsīr of 6:125 ❴. . . . He opens his breast to al-islām❵ in which he quotes first 49:7 ❴God has endeared to you al-īmān❵, implying the understanding of īmān for islām. He then gives another quotation from Ibn ᶜAbbās not found in our edition of the latter's tafsīr in which it is said that opening the breast means making it wide for al-tawḥīd and al-īmān in Him. (V, 100)

The specific relationship of īmān and islām is spelled out by Ibn Kathīr in his commentary on 49:14-17. Rather than indicating that the two are essentially different, he goes back to the familiar distinction that al-īmān is more specific [akhaṣṣ] than al-islām and says that this was the real content of the ḥadīth in which Gabriel described al-islām, al-īmān and al-iḥsān as progressing from the general to the more specific and most specific.[32] (VI, 390) As usual, however, it seems unavoidable that there is really a difference in kind as well as degree between the mu'minūn and the muslimūn of this verse, that

---

[32] See above, pp. 63-4.

being the inclusion of tasdīq in the response of the former. This is not in logical contradiction with Ibn Kathīr's earlier comments equating islām with īmān, for there he clearly means that the islām discussed in such verses as 5:3 and 6:125 is exclusive of the "non-taṣdīq" islām of the Arabs of Bani Asad and is that more specialized aspect which is īmān.

Like so many before him, then, Ibn Kathīr gives as the primary thrust of his understanding of islām clear evidence that it is man's personal response to God. Islām as dīn is tawḥīd and ikhlāṣ, and in its relationship to īmān, however that might be finally formulated, is shown to be related in terms of degree to the deepest expression of individual conviction. However it also seems apparent that in those passages in which he speaks of the role of Muḥammad in promulgating the dīn Allāh, he is intending an understanding of islām as a historical community. If we have been correct in interpreting his grammatical structure, we have a view of dīn and sharᶜ perhaps somewhat different from that of his predecessors. Ibn Kathīr wrote over seven centuries after the death of the Prophet, and it may well be that we are seeing here, made all the more evident in contrast to his dominant traditionalism, the beginnings of a more reified concept of islām. It also seems evident, however, that (as we have noted so often before) such a distinction was not clearly defined in his own mind, and that to whatever extent he may have intended a reified islām his primary understanding of dīn al-islām was as personal submission to God and profession of His oneness and unity.

IX

By the ninth century hijrī most of the Muslim world, especially the Arab portions, had for some time been in what orientalists like to refer to as the dark ages of Islam.[33] As far as we know from the written material left to us, there was very little creative effort in the realm of theology, and in tafsīr of the Qur'ān the dominant mode was a renewed emphasis on the traditionalism of the early centuries. It is not surprising that the shining light of this period, Jalāl al-Dīn al-Suyūṭī, is known not for innovative endeavor but for the exceptional depth of his erudition and ability to organize and classify the

---

[33]Von Grunebaum (Medieval Islam, p. 246) calls this the time "when Muslim science had been gripped by rigor mortis".

results of earlier scholarship.

From a Persian family who had some generations earlier resided in Baghdād, Abū'l-Faḍl ᶜAbd al-Raḥmān b. Abū Bakr b. Muḥammad Jalāl al-Dīn al-Khuḍayrī al-Shāfiᶜī was born in 849/1445 in the famous city of Suyūṭ in upper Egypt.[34] The details of his life are familiar to us through the biography of Sakhawī and Suyūṭī's own autobiography in Ḥusn al-muḥāḍarah; these have been summarized in Wüstenfeld's Geschichtschreiber.

Al-Suyūṭī's family had for nine generations occupied prominent positions in Suyūṭ in law, business, education and other respected professions of public service. His father was a serious student of the Qur'ān; it is apparent that the boy picked up this interest at an early age, for we find repeatedly recorded the fact that before eight years of age he had memorized the entire Qur'ān.[35] After the death of his father in 855 al-Suyūṭī was adopted by a ṣūfī friend.[36] One suspects that the influence of this association may have been considerable on the young boy, for he is reported to have had many dreams and visionary experiences and he even professed to have seen and talked with the Prophet Muḥammad over seventy times while awake.[37] In any case, his formal studies, under the most renowned teachers, concentrated on law, grammar, and tradition and resulted in a thorough familiarity with nearly all of the dominant branches of learning. Aside from his famous early mastery of the Qur'ān, he himself claimed to have memorized some 200,000 ḥadīths, saying, "Had I found any more I would have learned them, so perhaps there are not any more on the face of the earth!"[38] He held a succession of teaching positions, in 872/1467 becoming professor of law at

---

[34] Mubārak (al-Khiṭaṭ, XII, 105) gives al-Asyūṭ, a city well-known for many of its citizens, the most outstanding of whom was Jalāl al-Dīn.

[35] Al-Kattānī, Fihrist, II, 353; al-Suyūṭī, Ḥusn, I, 140; Ibn al-ᶜImād, Shadharāt, VIII, 52.

[36] Brockelmann, "al-Suyūṭī" in EI, IV, 573.

[37] Ibn al-ᶜImād (Shadharāt, VIII, 53-54) gives a variety of stories about these mystical experiences, including descriptions of visits with Khadījah, drinking the water of Zam-Zam without leaving Egypt, and receiving the personal assurance of the Prophet that he would dwell in paradise with no fear of punishment.

[38] Ibn al-ᶜImād, Ibid., VIII, 53; al-Kattānī, Fihrist, II, 303. Actually 200,000 is a modest figure in the light of such traditions as al-Bukhārī having chosen 6,000 for his Ṣaḥīḥ out of some 600,000 familiar to him, and the statement of Ibn Ḥanbal that one is qualified to be a mujtāhid if he learns 500,000.

the Shaykhūnīyah in Cairo, a position formerly held by his father.

Whether virtue or vice, it is certain that Jalāl al-Dīn al-Suyūṭī was not lacking in self-confidence. His professed ambition was to write in all the areas of Muslim learning and he seems to have done just that. His works are numbered at somewhere over five hundred, although he has been harshly criticized for his ambition in writing. Not only were many of these works extremely brief, really only pamphlets,[39] but he is even accused of rearranging material already written by other authors and giving it out as his own.[40] In a particularly caustic essay,[41] Goldziher discusses al-Suyūṭī's literary output, suggesting quite clearly that a good deal of his work was designed mainly to advertise the writer and to inform his contemporaries of his own unsurpassed greatness.[42] Quoting al-Suyūṭī as having said, "I am now the most learned among all of God's creatures, both in what concerns the pen and in what concerns the mouth", Goldziher concludes that such arrogance was in stark contrast to the Muslim idea of modesty in scholarship and indicates that it earned the irritation of some of the more modest believers.[43]

Be this as it may, there is still no question that it is for the depth of his knowledge and not the breadth of his ego that Jalāl al-Dīn al-Suyūṭī will long be remembered and studied. Whatever the opinion of some of his fellow scholars, the vast majority of people in his own day respected and revered him. His writings spread quickly to Syria, Asia Minor, the Maghrib and India[44] and with fame seems to have come an insistence on al-Suyūṭī's own part that it was God's mercy and aid which were his inspiration.[45] In 891/1486 he went from the Shaykhūnīyah to

---

[39]Al-Kattānī (Fihrist, II, 309) says that he could write three of these in a single day.

[40]Wüstenfeld, Geschichtschreiber, p. 228.

[41]"Zur charakteristik Ǧelāl ud-dīn Suyūṭī's und seiner literarischen thätigkeit" in SBKais. Ak., LXIX (1871), 7-28.

[42]Ibid., p. 8. As have others of the tafsīr writers examined in this essay, al-Suyūṭī claimed for himself the prerequisites to be the renewer [mujaddid] of his age.

[43]Ibid., pp. 23, 27.

[44]Wüstenfeld, Geschichtschreiber, p. 228.

[45]Mubārak (Khiṭaṭ, XII, 106) quotes Jalāl al-Dīn as having said that he could write well on any subject because God had given him the gift to do so.

al-Baybarsīyah, but because of some reputedly shady financial dealings he was relieved of this position by the sulṭān al-Mālik Ṭumān Bay.[46] He retired to the island Rawḍah where he remained until his death in 911/1505. It was to this place that many people used to come to pay honor to him; he was offered gifts and wealth from personages of high rank, but refused them all.[47] The esteem in which al-Suyūṭī was held can be seen in the custom of the people to have a special yearly religious service [mawlid] for him after his death, an honor paid only to those considered to have approached the realm of sainthood.[48]

Al-Suyūṭī's writings, as we have observed, are voluminous and cover a great many areas including philology,[49] history[50] and even some maqāmāt.[51] His primary interest, however, seems to have been the study of Qur'ān and tradition. The comprehensive al-Itqān fī ulūm al-Qur'ān is considered the definitive medieval Muslim work on Qur'anic sciences. Already translated into Urdu, this work is awaiting translation into a Western language. It was the first well-known thorough treatment of the problems and principles involved in exegeting the Qur'ān, codifying these principles [uṣūl al-tafsīr] long after they had been in operation.[52]

Collecting all of the traditions available concerning exposition of the Qur'ān, al-Suyūṭī compiled a large work entitled Tarjumān al-Qur'ān fī'l-tafsīr al-musnad. This work seems to be lost,[53] but we do have available a kind of abbreviation or condensation of it, al-Durr al-manthūr fī'l tafsīr al-ma'thūr[54] which instead of isnāds gives only the literary sources used.

---

[46] Wüstenfeld, Geschichtschreiber, p. 228; Brockelmann, "al-Suyūṭī" in EI, IV, 573.

[47] Ibn al-ᶜImād, Shadharāt, VIII, 53.

[48] Mubārak, Khiṭaṭ, XII, 106.

[49] One of the most important of his many works in this area is the large encyclopaedia, al-Muzhir fī ᶜulūm al-lughah.

[50] Badā'iᶜ al-zuhūr fī waqā'iᶜ al-duhūr (a world history); Ḥusn al-muḥāḍarah fī akhbār Miṣr wa'l-Qāhirah; Ta'rīkh al-khulafā'.

[51] See Brockelmann, "al-Suyūṭī" in EI, IV, 574.

[52] See Rahbar, "Reflections" in MW, LII (1962), 305.

[53] Nöldeke, Geschichte, II, 178; Brockelmann, "al-Suyūṭī" in EI, IV, 573.

[54] Teheran: al-Maktabah al-Islāmīyah, 1377 [1957].

This six volume work will provide one source of information from al-Suyūṭī in our quest for an understanding of the term islām.

The second object of our study in this essay is a work for which al-Suyūṭī is very well known in the Muslim world today, the Tafsīr al-Jalālayn.[55] This was written in cooperation with another Jalāl al-Dīn, namely his teacher al-Maḥallī (d. 864/1459), or more properly begun by the latter and completed by al-Suyūṭī.[56] The value of this tafsīr lies both in its brevity,[57] which renders it much more manageable for the average reader than the voluminous works of writers like al-Ṭabarī and al-Rāzī, and in its inclusion of syntactical explanations as well as legends of origin.[58] For our purposes it is often disappointingly brief, but using it in conjunction with al-Durr we shall attempt to assemble the elements of al-Suyūṭī's understanding of islām.

* * *

We observed earlier that unless an author stipulates otherwise, it seems safe to assume that the traditions he cites are those which he feels support his general understanding. In al-Durr al-manthūr we have little or no personal comment from al-Suyūṭī; we must attempt to glean his general intentions through surveying the traditions presented. This work becomes for our purposes a kind of supplement to the Tafsīr al-Jalālayn, which, as has been noted, is very concise and contains in the sections under consideration here no ḥadīth materials documented with isnāds.

The keynote of the understanding of islām in 3:19 ❬Truly al-dīn with God is al-islām❭ is tawḥīd, as we have seen so often before. By al-dīn, he says, is meant that dīn which has the approval of God [al-marḍá] and it is al-islām, "i.e. the revelation with which the Messengers instituted [by God] were sent concerning the profession of His unity [al-sharᶜ al-mabᶜūth bihi

---

[55]Tafsīr al-Qur'ān al-karīm. Damascus: al-Maṭbaᶜah al-Hāshimīyah, 1378 [i.e. 1379 (1959/60)].

[56]See Ḥājjī Khalīfah, Kashf, II, 358.

[57]"The writing is by means of brief expression [bi-taᶜbīr wajīz], but along with its small size it is great in meaning because in it they gave the essence of tafsīrs [lubba lubub al-tafāsīr]." (Ibid., II, 358).

[58]Nöldeke (Geschichte, II, 178) indicates that for these reasons this work is probably the most popular tafsīr among Muslims today.

al-rusul al-mabnīy ᶜalá'l-tawḥīd]." (Tafsīr, p. 56) This is stressed further when he says that the differing of those who have received the Book (the Jews and the Christians) is concerning al-dīn, in that some professed faith in God's unity [waḥḥada] while others rejected it [kafara]. The affirmation of tawḥīd characterizes those of the dīn al-islām, and its opposite, with all of the implications of the untranslatable verb kafara, characterizes those who because of their kufr cannot be of islām.

A final support of the stress on tawḥīd comes in the next phrase when al-Suyūṭī identifies the content of the knowledge that came to those receiving the Book specifically as al-tawḥīd. It is thus not surprising to find that in al-Durr concerning 3:19 he concentrates specifically on the relationship of this verse to the phrase in the preceding one, "There is no God but He". He lists a number of traditions that deal with the conditions prevailing at the time of the revelation of 3:18-19. The one instance in which we are given a specific treatment of islām is in the statement from Qatādah:

> Islām is witnessing that there is no God but God and the affirmation [iqrār] of what [the Prophet] brought from God. And it is the dīn Allāh which He Himself made incumbent and with which He sent His Prophets. And the saints [awliyā'] point to it. He does not accept other than it and does not recompense except by it. (II, 12)

Two things, then, are clear. (1) For al-Suyūṭī the stress is not on man but on God. To understand what is involved in man's submission one must focus on the oneness of God and see islām as man's affirmation of that oneness. Here again is the import of that potent phrase "dīn Allāh". This cannot be translated God's religion (in the sense that it is something possessed by God) but must be seen as the expression of man's response to God. (2) The dīn which is constituted by this affirmation has been the dīn of all those accepting the message of the revealed Books as brought by all of God's Messengers. Note again the use of rusul rather than rasūl, which is supported by a ḥadīth in al-Durr from al-Ḍaḥḥāk in which God says, "I have not sent a Messenger except with al-islām." (II, 12)

As has generally been the case in the commentary on 5:3 concerning the perfection of dīn, the completion of God's blessing and the choosing of islām as dīn, al-Suyūṭī understands this verse to be a reference to the completion of the regulations [aḥkām] and duties [farā'iḍ] of dīn after which no more will ever be revealed. (Tafsīr, p. 109) The traditions he quotes in al-Durr are again dealing largely with the asbāb al-nuzūl and with the fact that Mecca is now open to the mu'minūn and not the mushrikūn. A number of ḥadīths relate the reaction of the People of the Book (usually to ᶜUmar) to the revelation of this verse. One of these, from ᶜĪsá b. Hārithah al-Anṣārī, is worth noting here:

> We were seated in a group when a Christian said to us, Oh people of islām [yā ahla'l-islām], an āyah has been revealed to you which, had it been revealed to us, would have caused us to take that day and that hour as a feasttime. (II, 208)

The phrase of note, of course, is the "people of islām". This seems to be a clear instance of reification in which a Christian recognizes a particular group, of which he is not a member (presumably he has not designated himself a kāfir and thus one of the "renegade" People of the Book who would otherwise participate in the dīn al-tawḥīd [dīn al-islām]), and refers to it as al-islām. Such a usage in an early tradition, as we have seen in Muqātil b. Sulaymān and others, is not uncommon and seems to have characterized the period following the death of the Prophet more than later centuries.

Two other traditions cited here specifically mention islām. One is that in which the Prophet is supposed to have said that islām becomes twofold, fourfold, sixfold and finally is completed, after which ᶜUmar lamented the ensuing decrease. (Durr, II, 259) The other, given in the context of 5:3 as coming from Qatādah (Durr, II, 259) and in slightly different form under 3:85 as coming from Abū Hurayrah (Durr, II, 48-49), is the now familiar one about al-islām approaching God on the final day and saying, "Oh Lord, you are al-salām and I am al-islām." One wishes that al-Suyūṭī had added a few words of explanation of these two ḥadīths, both of which lend themselves to a variety of interpretations.

In the tafsīr al-Suyūṭī says that when God in 6:125 talks of opening the breast to al-islām, he means that He flings [yaqdhifu] into one's heart a light, for the reception and acceptance of which the heart is expanded, as is explained by a ḥadīth. (p. 125) The ḥadīth he obligingly provides in several renditions in al-Durr, and it is the well-known one in which the Prophet explains that the signs by which such an occurrence can be recognized are inclination toward the dār al-khulūd and salvation from the dār al-ghurūr and preparedness for death before the arrival of death. (III, 44)

In another ḥadīth which he gives from Ibn ᶜAbbās we find that the verse means the expanding of the heart to al-tawḥīd and al-īmān in Him, which two are correspondingly prevented from entering the heart of the one whom God wishes to lead astray. (III, 45) Here we see the coordination of tawḥīd, which al-Suyūṭī understands as the content of islām, with īmān, and in both these ḥadīths we have another indication of the personal and specifically internal nature of islām.

As we have found so often before, however, the assertions of the inner aspect of islām that come particularly with verses like 6:125 and 39:22 do not prevent the writer from making the clear distinction implied in 49:14 between the external submission of the Arabs of Bani Asad and the internal īmān of those who are truly sincere [al-ṣādiqūn]. Following the description of the ṣādiqūn in the verse, al-Suyūṭī says it is they who are sincere in their īmān, "not those who say 'we believe' and in whom is not found anything other than al-islām." (Tafsīr, p. 187) This is supported by traditions in al-Durr (VI, 99-100) indicating that al-islām is al-iqrār and al-īmān is al-taṣdīq, and that al-islām is the word [al-kalimah] and al-īmān the deed [al-ʿamal].[59] Al-Suyūṭī himself obviously sees no need to elaborate on the relationship or explain how, as did al-Rāzī and others, īmān and islām are both the same and different. He lets the traditions speak for themselves; the following one expresses well the connection between them:

> The Prophet said al-islām is the outward aspect [ʿalānīyah] of al-īmān in the heart, then he pointed with his hand to his breast three times, saying piety [taqwá] is here, piety is here. (al-Durr, VI, 100)

True to his calling as a traditionist and a traditionalist, al-Suyūṭī in these two works has presented a kind of synopsis of the general trends we have seen in the classical works of tafsīr. In the ḥadīths we find the understanding of islām, including occasional references to the specific dīn of Muḥammad, characteristic of the early period; in the Tafsīr, however brief, he is consistent with the classical interpretation that sees man's relationship to God in terms of His being and His unity. Here we have not the dīn of Muḥammad, but the dīn Allāh, the response of man to God.

X - XI

It should come as no surprise to the reader at this point to discover that the most popular and well-known commentaries of the tenth/sixteenth and eleventh/seventeenth centuries not only use early traditional material now very familiar to us, but that

---

[59]See above, p. 14.

they actually borrow whole passages of tafsīr from earlier commentaries often without changing so much as a word. This, as has been noted, was not seen in any sense as plagiarism, but was rather the praiseworthy adherence to time-honored interpretations of the Holy Word. Thus we find that two of the most famous commentaries of the tenth and eleventh centuries -- the Irshād al-ᶜaql of Abū'l-Suᶜūd and al-Ṣāfī of al-Kāshānī -- both borrow very heavily from al-Bayḍāwī's Anwār al-tanzīl of the seventh century. What is particularly interesting here is that the former two commentators came from very different backgrounds and represented very divergent persuasions, thus illustrating not only the strength of the traditionalism of this age but also the above-mentioned tendency of tafsīr writing to be less specifically sectarian than many of the other branches of the Islamic sciences. One of these writers was a Sunnī shaykh al-islām, the other a Shīᶜī mystic, yet both turned to a common source for a large part of their exegetical material.

Because much of these tafsīrs is repetitious of what we have already covered, it seems most convenient as well as instructive to look at them together, noting not only where they concur with al-Bayḍāwī but particularly where they differ from him and from each other. In an attempt to understand some of the reasons for both of these aspects, let us first consider the historical circumstances out of which each wrote.

Nearly a millenium having passed since the death of the Prophet, the Muslim community in the 1500's had spread far from its base in the Arab heartland. Politically it had undergone a great many changes and power struggles, in spite of which and around which developed a variety of structures for religious response. By the tenth/sixteenth century the center of power had moved away from the Arab world to the half-oriental/half-occidental capital of the empire of the Ottoman Turks.

The beginnings and development of the Ottoman Empire make a fascinating historical study, though too complex for consideration here. By the time Meḥmed II became ruler in 855/1451 the Turkish Anatolian emirates were fully subjugated and the Ottoman Turks were well established in southeastern Europe and the Western portions of Asia. Two years later Meḥmed took over Constantinople, a long-desired treasure which was not to be an unmixed blessing. The great culture and art of the city began to give way to corruption, and it has been suggested that in this moment of greatest glory actually began the decay of the empire.

This, however, was not to come for some time; after Selim I (picturesquely called "the Grim") came what was probably the zenith of the power and glory of the Ottoman Empire during the rule of Sulaymān I, known in the West as the Magnificent (ruled 926-982/1520-1566). Yet even by the end of Sulaymān's rule signs of decay were becoming apparent. The Janissaries were gaining more and more power, and control of succession to the throne was passing out of the hands of the sulṭān. The great upheaval that was to take place is characterized by Niyazi Berkes in The Development of Secularism in Turkey (pp. 18-19) as the breakdown in the traditional order. "The earliest symptoms of the disruption of the traditional order," Berkes says, "coincided with the approach of the Muslim millenium (corresponding to 1590 A.D.). Its coming had long been anticipated with grave apprehension. Many expected the event to signal the end of the world. The signs of disorder following the turn of the millenium confirmed such fears and produced a psychological state which lasted far beyond the event itself . . ."

The relationship between the organs of state and the religious structures in the Ottoman Empire was as complex and interesting as the rise of the empire itself.[60] While in theory church and state in Islam are one, as a reality this was short-lived. Certainly under the Ottomans a clear and careful separation was maintained, although with varying degrees of mutual respect and sanction. Crucial in the relationship between church and state were the men of knowledge, the ᶜulamā',[61] who included the ministers of religion [imāms], the juristconsults [muftīs] and the judges [qāḍīs]. It was the second of these who played the greatest role in co-ordinating the affairs of religion and state by interpreting the sharīᶜah, and the shaykh al-islām, the muftī of the highest rank, was a religious authority of considerable power and influence.[62] The shaykh al-islām was appointed to office by the sulṭān, and could be removed by him, yet at the same time the shaykh could depose the sulṭān by his own fatwá. In this way the ᶜulamā' kept firm control over the sulṭān and assured that he did not stray too far from the traditional dictates of established dogma.

---

[60] For a detailed study of this relationship, see Gibb and Bowen, Islamic Society and the West, I, pt. 2, especially chapter 8-9.

[61] Technical terms are given here in transliteration from Arabic rather than from the Turkish.

[62] See Berkes, Secularism, p. 15.

It was under Sulaymān the Magnificent that the shaykh al-islām gained his pre-eminent power, and it is here that we are introduced to the subject of our study of the tenth Islamic century, Abū'l-Suᶜūd.

That the empire maintained even some of its former glory under Sulaymān's inept successor Selīm II was due, in the opinion of many, to the continuing efforts of Abū'l-Suᶜūd and others.[63] Born in 896 or 898/1393 or 1395[64] in a village near Constantinople, Abū'l-Suᶜūd Muḥammad b. Muḥyi'l-Dīn Muḥammad b. Muṣṭafá al-ᶜImādī was the son of the teacher of Prince Bāyazīd Khān.[65] Of Kurdish origin, the father was particularly concerned with the understanding of the sharīᶜah and the ṭarīqah [ṣūfī brotherhood][66] and raised his son in an atmosphere of learning and piety.[67]

At the age of twenty-five Abū'l-Suᶜūd began a distinguished teaching career, going from one school to another until he finally reached one of the famous "eight madrasahs" established by Sulṭān Meḥmed II.[68] He then became a qāḍī in Brusa (939) and in Istanbūl (940) and was qāḍī ᶜaskar of Rumelia from 944-952.[69] In 952 the sulṭān promoted him to the above-discussed position of shaykh al-islām, a post he kept until his death in 982/1574.

---

[63] Joseph de Hammer (Histoire, IV, 3-4) notes that Western accounts of Ottoman history fail to take into consideration the obvious cause for the continuation of the prosperity of Sulaymān I's reign after his death: "En effet, la permanence de cet état florissant s'explique par le maintien dans leurs fonctions du grand-visir [Muḥammad] Sokolli et du moufti Ebousououd." Cf. Paul Horster (Zur Anwendung des islamischen Rechts im 16. Jahrhundert, p. 1): "Nur durch sie konnte das Reich während der Regierungszeit des unfähigen Sultans Selīm II. auf dieser unter Suleimān erreichten Höhe gehalten werden."

[64] The sources seem divided on this.

[65] Horster, Zur Anwendung, p. 2; Brockelmann, GAL, I, 438.

[66] The ṭarīqahs were wide-spread and very popular in the Ottoman Empire; on the whole they were tolerated by the ᶜulamā' and the more orthodox of the brotherhoods not only supported but included in the membership many, and eventually most, of the ᶜulamā' themselves. (See Gibb and Bowen, Islamic Society, I, pt. 2, 70-80.)

[67] Manuq, al-ᶜIqd al-manẓūm (on the margin of Ibn Khallikān, Wafayāt, II, 283).

[68] Ibid., p. 284; Schacht, "Abū'l-Suᶜūd" in EI_2, I, 152.

[69] Horster, Zur Anwendung, p. 2; Manuq (al-ᶜIqd, p. 285) tells us that the state of the fatwá in Rumelia was in turmoil, the position of law-making passing from hand to hand, and in a delightfully descriptive phrase says that the fatwá did not "settle on a roof with pillars under it" until Abū'l-Suᶜūd took office.

A close personal friend of Sulaymān I, Abū Suʿūd established himself quickly in a position of great respect and responsibility. Much of his success is attributed to the fact that he did not mix in the intrigues of Ottoman politics but concerned himself primarily with the pursuit of knowledge and the just application of the law. A prodigious worker, he is credited with having brought the sacred law [sharīʿah] into harmony with the administrative law [qānūn] to the extent that one could no longer speak of spiritual as opposed to worldly legislation.[70] No one regretted his death more than Selīm II, who had continued to honor him and his judgments as had his father. The shaykh al-islām's funeral was attended by all of the notables of state as well as great crowds of common people; one of the main streets of Constantinople took his name.[71]

As time-consuming as was Abū'l-Suʿūd's legal activity, he also enjoyed an excellent reputation as a poet as well as a commentator on the Qur'ān and author of a number of apologetic treatises. He seems to have been quite conservative and it is reported that while, in keeping with the general policies of the ʿulamā', he was in sympathy with the orthodox ṣūfī ṭarīqahs, he had little appreciation of the extremists and even ordered their execution.[72] His Qur'ān commentary generally exhibits these conservative leanings. Entitled Irshād al-ʿaql al-salīm,[73] it enjoyed real popularity in the Ottoman Empire and earned for its author a reputation as a competent mufassir. (Abū'l-Suʿūd also wrote separate commentaries on sūrahs 18, 48, and 67.) It is reported that after reading the first volume of the Irshād the sulṭān immediately raised the muftī's salary; upon completion of the second volume the salary was doubled.[74]

Despite the apparent worth of this tafsīr, however, it seems to be somewhat of an exaggeration to say, as several of the

---

[70] See M. Hartmann, "Die osmanische 'Zeitschrift der Nationale Forschungen'" in Isl., VIII (1918), 304-326.

[71] Ibn al-ʿImād (Shadharāt, VIII, 399) says that he was tall, thin and unpretentious, clearly exhibiting a concern for people along with qualities of leadership. He was both held in great awe and greatly revered.

[72] Schacht, "Abū'l-Su'ūd" in EI_2, I, 152.

[73] On the margin of Fakhr al-Dīn Rāzī's Mafātīḥ al-ghayb (Istanbūl: al-Maṭbaʿah al-ʿĀmirah, 1307 [1891], 8 voll. All volume and page references will be to this edition.

[74] De Hammer, Histoire, IV, 4-5; Ibn al-ʿImād, Shadharāt, VIII, 399.

sources have quoted, that in it Abū'l-Suᶜūd came forth with that which the mind would not permit [of which it could not conceive] and which ears have never heard.[75] In fact, at least in those portions of the commentary relevant to our study, he offers very little that we have not seen before, principally in the tafsīr of al-Bayḍāwī.

Before examining the Irshād in detail, we shall briefly consider the circumstances out of which Fayḍ al-Kāshānī composed his commentary, a work in many ways like that of Abū'l Suᶜūd and in other ways strikingly different.

Persia, out of which have sprung or through which have passed elements of nearly all of the forms of religiosity known to man, has been outstanding in Muslim history as one of the principal homes of both Shīᶜī and ṣūfī piety. It is appropriate, then, that for our study of the eleventh/seventeenth century we have a man who has been considered by his fellow Muslims to be one of the most important of the Shīᶜī writers as well as one of the greatest of the ṣūfī mystics, Fayḍ al-Kāshānī.

As the mystical approach has been only one of the many cross-currents in the religious life of Persia, so the Shīᶜah forms of worship have not always predominated in that country. It is interesting to note that each succeeding wave of rulers in Persia, from the time of the Sunnī Turks and the Shīᶜī Buwayhīs, has favored the branch of Islam not practised by its predecessors. Thus after the Buwayhī dynasties the Seljuks favored the Sunnīs, the Mongols the Shīᶜah, and the Tīmūrī rulers the Sunnīs.[76] By the time of the Ṣafavī dynasty, Shīᶜī doctrines had again been gaining strength in Persia, though by the early sixteenth century when the Ṣafavīyah took over, Persia was still mainly Sunnī.[77] It was not long, however, before Shīᶜī doctrines and practices gained sway over most of the country, a situation that still holds to this day.[78]

---

[75]". . . bi-mā lam tasmuḥu bi-hi al-adhhān wa-lam taqraᶜ bi-hi al-ādhān." (Manuq, al-ᶜIqd, p. 289) Cf. Ibn al-ᶜImād, Shadharāt, VIII, 399.

[76]See Donaldson, The Shi'ite Religion, pp. 291-93.

[77]"Between the Mongol invasion and the establishment of the Safavids Persia moved gradually toward Shīᶜism through both social, political and purely religious factors marked by the activity of certain Ṣūfī orders and several outstanding Shīᶜite theologians." (Seyyed Hossein Nasr, "Ithnā ᶜAsharī Shīᶜism and Iranian Islam", p. 100).

[78]At the present time some ninety-five per cent of all Iranians are Shīᶜī.

It is not surprising to find that with the political vicissitudes went the fortunes of the Shīʿī theologians and writers. We observed earlier that under Buwayhī rule were composed what are now known as the "Four Books" of early Shīʿī theology, written by al-Kulaynī, Ibn Babawayhī, and al-Ṭūsī.[79] Later under the protection offered by the Ṣafavī rulers a set of works was produced which has come to be known as the "three books", once more by a trio of writers with the name Muḥammad: (1) Muḥammad ibn Ḥasan ibn ʿAlī al-Ḥurr al-ʿĀmilī (d. 1100/1688), author of Amalu'l-Āmil; (2) Muḥammad ibn Murtaḍá Fayḍ al-Kāshānī (d. 1090/1680), whose work Kitāb al-wāfī is included in this group of three; and (3) Muḥammad Bāqir al-Majlisī (d. 1111/1699-1700), who wrote the famous Biḥāru'l-anwār.[80] These three works, along with the "Four Books" of the fourth and fifth centuries, form a core of Shīʿī theology, tradition and legal formulation.

The writer with whom we are specifically concerned, Muḥammad ibn Murtaḍá, more commonly known as Mullā Muḥsin-i-Fayḍ, was a native of Kāshān. His birth, according to calculations from references in his own writings, was about 1006/1597-8;[81] his death-date, of which we are more certain, is almost always given as 1090/1679-80.[82] He was an outspoken man, earning enemies as he harshly criticized some of the ʿulamā' and accused them of fisq and kufr. Yet in spite of his piety there were many who considered his own teachings as kufr because of their mystical-philosophical tendencies.[83] His general reputation seems to have been one of saintliness, however, and he was honored as a poet as well as theologian and philosopher. His tomb in Kāshān is revered as a holy place for the Shīʿah, to which many visitors come to pay homage.[84]

---

[79] See above, p. 77.

[80] Browne, A Literary History of Persia, IV, 358-59.

[81] Ibid., IV, 432. This is open to some question as it would have rendered him eighty-four at death, while some (eg. al-Khwānsārī, Rawḍāt, p. 516) indicate that he was at least ninety when he died.

[82] The reader is cautioned that the earlier edition of Brockelmann's GAL (II, 200) erroneously gives this date as 911/1505. This is corrected in the new edition (II, 413).

[83] Al-Baḥrānī (Lu'lu'at, p. 212) says that he came across one of al-Kāshānī's articles in which he calls for the unicity of being [waḥdat al-wujūd], describing the article as base [qabīḥah] and outspoken [ṣarīḥah].

[84] Al-Khwānsārī, Rawḍāt, p. 516.

Many tales are told pointing to the piety of al-Kāshānī and his family. One relates that when he wanted to go from Kāshān to Shīrāz to study with Mājid al-Baḥrānī his father at first refused permission, then decided to consult the Qur'ān. The augury, Q 9:123,[85] convinced him of the value of his son's trip.[86] The young man finally studied not only with al-Baḥrānī but with the famous Mullā Ṣadrá Muḥammad b. Ibrāhīm al-Shīrāzī (d. 1040-50/1630-41), whose son-in-law he later became.[87] Al-Kāshānī's works are recorded in some places as having exceeded eighty, in others as almost two hundred in number. In Arabic and Persian, they dealt with all of the traditional Islamic sciences. The fullest listing of his books and treatises, as well as biographical information, is to be found in the Persian Qiṣaṣu'l-ᶜulamā' of al-Tanukābūnī.

Despite his attentions to theology and tradition, however, al-Kāshānī's real fame came through his philosophical and mystical teachings. We noted above his stress on the unicity of being [waḥdat al-wujūd]; he was a great admirer of Ibn ᶜArabī and echoed in his writings many of the teachings of the famous Andalousian. (He is even reported to have copied much from Ibn ᶜArabī directly.)[88] Al-Wāfī, one of the "Three Books", shows in its explanation of ḥadīth definite ṣūfī leanings.[89]

---

[85] "It is not for the believers to go forth totally; but why should not a party of every section of them go forth, to become learned in religion, and to warn their people when they return to them, that haply they may beware?" (Q 9:123, Arberry translation).

[86] Al-Bahrānī, Lu'lu'at, p. 130; Browne, Literary History, p. 433. Another famous, though probably apocryphal, tale relates that al-Kāshānī was called upon by Shāh ᶜAbbās to meet with a foreigner who wanted to put the Muslim faith to the test. When Mullā Muhsin held hidden in his hand a rosary made from the clay of Husayn's tomb, the visitor identified the object as a piece of the earth of Paradise, and was promptly converted. (Donaldson, Shi'ite Religion, p. 301; Browne, Literary History, IV, 434).

[87] Henri Corbin (Terre Céleste, p. 183) testifies to al-Kāshānī's stature, saying: "Mohsen Fayz Kashānī, fut . . . un des plus brillants élèves de Mollā Sadrā et, après celui-ci, une des plus grandes figures de savants imāmites du XIe siècle de l'hégire."

[88] Al-Bahrānī, Lu'lu'at, p. 121. It should be observed, however, that this chronicler shows no great appreciation of either Ibn ᶜArabī, whom he calls a Zindīq, or of Fayd al-Kashānī, although he devotes some ten pages to a biography of the latter.

[89] Al-ᶜĀmilī, Amal al-āmil, p. 305. Al-ᶜĀmilī indicates that most of al-Kāshānī's works were written with a ṣūfī bent.

Traditionally, of course, the Shī^cah have been opposed to most of the elements of ṣūfī interpretation and there has been a long history of opposition to this kind of approach. It is true, however, that many Shī^cah have been attracted by elements of mystical thought, particularly in the later centuries. Undoubtedly aware of the dangers of ṣūfī identification, al-Kāshānī defended himself against the charges of mysticism, yet there is no doubt that many of his writings reflect strong ṣūfī influence.[90]

Al-Kāshānī's best-known Persian work is Abwābu'l-janān, a treatise on the necessity of prayer. In Arabic his fame rests primarily on the above-mentioned Kitāb al-wāfī and on his Qur'ān commentary al-Ṣāfī fī tafsīr kalām Allāh al-wāfī.[91] Completed in 1075/1664, the latter is, as Nöldeke says, a work that reveals the areas in which the teachings of the Shī^cah are touched with ṣūfī interpretation.[92] In addition to its reliance on al-Bayḍāwī, this tafsīr contains frequent references to the exegesis done in the fourth century by al-Qummī. Still in lithographed form, al-Ṣāfī has not yet received among Western orientalists the attention it deserves as the heir of the rich Shī^cī and ṣūfī teachings of Persia as well as the classical doctrines of Muslim traditionalism.[93]

* * *

As was indicated earlier, these tafsīrs follow so closely the Anwār al-tanzīl of al-Bayḍāwī, which in turn is based to a large extent on al-Zamakhsharī's Kashshāf, that their primary interest for us will be to note those areas in which they specifically differ. Such divergence is far more common in al-Ṣāfī, of course, particularly because of the author's Shī^cī and ṣūfī

---

[90] R. Strothmann ("Shī^ca" in EI, IV, 356-7) gives a brief but helpful summary of the mutual antagonisms between the Shī^cah and the ṣūfīs and philosophers. He cites al-Kāshānī's work Inṣāf fī bayān ṭarīq al-^cilm li-asrār al-dīn as the locus of his defense against charges of mysticism.

[91] Teheran, 1266 [1850], 1 vol.

[92] Geschichte, II, 181.

[93] That its importance has been recognized, however, is attested to by Arthur Jeffery ("The present status of Qur'ānic studies", p. 11); "For Shī^ca exegesis we are still largely dependent on the old standard works of al-Ṭabarsī, al-Qummī and al-Kāshānī."

interests.[94]

Abū'l Suᶜūd repeats almost word for word the comments of al-Bayḍāwī on 3:19 ❬Truly *al-dīn* with God is *al-islām*❭, saying that this is a sentence confirming the above affirmation that there is no God but He and that no *dīn* is acceptable to God except *al-islām*. However, where al-Bayḍāwī goes on to define *islām* as "*al-tawḥīd* and arming oneself with the *sharᶜ* that Muḥammad brought" (I, 197), Abū'l-Suᶜūd changes the last part of this to "embracing the noble *sharīᶜah* [*al-tadarruᶜ* *bi'l-sharīah* *al-sharīfah*]". (II, 628) This becomes even more significant when considered along with his succeeding comments on 3:19 ❬Those to whom the Book has been given did not differ . . .❭:

> This was revealed to the Jews and the Christians when they departed from *al-islām* which the Prophet brought [*alladhī* *jā'a* *bi-hi* *al-nabī*], denying his prophethood. (II, 628)

We have referred above to the investigations of W. C. Smith[95] concerning the usage of the various forms of *sharaᶜa* in classical Muslim writing. Our study of *tafsīr* thus far has confirmed his findings that *sharīᶜah* is generally seen as particularized and *sharᶜ* as absolute. Early Qur'ān commentators rarely used *sharīᶜah*, but tended much more to the usage of *sharᶜ*. It seems from Abū'l-Suᶜūd's choice of *sharīᶜah* as a specific substitution for al-Bayḍāwī's word *sharᶜ* that he wishes to convey the meaning of the more particularized group of regulations characterizing the community of Islam. This, of course, is not surprising to find in the *tafsīr* of one who was daily concerned with the application of laws. His use of the phrase "*alladhī* *jā'a* *bi-hi* *al-nabī*" in connection with *islām* itself in his remarks on 3:19 supports this. If *islām* for him is *tawḥīd* and arming oneself with the *sharīᶜah*, then he is referring to the *sharīᶜah* brought by Muḥammad, the specific regulations by which one carried out the will of God rather than to *sharᶜ* itself, God's absolute commanding of man. The distinction is subtle but real. It has been general among the *mufassirūn* to exegete 5:3 in terms of specific regulations, but not 3:19. Here, however, Abū'l-Suᶜūd

---

[94] That al-Kāshānī was willing to incorporate elements of *ṣūfī* interpretation into his work is a strong indication of the flexibility of his Shīᶜī stance. His willingness to rely to a great extent on what had by then become standard Sunnī *tafsīr* indicates again that he was attempting to transcend the purely Shīᶜī categories of interpretation, and brings into question the whole relationship of Shīᶜī doctrine to the larger Islamic tradition.

[95] "The concept of sharīᶜa"; see above, p. 111, n. 160; p. 123.

is defining islām clearly in terms of those requirements for man which are specifically a part of the community of Islam. In other words, islām, which is still man's act, is understood with an implication of communal reference generally not seen earlier in connection with this crucial 3:19 verse.

It is convenient for our study that of the eight Qur'ān verses mentioning islām 3:18-19 comes first in order, for it is in the tafsīr of this passage that we usually find statements most characteristic of the approach of the individual commentators. So we see in our first exposure to al-Kāshānī's thought that he is most clearly of a mystical persuasion, that he is a Shīʿī with the usual reliance on traditional Shīʿī exposition, and that the understanding of islām as dīn is inseparable from an understanding of the divine proclamation that "There is no God but He". In a presentation different from that of the previous commentators, he sets up an interesting structure in terms of the first three divisions of 3:18. Concerning the first ﴿God has borne witness that there is no God but He﴾ al-Kāshānī says:

> He explains His oneness [waḥdānīyah] to [some] people by His being manifest [ẓuhūr] in everything, making known His essence [dhāt] in every light and shadow, to [some] people by establishing a proof that points to it [His oneness], and to [some] people by revealing the āyahs by which it is expressed. (p. 91)

Al-Kāshānī's recognition of the unicity of being, here expressed as God's oneness shown forth in all things, is clear in this lovely passage. True to the mystical understanding, however, he indicates that only certain people can truly know God in this intuitive way; others need more explicit evidence such as the setting up of a proof or the direct guidance of God's special signs (by which he presumably means the verses of the Qur'ān as well as other tokens). This three-fold division is paralleled by the tafsīr of the following phrase ﴿likewise the angels﴾. These beings, he says, illustrate God's oneness

> . . . by affirming [bi'l-iqrār] through essence [dhātan] to [some] people, through action [fiʿlan] to [some] people and through speech [qawlan] to [some] people. (p. 91)

One of the particular characteristics of Islam is its tendency to classify people into various groups and categories. For the fuqahā' this has been a legal question, for the ṣūfīs a matter of religious instruction and of levels of knowledge. Al-Kāshānī expresses this tendency here by indicating that those who are able to come to a knowledge of God by His manifestation in every light and shadow can understand the affirmation of the angels in essence, while those requiring proofs are the ones needing an activist indication, and it is the ones to whom the *āyahs* are necessary that the angels affirm verbally. These divisions are not to be understood as detailed descriptions of reality, of course, but rather as a poetical expression of the levels at which God's creatures can come to knowledge of Him. This mystical apprehension is shown most clearly in the explanation of the third phrase of 3:18 ❴and the people of knowledge❵. These, he says, affirm God's oneness by faith.

> And the seeing clearly [*al-^{c}iyān* (which is what the angels do)] and the making clear [*al-bayān* (which is what God does)] resemble the becoming apparent [*al-ẓuhūr*] and the making apparent [*al-iẓhār*] in the unveiling [*al-inkishāf*] for oneself and the uncovering [*al-kashf*] [for others] by the testimony of the witnesses. (p. 91)

After quoting a *ḥadīth* concerning the final phrase of 3:18 ❴[It is He who] maintains justice❵, (it is interesting to note that here the people of knowledge, the Prophet and those who have been given guardianship [*al-awṣiyā'*],[96] also maintain justice), al-Kāshānī comes to the verse which is of particular interest for us. It would appear from the commentary, however, that ❴Truly *al-dīn* with God is *al-islām*❵ is of less direct interest to this *mufassir* than the previous verse, though the relationship between the two is clear. He seems to imply that since the fact of import is God's unicity and its manifestation in all things, man's *dīn* can of course be nothing other than the recognition of this. Thus with none of the elaboration of the *tafsīr* on the previous *āyah*, he says (as did al-Bayḍāwī):

> There is no *dīn* acceptable to God other than the *dīn al-islām* which is *al-tawḥīd* and arming oneself with the *shar^{c}* which Muḥammad brought. (p. 91)

Al-Kāshānī chooses to stick with *shar^{c}*, the term originally used in this particular definition by al-Bayḍāwī, rather than changing it to the "sharī^{c}ah" of Abū'l-Su^{c}ūd. We are, of course, left to wonder whether this was a conscious choice or if it simply did not occur to him to make the substitution preferred by the *shaykh al-islām*.

---

[96]The term *waṣīy* is the designation usually given by the Shī^{c}ah to ^{c}Alī himself (and *awṣiyā'* to the succeeding *imāms*), used in contrast to *khalīfah* which connotes the idea of physical succession only. The *waṣīy* is the one in whose favor the Prophet himself is believed to have spoken and *wiṣāyah* is thus the theological basis of the *imāmah*. The Sunnī term usually used for those considered to enjoy a special position of saintliness or nearness to God is *awliyā'*, applied to those whom the Shī^{c}ah consider the *awṣiyā'*. These terms have been interchangeable to some extent; al-Qummī used *awliyā'* to refer to the ^{c}Alawī line of *imāms*; both he and al-Kāshānī discuss the *wilāyah* (the latter also calls it the *imāmah*) of ^{c}Alī.

Then after all of the lofty poetical exegesis that has preceded, al-Kāshānī provides us with some very down-to-earth exposition when he quotes al-Ṣādiq in al-Kāfī as saying that "al-islām is before al-īmān because it is the basis of inheritance and marriage and īmān is that which earns one a reward." (p. 91) We shall find this idea repeated in the tafsīr of 49:14; what he apparently is saying is that the system of islām provides the formal structure for carrying out the practical arrangements of life, and it is into this that one is born and is automatically a muslim. Or, he might be indicating that islām is the act or fact of joining the ummah, the consequences of which are an assured basis for these practical arrangements. As we have observed before, the apparent ambiguity may well indicate that the two possibilities as we see them were not separate for al-Kāshānī (or al-Ṣādiq). Later on, when one comes to a fuller understanding of the meaning of God's revelation, says al-Kāshānī, one expresses affirmation of that revelation and thus proclaims that one has reached the stage of īmān. It may be, then, that for him at least one meaning of islām is that community of Muslims which by his time had established itself as a continuing group with a well-grounded legal and social structure. This is certainly not obvious, however, and in any case we can see that it is not the primary understanding for him since his initial definition of islām is in terms of tawḥīd and acceptance of shar^{c}. This is reinforced by his following reference to those to whom the book has come as not having differed "in al-islām". Obviously the other Peoples of the Book were not a part of that system whose regulations al-Kāshānī may have been mentioning when he spoke of inheritance and marriage.

The basic definition of islām given by both authors in the commentary on 3:85 ❴whoever accepts other than al-islām as dīn❵ comes directly from al-Bayḍāwī: "i.e. other than the profession of God's oneness [al-tawḥīd] and submission [al-inqiyād] to God's rule [ḥukm]." (Kashshāf, I, 217; Irshād, II, 736; al-Ṣāfī, p. 99) Unlike the others, Abū'l-Su^{c}ūd elaborates some by classifying among those who choose other than al-islām the ones who allege al-tawḥīd along with their shirk, such as the Peoples of the Book. While not really adding to the definition, it does reinforce the basic understanding of islām as the sincere affirmation of God's unity rather than verbal acknowledgement only. Both commentators echo al-Bayḍāwī's words that those whose dīn is unacceptable will be the final losers by spoiling the sound disposition [al-fiṭrah al-salīmah], and Abū'l-Su^{c}ūd includes the statement of the Kashshāf that this verse does not necessarily prove that islām and īmān are one.

We have seen that 5:3 has generally been the occasion for commentators to elaborate their understanding of the particular duties that God has enjoined on man. Abū'l-Suʿūd and al-Kāshānī are no exceptions, although the Shīʿī background of the latter makes his understanding considerably different from that of the Sunnī writers.

The author of the Irshād again adheres very closely to the tafsīr of al-Bayḍāwī, emphasizing that the completion of dīn means either victory over all religions (al-adyān) or determining the bases of doctrines and the analyses of the laws (al-sharā'iʿ). (III, 522) Perhaps the only point worth some mention, other than the fact that he continues to use the plural al-adyān freely, is that while al-Bayḍāwī gave as one understanding of the fulfilling of God's pleasure that He has completed al-dīn [bi-ikmāl al-dīn] (Kashshāf, I, 323), the shaykh al-islām adds "wa'l-sharā'iʿ", (Irshād, III, 523), taking another opportunity to emphasize that islām does involve the understanding and execution of specific laws and regulations.

This time with al-Kāshānī, however, we enter an area quite different from the tafsīr of al-Bayḍāwī. The only actual mention of islām comes at the end of 5:2 when in speaking of the despair of those who reject "your dīn", he says ⧉do not fear them⧉ means, do not fear "that they would claim victory over dīn al-islām and turn you away from your dīn." (p. 144)

Several interpretations are possible here. One could say that al-Kāshānī saw the verse to mean that the muslims were not to fear that their way of responding to God in tawḥīd and submission to His ḥukm and sharʿ would be supplanted by a better way. Or he may have understood that they were not to fear for the continuity of the particular community of the followers of the Prophet. Most likely, however, as we noted above, it would never have occurred to the commentator to choose between such alternatives. The dīn al-islām seems to mean here the way of submitting to God that characterized the members of the ummah and thus was also its name.

While most of the previous writers of tafsīr have discussed 5:3 by dividing it into the three clauses, al-Kāshānī quotes the the entire verse, then concerns himself primarily with the understanding of what is meant by the completion of dīn. This āyah was revealed, he says, after the Prophet established ʿAlī as a learned one [ʿāliman] for mankind on the day of Ghadīr

Khum[97] as he was leaving the Ḥajj al-Wadā^{c}. "It is the last obligation [*farīḍ*] that God revealed and after it He will reveal no other obligation." (p. 144) He quotes several Shī^{c}ī authorities, including al-Qummī, in support of the contention that God bestowed knowledge on ^{c}Alī and his progeny and on *al-awṣiyā'* (the *imāms*) one after the other. When this was done *dīn* was complete and grace fulfilled. We are left with the unspoken but certainly implied conclusion that *islām* includes for al-Kāshānī, and the Shī^{c}ah in general, acceptance of the authority of ^{c}Alī and his descendents. As we saw earlier with al-Qummī, this seems to be the general point of distinction between the Shī^{c}ī and the Sunnī understandings of *islām*.

In none of the *tafsīr* considered in this essay has there been any tendency whatsoever to interpret the *islām* in verses 6:125 and 39:22 as referring to the particular community of *muslims*. The very structure of the verses almost precludes any such understanding and it is rather to the implied relationship between *islām* and *īmān* that most commentators have devoted themselves. Both Abū'l-Su^{c}ūd (IV, 207-8) and Fayḍ al-Kāshānī (p. 182) repeat (with some minor variations in the latter) al-Bayḍāwī's entire *tafsīr* of 6:125. We can only refer the reader to the above notations on this portion of *al-Kashshāf* (see above pp. 125-26) and again raise the unanswerable question of whether or not they would have given a similar interpretation had they not been guided by the authority of tradition.

Similarly concerning 39:22 Abū'l-Su^{c}ūd (VII, 250) presents al-Bayḍāwī's discussion of *islām* as accepted by the soul [*nafs*] which in turn is related to the spirit [*rūḥ*], the heart [*qalb*] and the breast [*ṣadr*] (see pp. 125-26 above). Al-Kāshānī, omitting this passage, does quote al-Bayḍāwī that the opening of the breast means that one is able to take hold of *al-islām* with ease (p. 455). Yet he adds a distinctively Shī^{c}ī note with the comment taken from al-Qummī that the revelation came concerning *amīr al-mu'minīn*, namely ^{c}Alī. Skipping to his commentary on 61:7-8 we find the following interesting passage concerning those who wish to extinguish the light of God with their mouths:

> . . . they wish to extinguish the emirate [*wilāyah* of *amīr al-mu'minīn*] by their mouths. God is the fulfiller of *al-imāmah* by His saying ❴they believe in God and His Messenger and the light which We revealed❵ [64:8] and the light is *al-imām*. (p. 518)

---

[97]This day has become the occasion for a Shī^{c}ī festival honoring the moment at which the Prophet named ^{c}Alī as his successor.

Now if we put together al-Kāshānī's assertion on 39:22 that the opening of the breast to al-islām means widening and enlarging the heart for the light with the clear statement of 61:7 that the light is the wilāyah or imāmah of ᶜAlī, we have added support for the understanding he conveyed on 5:3 that acceptance of the role and authority of ᶜAlī in the direction of religious life is a real part of the meaning of islām.

As usual, the understanding presented in these verses of islām as reception of the light of God, with all that that involves, stands in apparent contrast to the implications of 49:14-17. Again we hear the echo of al-Bayḍāwī's (and al-Zamakhsharī's) words when both Abū'l-Suᶜūd and al-Kāshānī define islām as "being led [al-inqiyād] and entering into peace [al-silm] and giving witness to the testimony [al-shahādah] and ceasing fighting", and al-īmān as "confirmation [al-taṣdīq] with trust [al-thiqah] and peacefulness [tuma'nīnah] of the heart". (Irshād, VIII, 607-8; al-Ṣāfī, p. 491) Abū'l-Suᶜūd gives a bit more detail in his discussion of the relationship of islām and īmān, but in general follows the discussion given by al-Bayḍāwī, ending with the summary statement that while the Arabs of Bani Asad claimed īmān as a favor, in reality such favor can be from God alone and that by which these people were characterized in reality was [an] islām [fī'l-ḥaqīqah islām]. (Irshād, VIII, 710) As with the cases above where al-Zamakhsharī and al-Bayḍāwī used islām without the article, it seems insupportable to suppose that anything other than the individual act of submission is involved, however superficial this may be understood in contrast to al-īmān.

Clearly in 49:14-17 islām involves the outward acts by which one was permitted to join the muslim community, namely not fighting but remaining at peace with them and giving the verbal testimony that there is no God but God (this may also have included the testimony that Muḥammad is the Prophet of God). Al-Kāshānī emphasizes this by repeating the statement given above on 3:19 that islām is before īmān and in it one inherits and marries, while by īmān one is rewarded. Again we have the suggestion that for this writer the act of submission and the name of the group one enters upon submitting are indistinguishable. That he is principally concerned, as was Abū'l-Suᶜūd, with the act itself, however, is indicated in his following words of clarification:

> And the individual [ᶜabd] can be a muslim before he is a mu'min but cannot be a mu'min unless he is a muslim. For islām is before īmān and it is a partner of [yushāriku] al-īmān. If a person commits one of the grave sins or one of the small sins which God has forbidden

> he is outside of īmān [khārijan min al-īmān], the name of īmān fallen from him, and the name of islām established upon him [thābitan ᶜalayhi]. (p. 491)

This does not mean, of course, that when īmān is forfeited islām then begins; it is rather that islām may continue even after one is outside of īmān. If any further proof is needed of the distinction between these two terms, al-Kāshānī cites the tradition that islām is external [al-ẓāhir], making incumbent on people what have come to be known as the five arkān. "This is al-islām, and al-īmān is the (intimate) knowledge of this matter [maᶜrifat hāthā'l-amr]. Furthermore, if one confesses it and does not know [i.e. understand] this command, he is a muslim and he is misguided [ḍāll]." (p. 491)

Nothing could be clearer than this distinction, and for the first time since his discussion of 3:19 we find some hint of al-Kāshānī's ṣūfī inclination. Islām involves those specific external acts by which one associates himself with the community of muslims. (It is surprising to note how seldom in the other tafsīrs we have studied that the five arkān have been specifically enumerated as they are here.) Īmān, on the other hand, is equated with knowledge [maᶜrifah], by which the mystic understands that special insight into the nature of God's manifestation characterized by various levels of attainment. These levels have been described beautifully in his commentary on 3:18, as we saw above. Islām is performance of what is commanded, and īmān is the perception and understanding of the real content, and intent, of that command. Al-Kāshānī's last words above are an unequivocal statement of the difference between islām and īmān when he concludes that if one cannot be said to possess īmān, cannot really understand the command although he confesses it, he is characterized only by islām and while certainly not doomed is nonetheless misguided.[98]

The tafsīr of Qur'ān 61:7-9 often proves to be a kind of conclusion to the understanding of an author's thought on dīn and islām, much as the commentary on 3:19 usually gives a good introduction. Here we find Abū'l-Suᶜūd continuing to quote al-Bayḍāwī, particularly in speaking of islām as that which leads one to the joy of this world and the next (VIII, 198) and the putting out of God's light as meaning extinguishing "dīnahu aw-kitābahu aw-ḥujjatahu". (VIII, 199) We might press the

---

[98]See Izutsu, The Concept of Belief (pp. 35-36), for an historical discussion of the position taken by different groups of Muslim theologians concerning the relationship of the one who commits grave sins to īmān and islām.

point that by putting "His dīn" in apposition to two objective genitives, His Book and His proof, al-Bayḍāwī and Abū'l-Su^c^ūd intend "God's religion" rather than "man's service [dīn] of God". Even if this were the case, however, it would be difficult to argue that the intention is a reified group dīn rather than a metaphysical reality, although for Abū'l-Su^c^ūd especially there has been considerable stress on the practical legal aspects of dīn al-islām. It is interesting to note in this connection the change that has taken place in the tafsīr of 61:9 ﴿. . . that He may make it predominate over all dīn﴾. We have already seen that while earlier commentators continued to use dīn in the explanation, after al-Zamakhsharī the change to adyān has generally prevailed. We also find that while al-Ṭabarī spoke of this victory coming at the descent of ^c^Īsá b. Maryam, al-Zamakhsharī, here quoted by Abu'l-Su^c^ūd, indicates that God has already accomplished it,

> so that there does not remain [lam yabqa] a religion among the religions [dīn min al-adyān] except it be overcome and vanquished by dīn al-islām. (VIII, 199)

As with al-Zamakhsharī, we can only speculate as to whether Abū'l-Su^c^ūd intends dīn in the reified sense or not, although for a shaykh al-islām under Sulaymān the Magnificent in one of the most glorious periods of Ottoman history it is not difficult to imagine that he considered the Islamic religion, with all of its legal specifications, to have been proven superior in every way to the religions with which it had historically come into confrontation. Again, however, these are only hints as to what Abū'l-Su^c^ūd really meant; it is particularly difficult to discern his intention when so much of his material is repetition. Yet it would seem that with the emphasis on the sharā'i^c^ and these suggestions of islām in relation to al-adyān that we may well be seeing the beginnings of that more reified understanding of islām of which we shall find clearer examples in the tafsīr of the twentieth century.

In commenting on 61:7, Fayḍ al-Kāshānī brings us full circle back to his original definition and understanding of islām. He begins by saying as did al-Bayḍāwī that there is none more sinful than the one who makes a claim of falsehood against God after having been called to external [al-ẓāhir] islām, (p. 518) and from the tafsīr of 49:14 we assume he means the islām by which one formally acknowledges membership in the muslim community through performance of the prescribed duties. Again following al-Bayḍāwī, in discussing 61:9 in which God says He will make dīn al-ḥaqq victorious over all dīn, he says that this dīn, which has already been identified with islām, is the true attribution of unity to God [maḥḍ al-tawḥīd] and refusing to associate any other with Him [ibṭāl al-shirk].

What he seems to be saying throughout this tafsīr is not, as it might appear, that in one sense islām is the external performance of those obligations by which one identifies with the muslim and in a other sense it is the inner affirmation of God's unity and acceptance of His sharᶜ. The tawḥīd and arming oneself with the sharᶜ are also very much a part of the external [ẓāhir] islām which he so carefully has distinguished from īmān in 3:19 and 49:14. It is clear from his discussion of 6:125 that he does not mean by saying islām is ẓāhir that it cannot be sincere. Islām is tawḥīd, and the expression of it is in the saying of the shahādah which he indicates is the first requirement of islām. He does not specify it, but we may infer that there are various degrees of personal commitment involved, ranging from the islām described in 6:125 to that of the Arabs of Bani Asad.

In one sense we can say that in stressing islām as the basis for such legal particulars as marriage and inheritance, al-Kāshānī is strongly emphasizing its group, i.e. reified, usage. Yet he never distinguishes this from the personal individual act by which one acknowledges himself to be a member of that community. His real point is that this islām, though linked with īmān, is really different from it. Islām is the expression of tawḥīd, but īmān is the comprehension [maᶜrifah] of the command of Him about whom one acknowledges unicity according to the understanding of His essence that has been granted to one by God.

XII

It is significant -- and unpremeditated insofar as the design of this essay is concerned -- that with the passing centuries the best-known exegetes of the Muslim world have represented areas increasingly distant from the old centers of Arab power in Arabia, Syria and ᶜIrāq. Thus investigation of the last few centuries has taken us from Egypt to the heart of the Ottoman empire in what is now Turkey and to Persia. For the twelfth/eighteenth century we move even farther to an area in which at least one individual was beginning to feel the stirrings of what was later to take the shape of active reform. The place is India, the person is Shāh Walī Allāh of Delhi.

In considering the work of al-Dihlawī we are departing from our general theme in two ways. In the first place, he wrote no tafsīr as we have come to understand Qur'ānic exegesis in terms of specific interlinear commentary. He was, however, devoted to the study of the Qur'ān and principles of exegesis. Although in the strict sense of the terms he was neither modern nor an exegete, he is cited by J.M.S. Baljon in Modern Muslim Koran Interpretation (p. 3) as "the man who discerned the signs of his times", a precursor of modern commentary. Taking his major work as a tafsīr in the loose sense of the word (a freer understanding of which characterizes much of what is considered exegesis in the fourteenth/twentieth century) we shall attempt to trace some of the themes that have emerged in the study of the concepts islām and dīn in the writings of previous mufassirūn.

The second way in which a study of Walī Allāh is a change from the pattern of this study is that he is not a traditionalist in the sense characterized by the other commentators of the seventh/thirteenth century period. That is, while pledged to the study of ḥadīth and tradition, and indeed supremely convinced of their importance, he does not accept the conclusions of centuries of theologians without exercise of his own powers of rational criticism. There are exegetes from his century, of course, who did follow the mode exemplified by the others of the "middle ages" of Islam.[99] Aside from the fact that these others are relatively little known and little read, in general they are rather uninteresting by virtue of their apparent failure to provide much of any material not seen before (at least as concerns the passages of relevance to our study). We are therefore going to digress from the pattern of interlinear commentary for one century's consideration in order, hopefully, to provide some fresh insights into the general theme and particularly to take the opportunity to become acquainted to some small degree with the thought of one of the outstanding thinkers and writers of the history of Islam.

It is readily apparent that a few pages can only begin to introduce a man who has been described as pre-modernist, fundamentalist, conservative, socialist. Aziz Ahmad calls him "the common fountain head of Deoband orthodoxy and of Aligarh modernism",[100] one whose fundamentalism "heralded the first thaw which

---

[99] Such a mufassir was Sulaymān ibn ᶜUmar al-Jamal (d. 1204/1790), whose commentary al-Futūḥāt al-ilāhīyah is replete with repetition of the tafsīr of preceding centuries.

[100] Islamic Modernism, p. 198.

melted, to some extent, the frozen and rigid mass of traditionalist orthodoxy in Indian Islam and pointed the way simultaneously to two mutually incompatible directions, revivalist conservatism and rationalist modernism."[101] That Walī Allāh himself saw rationalism and conservatism not only as compatible but as essential to each other is abundantly clear in his writings.

Al-Dihlawī's life must be seen against the background of a tumultuous political situation in India. Indo-Muslim society was entering a period of sharp decline after the glorious days of Moghul power and influence. Following the death of Emperor Awrangzīb ᶜĀlamgīr in 1119/1707 the efforts of that ruler to enforce the _sharīᶜah_ were discontinued and his successors were notoriously weak and ineffective.[102] Walī Allāh watched India sink into a time of increased internal chaos and strife under the rule of ten emperors after ᶜĀlimgīr. Added to these internal problems was the arrival of European powers in India, particularly the British in Bengal and Behar. Walī Allāh saw in his own land conditions that led him to be concerned over the double threat of internal deterioration and external overlordship.[103] To this was added through his travels an awareness of the deteriorating conditions of other areas of the Muslim world. Out of this situation grew his intense interest in redefining the bases of morality and coming to a renewed understanding of the fundamentals of _dīn_ as outlined in the Qur'ān and _ḥadīth_.

Most sources indicate that Aḥmad bin ᶜAbd al-Raḥīm al-ᶜUmarī al-Dihlawī was born four years before the death of Emperor ᶜĀlamgīr, in 1115/1703. His own Persian autobiography, however, gives the date as 1110/1698.[104] It is reported that his father, a master of the _ṣūfī_ Naqshbandīyah (who was sixty years old at the time), was informed of the impending birth of his only son by the occurrence of a variety of auspicious signs.[105] At the age of five, Walī Allāh finished reading the Qur'ān and moved to Persian works, at ten he began independent study and by fifteen

---

[101] _Ibid._, p. 2.

[102] Rahbar, "Shāh Walī Ullāh and ijtihād" in _MW_, XLV (1955), 346.

[103] Cf. Smith, _Islam in Modern History_, pp. 51-53.

[104] Hussain, "The Persian autobiography of Shāh Walīullah" in _JASB_, VIII (1912), 161. Cf. al-Kattānī, _Fihrist_, who in I, 125 gives 1110 and in II, 436 gives 1114.

[105] Ṣiddīq Ḥasan, _Abjad al-ᶜulūm_, p. 912.

was considered learned in logic, philosophy, astronomy, mathematics, fiqh, uṣūl, ḥadīth, tafsīr and taṣawwuf.[106]

Extremely important to Walī Allāh's early training, and consequently to his emerging theology, was the heritage of ṣūfī mysticism from his father. At the same time that he was completing his regular course in the traditional areas of study, he says in his autobiography, "[I] devoted myself to occupations of the ṣūfī, specially (sic) those of Naqshbandīya saints. With regard to tawajjuh (meditation), talqīn (instruction), learning the mode of religious rites, and putting on the garment of the ṣūfī I equipped myself . . ."[107]. At the death of his father, when he was only seventeen, he was allowed the privileges of bayᶜah (initiating others into the order) and irshād (spiritual instruction).[108] He remained a ṣūfī throughout his life, devoted to purging his land of the hypocrisy and sham of many of its mystical orders. We are told that he continued to have frequent experiences of mystical awareness.[109]

When his father died, Walī Allāh took his place as lecturer at the Madrasah Raḥīmīyah at Delhi. In 1143/1731 he left for the ḥijāz on pilgrimage.[110] Here over the course of fourteen months he developed his growing interest in the sciences of ḥadīth and jurisprudence and declared himself, as have others of the mufassirūn of this study, to be the mujaddid or reformer of his age. Again we see the direct influence of his mystical orientation as he is said to have received guidance from the Prophet and from God Himself.[111] (A question of considerable interest, but one on which little light has been thrown, is whether or not he came into contact with the Wahhābīyah while in Arabia.) After returning to Delhi his popularity as a teacher grew to such an extent that a new madrasah was constructed for him at the Imperial Palace where he continued to instruct until his death in 1176/1763.[112]

---

[106] Ḥasanal-Maᶜṣūmī, "An appreciation of Shāh Walīullah" in IC, XXI (1947), 342; Husain, "Persian autobiography", p. 162.

[107] Husain, "Persian autobiography", p. 163.

[108] Ibid., p. 165.

[109] Ṣiddīq Ḥasan (Abjad, p. 912) describes several of his apprehensions of tawḥīd in which the knowledge of existence descended on his heart.

[110] al-Kattānī, Fihrist, II, 436.

[111] Ḥasanal-Maᶜṣūmī, "An appreciation of Shāh Walīullah", pp. 343-4.

[112] Ibid., pp. 344-5.

He is conceded to have been one of the most learned men of his time, his influence extending to the formation of what is considered the Walī Allāh school of fundamentalism/reformism.[113] Primary in his consideration were the two basic sources of the Qur'ān and _ḥadīth_ materials. It is said that he resurrected _ḥadīth_ and _sunnah_ in India after they had long since been dead, that under him the dead branch of the study of traditions became infused with new life.[114] Closely related to this was his interest in _fiqh_. He saw about him a people for whom the fundamentals of the _sharīᶜah_ had become increasingly unimportant. To the study of the _uṣūl_ of _fiqh_ and _ḥadīth_ he carried the tool of reason, realizing that the centuries of _taqlīd_, blind following of the dogma of the ages, had helped to deaden the spirit of Muslims in his own country and elsewhere.[115] He was convinced that a rational approach to the teachings of the Qur'ān would help to bring about the social, political and economic reforms so badly needed in the Muslim world.

Al-Dihlawī belonged to the Ḥanafī school of law, which he considered to be the most flexible of the four. His goal was a common meeting-ground between them in which the rational study of _fiqh_, _ḥadīth_ and Qur'ān would result in a reconciliation of differences. (Rationalism, however, did not carry him to the extreme of eliminating the obligations of the law.[116]) He wrote two commentaries on _ḥadīth_, one in Persian and one in Arabic, maintaining that the most authentic of the collections is the _Muwaṭṭa'_ of Imām Mālik rather than works of al-Bukhārī or Muslim.[117]

Of the nearly fifty works to his credit, many consider his translation of the Qur'ān into Persian, _Fatḥ al-raḥmān bi-tarjamat al-Qur'ān_, to be the most important. (Unfortunately not all of his countrymen approved of this project, some labelling it

---

[113]Walī Allāh's legacy is a fascinating study, particularly in such areas as the contrast of his teaching with that of Ibn al-Wahhāb, his direct influence on thinkers like Sayyid Aḥmad Khān, and the development of the theological school at Deoband.

[114]al-Kattānī, _Fihrist_, I, 125 and II, 437. Actually ᶜAbd al-Ḥaqq Muḥaddith of _Dihli_ preceded him in this.

[115]We shall find this theme reiterated with great clarity in the writings of Muḥammad ᶜAbduh in the fourteenth/twentieth century.

[116]See Rahbar, "Shah Walī Ullāh and ijtihād", p. 346.

[117]al-Kattānī, _Fihrist_, II, 437; cf. Isḥāq, _India's Contribution to the Study of Ḥadith Literature_, pp. 172-74.

bid^c^ah, innovation, an accusation which did little to discourage Walī Allāh.[118]) He also set out his own statement on matters concerning the interpretation of the Qur'ān in a brief and concise work entitled al-Fawz al-kabīr fī uṣūl al-tafsīr. Only about one-twentieth the size of al-Suyūṭī's Itqān, this Persian work deals critically with the science of Qur'ān exegesis.

The writing generally considered to be his magnum opus, and that with which we are dealing in this essay, is the Arabic Ḥujjat Allāh al-bālighah.[119] A kind of encyclopaedia of Islamic sciences, it treats not only the fundamentals of dīn but a variety of other subjects including metaphysics, politics and economics. Underlying all of it is his emphasis on the rational basis of the ordinances of God. In this essay we shall examine only certain sections, determined by table of contents rather than, as usual, by commentary on specific āyahs. Our aim, however, will be the continuing development of the understanding of dīn al-islām as it relates to and grows out of the interpretation of the verses of the Qur'ān.

It is not the purpose of this essay to evaluate the success of Walī Allāh's endeavors or of the movement that bears his name. Let us rather acknowledge him as an engaging thinker and personality, a fresh breeze blowing over the centuries of repetitious commentary, and thereby more than worthy of our attention at this point in our historical survey.

* * *

As the only work considered in this essay that is not an interlinear tafsīr, the Ḥujjat Allāh presents some problems in analysis not usually encountered. The most obvious is that to lift his comments on islām out of the context of his thought as developed throughout the two volumes of this work is perhaps to risk an injustice not so likely with the traditional tafsīrs. His discussion of īmān, islām and dīn is set against the background of a detailed sociological structure, for a complete understanding of which it really is necessary to consider the entire work. Keeping in mind the limitations of this kind of analysis, however, we shall attempt to trace a general understanding

---

[118] Hasanal-Ma^c^sūmī, "An appreciation of Shāh Walīullah", p. 348; see also Rahbar, "Reflections on the tradition of Qur'anic exegesis" in MW, LII (1962), 305.

[119] Cairo: Idārat al-Ṭibā^c^ah al-Munīrīyah, 1352 [1933], 2 voll.

of Walī Allāh's views on the meaning of islām and the closely related terms dīn and īmān.

The first and most obvious thing to be noted about Walī Allāh's treatment of the term islām in Ḥujjat Allāh is that it is brief. That is, in the course of an essay of over four hundred pages he uses this word fairly infrequently, and rarely gives us much of an explicit understanding of how he takes its meaning. We have observed in his biography that his concern with social improvement as well as with returning to the fundamentals of dīn have led him to be characterized as a forerunner of modernism. In this infrequency of islām either as noun or adjective (islāmī), however, the Ḥujjat Allāh is certainly not akin to modern writings, almost all of which abound with uses of the word. Yet we shall see that in other ways, particularly in the understanding of dīn, there are strong elements of similarity between his writing and that of the fourteenth/twentieth century.

The two parts of this work are concerned with general principles [al-qawāᶜid al-kullīyah] and with what Walī Allāh calls the interpretation of the secrets of the traditions [asrār al-aḥādīth].[120] The general principles, he says, are the basis for the sharāʾiᶜ [derivative laws], and were generally accepted by the groups [milal] existing at the time of the Prophet. Included in the first section are discussions of righteousness and sin [al-birr wa'l-ithm] and of sectarian politics [al-siyāsāt al-millīyah], and in the second section are the policies of the community [al-ummah] regarding laws and punishments, and the method of deducing laws from the speech of the Prophet.

With the aid of his detailed and very extensive table of contents, one is able to ascertain with relative ease those sections of interest to the unfolding of this essay. We shall deal with these relevant areas under two general headings: Walī Allāh's commentary on the relationship of islām and īmān (in which section we do find fairly frequent occurrence of the maṣdar islām) and his development of the theme of the meaning and continuity of dīn.

In the section entitled "Among the varieties of al-īmān" (I, 162-69) we are introduced most specifically to his ideas on islām. He begins with a statement in which it is clear that islām is not to be seen as reified. Indicating that the Prophet was sent to mankind in order that his dīn become triumphant over

---

[120]He discusses the organization of the book in the introduction (I, 7-12).

all religions [li-yaghliba dīnuhu ᶜalá'l-adyān kullihā], he says:

> There existed in his dīn [different] kinds of people, necessitating the distinction between those taking al-islām as their dīn [yadīnūna bi-dīn al-islām] and others, moreover between those who were guided by the guidance with which he was sent and others in whose hearts the joy [bashāshah] of al-īmān had not entered. (I, 162)

It seems that within the group of the followers of Muḥammad were several divisions: those who accepted islām and those who did not, those who were guided to al-īmān and those who were not. Continuing with this discussion, he says that īmān, therefore, is of two kinds. One kind of being a mu'min is that with which the mundane Islamic regulations [aḥkām al-dunyā] have to do. The member of the community is protected by the laws of that community: ". . . the protection of blood and property, and its jurisdiction is over externals in al-inqiyād." If people witness to the one God, pray ṣalāt and pay zakāt, then they are protected insofar as their lives and property are concerned "except by the ḥaqq al-islām."[121] (I, 162) In other words, their lives and properties are safe except by "due process" of Islamic law. He quotes several traditions showing that a formal member of the community should not be denied recognition as a Muslim no matter how insincere his membership might seem to be, ending with this statement: "It is part of the basis of al-īmān to refrain, concerning the one who says there is no God but God, from calling him a kāfir because of a sin or removing him from al-islām because of a deed." As we have seen again and again, particularly in the early tafsīrs and in the ḥadīth, there is often no clear-cut division between personal and communal islām, or indeed between islām and īmān.

The second kind of īmān, he says, is that with which are involved

> . . . the judgments of the hereafter concerning salvation and triumph by degrees. And it comprehends every conviction and every action acceptable to God and every virtuous character of the Lawgiver is to call everything of it an īmān in order that it might be serious stimulation to man to pursue its particular detail. (I, 162)

He then quotes, among others, the ḥadīth that says that the muslim is the one from whose tongue and hand the muslims are safe, indicating as before that there are many divisions in this [wa-lahu shuᶜab kathīran]. This is like the example of the tree "of which it is said that the branches and limbs and leaves and

---

[121] See Ibn Ḥanbal, Musnad, V, 232.

fruits and flowers altogether are a tree". But if some of the leaves fall and the limbs get broken or the fruit is harvested, then it is called [not simply a tree but] a deficient tree. If, on the other hand, the tree is torn out of the ground, then the root itself is gone. The tree is the analogy for all of the people in Muḥammad's dīn, whose faith is of differing kinds, in the last instance not real but only nominal. It was necessary for the Prophet to establish two grades [jaᶜalahā al-nabī ᶜalá martabatayn] in relation to the group as a whole. The first of these is described by the ḥadīth that islām is built on five things: the two testimonies, prayer, almsgiving, fasting and pilgrimage. As for the rest of the people, applicable to them is the saying that al-īmān is seventy and some sections, the most important of which is saying that there is no God but God and the least important to remove harm from the road. (I, 163) He continues with a variety of examples and traditions to develop this theme.

There are several points of interest for us here. The first, as we have noted, is that in the strictest sense he seems to be saying that the dīn of the Prophet includes both those who submit in islām and those who do not. Īmān, therefore, comprehends both those who perform the arkān and those who exhibit other degrees of allegiance, all combining to make the tree which is the community of Muḥammad. Secondly, it is clear that islām and īmān, and correspondingly dīn, have both an individual and a group meaning, and that generally they cannot be understood with one meaning exclusive of the other.

Later in this discussion he elaborates on the same theme when he quotes again the saying of Muḥammad that islām is built on five things:

> These five things are the pillars of al-islām and whoever does them and does not do other than them of the obediences has saved his neck from punishment and he is worthy of the garden . . . he specified the five as pillars because they are the most famous of the acts of devotion [ᶜibādāt] of the people. And there is no millah from among the milal that has not taken them and made them a requirement like the Jews, Christians, and the Magians and the rest of the Arabs, the difference being in the way in which they performed them. Because in them is what is sufficient. (I, 162-63)

It is interesting that in the centuries of tafsīr we have considered there has been relatively little of the emphasis on the pillars or arkān so important in the ḥadīths themselves. Yet for Walī Allāh they seem to play a dominant role. Undoubtedly the factor of the social situation out of which he was writing is an important consideration here. Conditions in India, as we have seen, were deteriorating, and the hypocrisy of many of the leaders of the ṣūfī orders probably contributed to the moral downswing of the Muslims. Here in the very foundations of the sunnah was the opportunity to stress the behavior according to which one walks the straight path.

The reader is left in no doubt about his understanding of dīn as including the muslims and the non-muslims when he goes on to say:

> When the mission [of Muḥammad] became public, and people were entering the dīn Allāh in crowds, it was inevitable that there would be a ẓāhir sign by which a distinction is made between that which is acceptable and the contrary. Around this revolves the judgment of al-islām [wa-ᶜalayhā yudāru ḥukm al-islām] [i.e. the decision as to one's being muslim] and by it the people are held responsible. (I, 164)

On the basis of this external sign depends the applicability of Islamic ordinances and punishments. The evidence seems to indicate, then, that by the dīn of the Prophet, which he also calls dīn Allāh, Walī Allāh means the community system of Muḥammad's followers, rather specifically a group notion. It is interesting to observe that while dīn Allāh has heretofore been more plausibly understood as man's response to God, here it seems to be an implication of God's (and the Prophet's) religion. Islām for him is this but also is more exclusive, apparently referring to the personal submission of man and at the same time to the collective group of those who evidence the five primary obediences, the arkān, thus witnessing that they are those into whose hearts the joy of īmān has entered.

As we noted earlier, this discussion of islām occupies relatively little of Walī Allāh's attention in the Ḥujjat Allāh. What does appear to concern him greatly, however, is the development of the theme of the one universal dīn. Although he specifically correlates this with islām only infrequently, it is worthwhile considering his main ideas precisely because they are so similar to what characterizes the modern understanding. The essential difference, and it is an interesting one, is that while Walī Allāh talks about al-dīn, modern writers and commentators would be much more likely to say dīn al-islām, or al-dīn al-islāmī.

Among several chapters relating to this theme is the one entitled "Clarification that the root of religion is one and its regulations and ways are different". (I, 86-91) This he begins with verses 42:13 and 23:52-53 of the Qur'ān:

﴾He has enjoined for you by way of al-dīn what He commanded to Nūḥ and what We have revealed to you and which We enjoined upon Ibrāhīm, Mūsá and ᶜIsá to establish al-dīn and not have divisions in it.﴿ Mujāhid said: We have made incumbent upon you, O Muḥammad, and upon them one dīn. And God said, ﴾This community of yours is one community and I am your Lord, so keep your duty to Me. For they have cut off their affair into sects, each party rejoicing in its tenets.﴿ This means that the millat al-islām is your millah . . . (I, 86)

By apparently equating "this community of yours is one community" with "the millah of islām is your millah", he seems to be saying not that dīn = islām as we have seen in other commentaries, but that several milal, of which islām [Islam] is one, equal or participate in one dīn. Millah is generally understood as having a somewhat reified reference, and this seems to be the case here as is evidenced in the title of the bāb. Thus he repeats here: "Know! that the source of dīn is one [aṣl al-dīn wāḥid] . . . and that the differences are in the regulations [sharā'iᶜ] and the procedures [manāhij]." Regulations and procedures are generally discussed with reference to a group. But again he makes it clear that it is impossible to draw a line between the organization and the individual response of the muslim when he elaborates on that in which all the Prophets were in agreement. He does not say "dīn is. . ." but rather "the source of dīn is. ." leaving open the possibility that what he really means is the source of individual response as well as the source of that which is the basis of the group millah identified as islām. Thus he says,

> The Prophets all agreed on the tawḥīd of God in servanthood [ᶜibādah] and seeking help [istiᶜānah] and exaltation (above all objects of experience) [tanzīh] of Him away from all that is not suitable to Him, forbidding heresy in regard to His names . . . (I, 86)

He continues for several pages to elaborate on the source or basis of dīn, the elements of which constitute the arkān we saw above as well as a variety of other regulations. Again in the description of how this basis becomes perverted we see the relationship of the individual acts to the community described by millah. "Know that the Ḥaqq [truth] Himself, when He sent a Prophet to a people to establish the millah for them by his tongue, [the Prophet] did not leave in it any crookedness." (I, 122) It is the successors of the disciples who became negligent and began to mix untruth with truth. The Prophets themselves added things on to the millahs of the Prophets preceding them, but did not subtract or change much. Our Prophet, however, has added to, subtracted from, and changed the dīn, returning all to its original form.

So concerned is Walī Allāh with this theme of unity in the ummah that he gives us an unusual and quite fascinating explanation of the relationship of those who are unable to function as "full muslims" to the community of islām. Those of sound disposition and pure nature whom the Islamic call never reached in the first place, or to whom it came in such a way that doubt still remained, are never really subject either to the blessings or damnation of eternal judgment; in death they return to a condition of blindness, neither to punishment nor to recompense, "until their bestiality [bahīmīyah] is rescinded and there shines upon them something of the gleams of the angels . . . " (I, 117) However there are those whose intelligence is deficient [naqaṣat ᶜuqūluhum] -- like most boys, insane, fallāhīn and slaves as well as those who are reasonable under ordinary circumstances but become irrational in crises -- and for them the situation is similar to that of the black slave woman who, when asked by the Prophet where God is, pointed to the sky. In other words, while they are incapable of islām in the full sense

> . . . what is expected of them is that they resemble (imitate) the muslimūn so that there may be a unity of the ummah [lit. that the word may not be divided into groups]. (I, 117)

In the chapter entitled "The need for a dīn to abrogate the adyān" (I, 117-119) we seem to have a suggestion of the necessity of a universal dīn to supercede the religious pluralism described in the first line as "the milal found on the face of the earth". In this chapter there is an increasing emphasis on the unique position and mission of the Prophet Muḥammad, a trend that is to dominate the writing of the twentieth century (as is the idea of universal dīn). All of the milal have been convinced, of course, that their head was truthful and indeed perfect, unequalled in establishing regulations and manifesting the supernatural. Their people have been ready and willing to fight for these convictions. The problem has come in the natural tendency of men to pervert elements of the original millah, changing the regulations or becoming careless in their observance, with the result that the milal fight with one another and ascribe to the others falsity, thus obscuring the truth common to all. It is interesting that Walī Allāh describes "the condition of the jāhilīyah and the confusion [iḍṭirāb] of their adyān." From a preceding reference to the Indian work Kalīlah wa-dimnah, and the mixture of milal that it describes, it seems that he includes in jāhilīyah the Peoples of the Book as well as the various groups in India in pre-Islamic times. Into this scene has come the imām who is to collect the [various] communities [al-umam] into one millah.

> He requires other principles than those that have previously been mentioned, among them that he call a people to the wise sunnah and purify them and correct their condition and gather them up to himself to the utmost of his ability so that he can attack the people of the world and scatter them to the horizons. Thus God says [3:110]: ⟨You are the best ummah brought forth to people⟩. (I, 118)

This imām, of course, is the Prophet Muḥammad.

In one sense the discussion of dīn from here on seems to be with an increasingly reified understanding, meaning the specific religion of the followers of Muḥammad as they faced the social and political situation of the world in the early period of historical Islam. Thus Walī Allāh says that the establishment in the world of a millah which orders the good and forbids the evil was contingent upon the disintegration of two major powers: Khusraw the ruler of ᶜIrāq, the Yaman and Khorasān; and Caesar, the ruler of Syria and Asia Minor. God ruled the disintegration of their empires and notified the Prophet that when Khusraw is overcome there will be no Khusraw after him and likewise no Caesar after Caesar's defeat. In another sense, however, we can understand by this that the new actual religious understanding and system introduced by Muḥammad is at the same time the ideal and true self-surrender to God, which is destined (at a particular historical moment) to supercede the man-made political (and religious) systems then extant.

After this historical discussion in which dīn, millah and islām are portrayed not only as a religious but a political unity, Walī Allāh returns us specifically to the theme of dīn as involving personal decision and response. First he quotes Abū Bakr that "this dīn will overcome all the adyān, not leaving a single one" (I, 119) but that it will have overcome it with mighty might or with humiliating humiliation. Then the people will be transformed [yanqalibu] into three divisions: those who are led to religion outwardly and inwardly [munqād li'l-dīn ẓāhiran wa-bāṭinan] (I, 119), those who are led externally in spite of themselves, and the kāfirs. Ultimately the distinction among these three, particularly between the first two, rests on the degree of individual commitment involved. Again, however, understanding of the kāfir as an individual denier of the faith is inseparable from the kāfir who is denied membership in the community.

Several things, then, stand out as distinguishing Walī Allāh's interpretation of dīn al-islām from that which we have seen before. In the first place is his inclusion in the *dīn* of the Prophet both of those submitting in *islām* and of those unable to do so. Secondly is the interesting inclusion into the community of *islām* itself both of those willing and able to attest to their faith in the acceptable way -- principally by performance of the *arkān* -- and in a kind of affiliated fashion of those for whom such attestation is not completely possible. Previous *tafsīrs* have generally conceded that all of the Prophets have come with the truth of *islām*, despite the later perversions accruing to the practices of their communities. Walī Allāh is different here not so much in kind as in degree -- like the modern commentators he develops the theme of *islām* as universal *dīn* far more than did his predecessors. Unlike the later writers, however, he does not, as we have noted, constantly identify this *dīn* as *islām*, perhaps due to the fact that his country was only in the beginning stages of the confrontation with the modern world which may well have been a major factor in the stress of the moderns on the religion of *islām*. (We shall consider this issue in greater detail in the next chapter.) On the whole, however, perhaps the most striking element of Walī Allāh's narrative, and that which ties him closely to the traditional material of the previous centuries, is his constant intertwining of the concepts of a personal and a group *dīn*; they are two facets of one idea. A final fact to be noted, and again the implications of this will be developed more fully later, is that while his references to *islām* as a religious community are frequent and apparent, they are always (in the sections considered here) in connection with the early *ummah* of the Prophet of God and never refer to the specific Muslim community of the twelfth/eighteenth century of which Walī Allāh himself was a part.

XIII

We come now to the close of the second period of *tafsīr* writing, that which began with the seventh/thirteenth century of al-Bayḍāwī and ends in the thirteenth/nineteenth century. The general character of this commentary has been traditional, highly repetitious of what has preceded and disinclined toward the kind of rationalist speculation typifying the works of such writers as al-Zamakhsharī and even al-Rāzī. (The selections from Shāh Walī Allāh provided an interesting, though not radical, diversion from that pattern.) It is appropriate, then, that thirteenth century *tafsīr*, particularly that which is representative of the earlier part of that century, should prove itself to be the epitome of traditionalism, appearing in retrospect to be a kind of last ditch stand against what we now see as the close-pressing influences of modernism.

Two exegetes stand out as the best known and most widely read of this period: al-Shawkānī of the Yaman and al-Ālūsī of Baghdād. Both are traditionists as well as traditionalists, yet there is a clear difference in the way they approach the problem of interpreting the Qur'ān passages.

Slightly older than his contemporary, Muḥammad b. ᶜAlī b. Muḥammad b. ᶜAbd Allāh al-Shawkānī was born in 1172/1760 and studied in Ṣanaᶜā where he remained as teacher, qāḍī, and eventually muftī.[122] Studying first under his father and then under a succession of famous teachers (attested to in his biography), he was soon considered a master of the traditional sciences of fiqh, ḥadīth, and the like.[123] Apparently not considering himself exclusively associated with any one of the schools of law,[124] he was primarily dedicated to the strict study of traditions. His Nayl al-awṭār, a collection of ḥadīths, is felt to be one of the best and most comprehensive works of his day on sunnah and its fiqh; al-Kattānī calls him the imām, the last of the traditionists of the East [khātimat muḥaddithī al-mashriq].[125] Appointed in 1229/1813 as court judge by Imām al-Manṣūr b. al-ᶜAbbās, ruler of al-Yaman, he remained in that capacity until his death in 1255/1839.[126]

Al-Shawkānī's tafsīr, Fatḥ al-qadīr al-jāmiᶜ,[127] is of scholarly interest primarily because he has made use of sources now unavailable to Western historians.[128] In this work is exemplified his intense concern with rejecting all that is built on analogy [qiyās, munāsabah] or independent opinion [ijtihād] or

---

[122]Zabārah al-Yamanī, Nayl al-waṭar, II, 297.

[123]Al-Shawkānī, Itḥāf, p. 188 (from a biography by Ḥusayn al-Yamanī).

[124]". . . er hielt sich zu keiner der anerkannten Maḏāhib . . ." (Brockelmann, GAL, S II, 818).

[125]Al-Kattānī, Fihrist, II, 408.

[126]Al-Shawkānī, Itḥāf, p. 119.

[127]Cairo: Muṣṭafá al-Bābī al-Ḥalabī, 1384-5 [1964-5], 5 voll.

[128]Jeffery, Materials, p. 2. Jeffery's concern with Fatḥ al-qadīr is in its application of variants on the consonantal text of the ᶜUthmānic redaction of the Qur'ān.

deduction [takhrīj].[129] Al-Shawkānī was of the opinion that theoretical analysis and personal opinion are too easily entered upon and that too much of the history of Muslim thought has been characterized by accepting what one pleases and discarding that toward which one is not inclined.[130] In the realm of the sunnah of Muḥammad, however, no one is allowed to tamper, and it is this area with which al-Shawkānī is supremely concerned. We can gather from the sources that not all of his choices of acceptable traditions were applauded by his contemporaries; he apparently made what were considered to be poor selections in terms of validity, contrary to what had been accepted by the ijmāᶜ of the community.[131] The point of interest for us is that it was these traditions alone, rather than them in conjunction with the analysis of the tafsīr of intervening centuries, that he chose to fill the pages of his Qur'ān commentary. The situation is somewhat different with al-Ālūsī.

If we consider "modern" to be a category of time, then on a continuum of fourteen centuries the Qur'ān commentary of Abū'l-Thanā' al-Ālūsī, written in the 1200's/1800's, must certainly be said to be modern or very close to it. When al-Ālūsī is referred to in Western surveys of tafsīr literature it is generally in a discussion of modern commentary.[132] Yet if modern is seen rather as a type of interpretation reflecting a new approach to the exegesis of the Qur'ān, then al-Ālūsī is clearly pre-modern, specifically traditional. The importance of his commentary, Rūḥ al-maᶜānī fī tafsīr al-Qur'ān[133] lies in its author having collected and organized an immense amount of material from earlier exegesis, some of it not readily available in the commentaries which we have seen to be the classics of Muslim scholarship.[134]

---

129 Zabārah al-Yamanī, Nayl, II, 299. Takhrīj has the technical meaning of determining the authenticity of a writer's sources.

130 Zabārah al-Yamanī, Nayl, II, 299.

131 See al-Kattānī, Fihrist, II, 408.

132 Birkeland, "The Lord guideth" in Skrifter (1956), pt. 2, 1-140; Blachère, Introduction, p. 222.

133 Būlāq: al-Maṭbaᶜah al-Kubrá al-Mīrīyah, 1301-10 [1883/4-1892], 9 voll.

134 "There is an abundance of new material available, and in particular the large commentary of al-Alūsī (sic) . . . which, though it is the work of an author of the nineteenth century, gathers up most of the results of earlier exegetical works." (Jeffery, "The present status of Qur'anic studies", p. 13).

Abū'l-Thanā' Maḥmūd Shihāb al-Dīn (1217-70/1802-54) was one of the most famous representatives of the family al-Ālūsī of Baghdād. His father, a descendant of the Imām al-Ḥusayn, was head instructor at the principal mosque of Baghdād and his mother also came from a learned and respected lineage.[135] Abū'l-Thanā', like so many of the commentators of our study, seems to have been a prodigy, studying the fiqh of the Ḥanafīyah and the Shāfiᶜīyah at the age of seven.[136] By the time he was thirteen he was well established as a teacher and author. He was soon considered to be one of the eminent authorities of ᶜIrāq in tafsīr and iftā' and in 1248/1832 became the muftī of the Ḥanafīyah.[137] All did not go smoothly for him with the Turkish authorities, however, and by order of the Pāshā of Baghdād he was deprived of office.[138] Two years later, after a sermon in which he particularly praised the Turkish rule (followed by a work entitled Proof for the Obedience of the Sulṭān), he was again restored to office and full favor.[139] His troubles soon began again, however, and he found himself in such bad financial straits that he was forced to go to the sulṭān to plead his case.[140] This time he won the approval of the authorities by showing the sulṭān his completed work on the tafsīr of the Qur'ān. He remained in a position of comfort and respect until his death in 1270/1854.

Rūḥ al-maᶜānī, as we have noted, is a collection of exegetical materials from a variety of sources. He makes no attempt to distinguish between ḥadīth having what have been considered by the Sunnī traditionalists as reliable isnāds, and those that could not claim such documentation. Too, he provides an interesting mixture of ḥadīths from the ancestors [salaf], speculations of the theologians [mutakallimūn], direct quotations from Shīᶜī tafsīrs and some mystical [ṣūfī] interpretation. Coming as his work does at the end of a long line of tafsīrs, it is relatively easy for us to determine from where he drew the bulk of his material.

---

[135] Zaydān, Mashāhīr, II, 175.

[136] Al-Atharī, Aᶜlām, p. 22.

[137] Zaydān, Mashāhīr, II, 175.

[138] Al-Dasūqī, Fī'l-adab al-ḥadīth, I, 59.

[139] Al-Atharī, Aᶜlām, p. 23.

[140] Al-Atharī (Ibid., p. 24) says that hunger and thirst nearly drive him to eat the mat on the floor and drink the ink with which he was writing his tafsīr!

The basic point of difference between these two, then, is that while al-Ālūsī presents long passages from earlier *tafsīrs* (his commentary is little more than an arrangement of such selections), al-Shawkānī avoids historical commentary, which he feels to be too interpretive, and in the main gives us what he considers pure traditional material from the *sunnah*. In the fourteenth/twentieth century we shall see reason elevated to a position of supreme importance, as it was to a great extent in the thought of Shāh Walī Allāh; in both of these *tafsīrs* of the nineteenth century it is the strength of tradition, in the several ways in which this is interpreted, that predominates.

* * *

Our discussion of the *tafsīrs* of al-Shawkānī and al-Ālūsī will be by way of a quick summary rather than a detailed analysis precisely because the material is by now quite familiar to us. We already have seen most of the *ḥadīths* (and those not seen are still very much in keeping with the general tenor of early traditional material) and most of the passages in al-Ālūsī's commentary are directly out of *tafsīr* that we have read once or even several times before.

Thus concerning 3:19 al-Shawkānī discusses the *fatḥa-kasrah* controversy and the opinions of al-Kasā'ī, explains that the majority feel that *islām* has the meaning of *īmān* though their source is different as expressed in the *ḥadīth* about Jibrīl (see above, pp. 12-13), and quotes the familiar words of Qatādah that "*al-islām* is testimony that there is no God but God, and *iqrār* of what comes from God, and it is the *dīn* of God which He Himself enjoined." (I, 325-6)

Al-Ālūsī begins with these same words from Qatādah, then offers us a long string of passages taken from such works of *tafsīr* as that of al-Qummī, al-Ṭūsī, Abū Su^{c}ūd, al-Bayḍāwī and others. (I, 540-42) (These are not specifically acknowledged, but are certainly recognizable.) We saw previously that al-Ālūsī preferred not to identify himself with any particular school or *madhhab*; this may well lie behind his unusual combination of materials from a wide variety of traditions. Thus we have the *ḥadīth* from *amīr al-mu'minūn* (^{c}Alī) which draws the chain of relationship through *islām*, *taslīm*, *yaqīn*, *taṣdīq*, *iqrār* and *adā'*. (See above, pp. 82-83) He also discusses the opinions of al-Kasā'ī, drawing together this as he does all of the material that he presents with extremely detailed grammatical analyses. If al-Ālūsī himself has made any notable personal contribution apart from the magnitude of his effort in gathering together all of this material, it is in his lengthy attempts to present every conceivable possibility of grammatical interpretation of the verses of the Qur'ān. (It must be said that some of these interpretations stretch the imagination, and the Arabic, rather beyond the realm of probability.) He discusses the understanding of islām by īmān, by the sharīᶜah, by knowledge of the regulations [aḥkām]. In connection with the last he indicates that the being [kawn] of dīn al-islām is confined to time because the regulations of the Lawgiver are changed and substituted according to man's interests and circumstances. (I, 530) In this is the only hint he gives of a plural understanding of islām, and the implication is not of a reified Islam but of the (now familiar) relationship between individual and group in one expression. We do not find, as in Walī Allāh and even more in the writers immediately to succeed al-Ālūsī, stress on the theme of islām as universal dīn.

Al-Shawkānī devotes most of his discussion of 3:84-5 (I, 357-58) to the understanding of what it means to submit out of obedience [ṭawᶜ] or unwillingness [karh], equating islām in the latter sense with istislām. We saw in the tafsīr of Ibn ᶜAbbās that one interpretation of "willingly" means those born in al-islām, the connotation being that one is born into the group of muslimūn, yet again with no clear distinction made between the individual act and the group itself. Al-Shawkānī echoes this when in connection with ⁅to Him submits whosoever is in the heavens and the earth⁆ he repeats the interpretation that "as for those in the heavens it is the angels, and as for those on earth it is those born into al-islām [wulida ᶜalá'l-islām]." (I, 358) Al-Ālūsī is briefer, offering in terms of definition only that islām is tawḥīd, inqiyād, and the sharīᶜah of the Prophet, the tafsīr of this verse being that whoever seeks other than the regulations enjoined by God through His Prophet will find his dīn unacceptable. (I, 622-23) Again we have a highly personal interpretation.

Both al-Shawkānī (II, 10-11) and al-Ālūsī (II, 248-49) view Qur'ān 5:3 in the traditional way by discussing the completion of the regulations of what is permitted and forbidden, the conditions of descent of the āyah (Friday, Yawm al-ᶜArafah, etc.), the defeat of the kāfir at Mecca and destruction of their places of sacrifice. In the latter we read: ⁅And I have chosen for you al-islām as [a] dīn⁆, meaning I have selected it for you from among the adyān and it is al-dīn with God and no other [is] (a passage we have seen several times before). Al-Shawkānī says that this means:

> I have informed you of my approval of it for you. God does not cease approving [lam yazal rāḍiyan] al-islām for the community of His Prophet. There is no great benefit in the specification of this approval for this day if we take it at its face value [i.e. if we take it to mean only that particular day]. [The real meaning is] that He approved for you al-islām which is for you this day a dīn remaining to the end of the days of the world. (II, 11)

One senses a certain difference between what is characterized here and the eternal religion described at such length by al-Dihlawī and which is elaborated by the modern commentators. The latter is the ideal religion revealed to all the Prophets, actualized by the community of the Prophet and appropriate for all peoples of all ages -- with a distinctly plural connotation. Here in the context of the regulations and duties now made complete the emphasis is on dīn as the individual performance of these duties, the personal relationship of man to his Lord. The distinction is subtle but real and hopefully will be made clearer when we come to the interpretations of Muḥammad ᶜAbduh and Rashīd Riḍā -- and even more by Sayyid Quṭb -- in the next century.

The tafsīr of the next three verses in both of these writers -- 6:125, 9:74 and 39:22 -- is, not surprisingly, centered on the understanding of islām as a condition of the heart, generally in opposition to the concept of kufr or rejection of faith. (Fatḥ al-qadīr, II, 160-62; II, 383; IV, 458-59 and Rūḥ al-maᶜānī, II, 570-71; III, 339; VII, 397). Both quote the metaphor of a light being thrown into the breast, the signs of which are inclination toward the house of eternity and leading away from the house of deception. Al-Ālūsī apparently borrows from al-Bayḍāwī when he discusses the connection of the soul [nafs] and the heart to the rest of the body. "And the nafs is that which is qualified by al-islām and al-īmān." (VII, 397)

Presenting the usual discussion of the asbāb al-nuzūl concerning 49:14-17, al-Shawkānī (V, 67-69) and al-Ālūsī (VIII, 197-99) are in agreement with the great majority of mufassirūn who support the apparent distinction given in the verse itself between islām and īmān. Thus the former quotes al-Zajjāj that

> al-islām is evidencing submission [iẓhār al-khuḍūᶜ] and acceptance of that which the Prophet brought, and by that blood is spared; and if along with that evidencing is conviction [iᶜtiqād] and confirmation [taṣdīq] of the heart, then it is al-īmān and the possessor of it is a mu'min. (V, 68)

Al-Ālūsī gives the familiar distinction first seen in al-Zamakhsharī that al-īmān is "confirmation [taṣdīq] with trust [thiqah] and peacefulness [ṭuma'nīnah] of the heart" while islām is "being led [inqiyād] and entering into peace [silm] and it is the opposite of war . . ." (VIII, 197) In neither of the fairly lengthy commentaries on these verses is there anything new and different. Al-Ālūsī, like al-Zamakhsharī, takes the opportunity provided by the distinction in this verse to give another detailed grammatical analysis.

In 61:7-9 both al-Shawkānī (V, 220-21) and al-Ālūsī (IX, 63-64) stress that the one inventing the lie was never really accepting of al-islām as defined as "the best of the adyān and the most noble of them", the dīn al-ḥaqq brought by the Prophet. For the latter the light of God is defined as this dīn al-ḥaqq, and al-Shawkānī summarizes the several interpretations of nūr Allāh as "the Qur'ān, or al-islām, or Muḥammad, or the arguments and proofs, or all of these things . . ." (V, 221)

Such a condensation of the above passages as we have just presented would certainly be inadequate and an injustice to the writers in question were it not for the fact that we are already so familiar with the material that they give. For the modern Western writers one of the basic requirements of scholarship is originality. For the traditionalists of whom al-Shawkānī and al-Ālūsī were representative, presentation of that which has been adjudged true and approved by the community is the only acceptable mode of procedure.

With these collections of tradition, then, we come to the close of the period of Islamic scholarship in which ijtihād was, for the most part, considered reprehensible and repetition a virtue. The next several decades after al-Ālūsī were to herald the clear beginnings of a new era in tafsīr and a new way of approaching the funadmentals of dīn as expressed in the words of the Qur'ān and the sunnah of the Prophet.

FOUR: NEW DIRECTIONS IN "TAFSĪR"

> Truly speaking, the entire history of Islam is one of exegesis of the Qur'ān; and it is only by viewing the entire history of Islam in its relation to the Qur'ān that we can attain any unity of perspective on that history.[1]

These words, written by a twentieth-century Muslim,[2] reflect the general approach of modern scholars to Qur'ānic study. Standard tafsīr up to the last century undertook a passage-by-passage explication and interpretation of the sacred Book as we have seen in the painstaking endeavors outlined in the above chapters. Beginning in the late eighteen hundreds, however, a new kind of tafsīr emerged -- one in which the commentators, rather than specifically explaining the lines of the text, attempted to use the text as a support and foundation for their own ideas.[3] Modern interpretation of the Qur'ān is often incorporated into, and often the basis of, what can be seen as the contemporary counterpart of the classical works of the theology and philosophy of Islam.

Many Western writers have been critical of the tafsīr of the late nineteenth and the twentieth centuries as being too defensive, unrealistic in its attempt to prove that all of the results of contemporary scientific endeavor are already to be found in germinal form in the Qur'ān.[4] The general trend of

---

[1]Rahbar, "Reflections" in MW, LII (1962), 298.

[2]Rahbar has since converted to Christianity.

[3]One can argue, of course, that this is what has always been done, that interpretation is subjective by definition and that in the long run there is really no difference between exegesis and eisegesis. The point here is that the intent, and therefore the form, is often different in modern commentary from the interlinear tafsīr that we have come to expect.

[4]Kenneth Cragg (Counsels, pp. 169-70) speaks of the practice of some liberals of using the content of the Qur'ān for their own means. "Cruder forms of this habit of mind are sometimes founded on a concept of Quranic prescience . . . What sciences have established and applied, even material ones like hygiene and metallurgy, may be read into the words of the Qur'ān." Blachère (Introduction, pp. 222-24) talks about the disappointing (décevant) aspects of modern commentary: ". . . reprenant la conception du CORAN en tant que somme de toutes les connaissances humaines, elle pose comme principe que le "Livre d'Allah" contient l'énoncé de toutes les grandes découvertes modernes, aussi bien en astronomie qu'en physique, en chimie ou dans les sciences naturelles."

this commentary has been toward demonstrating that the essence of islām is its universality and that in the verses of the Qur'ān is to be found an understanding of life and reality that is applicable to every age and time. Whether attempting to see the Qur'ān as the precursor of modern science, psychology and technology, or portraying the Prophet as the possessor of (almost) unique qualities of leadership and personal dynamism, the basic aim of modern tafsīr and dogmatic writing often has been the attempt to reinterpret scripture in the light of the modern situation. As a result, it has been characterized by the use of reason over legend, an avoidance of interpretation in terms of the magical or miraculous, and increased use of principles of psychology.

It is not surprising to find that over the past century there have been a variety of writings by Muslims on principles of exegesis of the Qur'ān. While the Itqān of al-Suyūṭī was concerned mainly with classifying the methods already in operation, modern criticism of the history of tafsīr usually concerns itself with an attempt to explain where classical commentary "went wrong", with a clear exposition of what should serve as the bases of exegesis. In the Taḥrīr fī uṣūl al-tafsīr, for example, Sayyid Aḥmad Khān (1817-1898) sets forth fifteen such axioms in an attempt to reconcile the understanding of the Qur'ān with the science of his day.[5]

Another very influential modern thinker who has enunciated his dissatisfaction with earlier Qur'ān tafsīr is Mawlānā Abū'l-Kalām Āzād (1888-1958). In his popular Tarjumān al-Qur'ān he states:

> When we look back into the history of the commentators of the Qur'ān from the earliest centuries of Islam right up to the close of the last century, we find that the standard of approach to the meaning of the Qur'ān has steadily deteriorated. This was the result of a gradual decadence in the quality of the Muslim mind itself. When the commentators found that they could not rise to the heights of the Qur'ānic thought, they strove to bring it down to the level of their own mind. (I, xxxi-xxxii)

Enumerating what he feels to have been the factors contributing to this state of affairs (I, xxxii-xxxviii), he mentions the intrusion of philosophical speculation from Greece and Persia; a distortion of the natural simplicity of the Qur'ān by textual criticism, footnotes and indices; the influence of

---

[5] Translated by Daud Rahbar, "Sir Sayyid Aḥmad Khān's principles of exegesis" in MW, XLVI (1956), 104-112, 324-335.

Jewish lore on interpretation; an increased use of later over earlier *ḥadīth* materials; the investment of simple Arabic words with new philosophical meanings as well as linguistic misinterpretations of original Qur'ānic words and phrases; and the effect of the varying political and doctrinal atmosphere of succeeding generations. Āzād also points to a practice which no one familiar with the historical progression of Qur'ānic interpretation can miss -- the tendency, even habit, of commentators to lean heavily on the work of their predecessors, thereby frequently perpetuating inaccuracies. In a final damning observation Āzād states that

> The prevailing ineptitude of scholars in the succeeding periods of Muslim history let every form of idiosyncracy prosper; so much so, that only those commentaries came into fashion and were read with zest which bore no trace whatever of the touch given to the interpretation of the *Qur'ān* by the earliest band of commentators. (I,xxxviii)

Āzād's own commentary is an attempt to return to the original meaning of the Qur'ān by presenting that which is universal in its teaching.

Many others could be cited for their contributions to a modern understanding of Qur'ānic exegesis. Sometimes, as in the above, their principles are stated with reference to *tafsīr* of the text itself. More often, however, their understanding of the importance and relevance of the Qur'ān and how it should be examined are a part of a general consideration and exposition of the basic elements of Muslim faith.

XIV (a)

Because the fourteenth/twentieth century does provide, to a great extent, some new directions in commentary on the Holy Book, we will again consider in detail two different *tafsīrs*. If this deviation from the pattern of our essay was defensible for the previous century because commentary in general was so repetitive of traditional writing, it is justifiable here because some marked and interesting changes are to be observed.

The first work under consideration here might be seen as occupying a kind of half-way position between the modern writings scarcely recognizable as *tafsīr* in the sense we have come to expect and the classical commentaries following the structure of interlinear exegesis. This is the *Tafsīr al-manār* of Muḥammad ᶜAbduh (and Rashīd Riḍā). Unlike many of the other modern works, it does comment on all of the verses of the Qur'ān (insofar as this work was completed) in their accepted order. That the *tafsīr* also shares many of the qualities of contemporary commentaries and apologetic writings will readily be apparent. This work is especially interesting both as a kind of meeting-place between old and new, and to the extent that it represents the orientation and thought of one of the best-known and most controversial[6] of those who have spearheaded the movement to understand the fundamentals of Islam in the modern age. Primarily a reformer, ᶜAbduh concerned himself in a variety of ways with what he saw as perversions of the true *dīn* as practised by the ancestors [*al-salaf*] and with an attempt to rectify them. The extent to which he succeeded is debatable; that he planted the seeds of further attempts at reinterpretation and reform is not.

Secondly, we will consider a commentary somewhat different in content from the *Tafsīr al-manār*. This is *Fī ẓilāl al-Qur'ān* of Sayyid Quṭb. This recently executed Egyptian reformer was particularly concerned with the social implications of *islām*, an interest we shall find frequently illustrated in his writing. If ᶜAbduh and Riḍā represent a half-way mark between traditional and modern, Sayyid Quṭb can be seen as "fully modern", his commentary as well as his other writings expressing some of the major concerns of contemporary Muslim thinkers. We shall look first at the *tafsīr* of ᶜAbduh and Riḍā, then consider how their commentary compares with the work of Sayyid Quṭb.

The details of ᶜAbduh's life, particularly his relationship with Jamāl al-Dīn al-Afghānī, are generally well-known and readily available in a number of thorough biographical sketches.[7] Born in 1266/1849 in lower Egypt, at an early age he began theological studies at the mosque school in Ṭanṭā. His interest was unaroused, however, and it was not until he became exposed to the mystical approach that his enthusiasm for religious study came to the fore. In 1865 he entered the Azhar Mosque, devoting himself in the meanwhile to asceticism and the pursuit of mystical understanding. Then in 1872 he came into contact with the fiery al-Afghānī, with whose philosophy and fortunes he was to

---

[6] ᶜAbduh was controversial in his own life-time in Egypt; he is perhaps even more so in retrospect. In general he is held in higher esteem by his fellow Muslims than by Western students of modern Islamic developments, some of whose assessments will be cited later.

[7] The most complete biography is that of his pupil and associate Muḥammad Rashīd Riḍā, *Ta'rīkh al-ustādh al-imām* (see bibliography). See also Jomier, *Le Commentaire Coranique du Manār*, pp. 1-45; Adams, *Islam and Modernism in Egypt*, pp. 1-103.

become deeply involved. Through al-Afghānī ᶜAbduh was introduced to the outlook of Europe and awakened to an interest in the situation of Islam in the contemporary world.

He continued for some time to approach his study from the mystical view-point; it was almost as that of a pīr or master that he accepted the influence of al-Afghānī in his life.[8] Gradually he became actively involved with more pragmatic concerns and in 1876 began a career in journalism which was to bear most influential fruit. After a brief period in which he was in political disfavor, ᶜAbduh in 1880 became editor of the official al-Waqā'iᶜ al-Miṣrīyah, which soon turned into the chief advocate of liberalism. The vissicitudes of his career are too detailed to follow here and are easily available from other sources. Suffice it to say that while al-Afghānī advocated revolutionary reform, Muḥammad ᶜAbduh became the spokesman for the theory of gradual reform based primarily on progress in forms of education.[9] In 1884 he and al-Afghānī founded the society al-ᶜUrwah al-Wuthqā, which supported a short-lived publication of the same name, for the propagation of Muslim nationalism. After this ᶜAbduh left al-Afghānī and devoted himself more completely to his interest in theological reform. A period of exile from Egypt ended with his appointment as state muftī in 1899, which position he held until he died in 1905. Through this post he was able to introduce reform in the religious courts. It was during this last period of his life that he published some of his most important works, including Risālat al-tawḥīd and al-Islām wa'l-naṣrānīyah. It was also then that he entered into close association with the editor of the monthly review al-Manār, Shaykh Muḥammad Rashīd Riḍā.

Riḍā (1282/1865-1354/1935) was a Syrian from the city of Tripoli (now in Lebanon). Famous for his ideas on the caliphate, his importance for us lies in his association with ᶜAbduh in the

---

[8] Elie Kedourie (Afghani and ᶜAbduh, pp. 9-12) discusses the apparent idolization of al-Afghānī by ᶜAbduh, and the mystical doctrine of waḥdat al-wujūd [the unicity of being] that dominates the latter's earliest writings.

[9] Summarizing the intentions of the movement of Arab modernism of which he sees ᶜAbduh as a chief spokesman, Cragg ("The modernist movement", pp. 156-7) says that it should be seen as "the desire to demonstrate in practical terms and in response to particular concrete issues that Islam is adequate to the needs and demands of the present . . . . [This] was the great conviction of Muḥammad ᶜAbduh in Egypt . . . . He sought to harness the fervent impetus of Jamāl al-Dīn al-Afghānī's political Pan-Islamism into interior intellectual tasks . . ."

composition of the Manār commentary on the Qur'ān. Exposed to a European education earlier than ᶜAbduh, in the long run he was less attracted by Western thought than his teacher and associate. He became very involved in the politics of Syrian nationalism and was elected President of the Syrian National Congress in Damascus.[10] In Egypt he founded and edited the journal al-Manār through which he expounded his political and theological ideas (and those of ᶜAbduh) from 1898 until 1935. A much more voluminous writer than ᶜAbduh, he devoted himself vigorously to a reinterpretation of the principles of Islam largely based, by his own assertion, on the teachings of his mentor. It was through the pages of this journal that the Qur'ān commentary of ᶜAbduh first came to view.

We are told that in the beginning Muḥammad ᶜAbduh did not want to undertake a tafsīr of the Qur'ān, feeling that the many commentaries already written -- some well done and others inferior -- should suffice.[11] But at the insistent urging of Riḍā he decided to make exegesis of the Qur'ān the subject of a lecture course at al-Azhar. From notes on these lectures Riḍā compiled the interlinear tafsīr, approved and revised by ᶜAbduh, first published in al-Manār in 1900 and attributed to Muḥammad ᶜAbduh. (It is for this reason, of course, that the full work we now have goes by the title of Tafsīr al-manār.[12]) As ᶜAbduh was never able to complete the commentary past sūrah 4:125, Riḍā himself continued it in what he intended to be a style and content with which his teacher would have been in full agreement; ᶜAbduh until his death had given complete assent to everything printed in his tafsīr. (However by 1905, when he died, only one and a half sūrahs had been edited.[13])

---

[10] For a discussion of the political views of Rashīd Riḍā, particularly as they relate to the theory of the caliphate, see Kerr, Islamic Reform, chapter 5.

[11] See Jomier, Le Commentaire Coranique, pp. 45-47. This is not to say that ᶜAbduh was uninterested in Qur'ān commentary; it was one of the continuing concerns of his life. Mentioning a discussion in 1869 between ᶜAbduh and al-Afghānī on orthodox and ṣūfī interpretation of certain passages, Adams (Islam and Modernism, p. 33) comments: "Taṣawwuf and tafsīr! -- mysticism and Ḳur'ān interpretation -- the two subjects at that time most dear to the heart of Muḥammad ᶜAbduh."

[12] Tafsīr al-Qur'ān al-karīm, tafsīr al-manār. Cairo: Dār al-Manār, 1367-1375 [1948-1956], 12 voll.

[13] Jomier, Le Commentaire Coranique, p. 51.

Ideally, then, the reader of the Tafsīr al-manār could assume that everything he reads is, or would be, the word of Shaykh Muḥammad ᶜAbduh. In fact, however, the words are those of Rashīd Riḍā, and despite his claim to faithful reproduction of speech and thought, it seems difficult to suppose that many of the ideas are not also peculiarly his, subject as they may have been to influence from his master. In discussing the commentary, therefore, we shall ascribe authorship to Riḍā, indicating clearly those passages coming directly from ᶜAbduh (easily identifiable as they are introduced by the phrase "qāla al-ustādh al-imām",[14] in contrast to the comments which Riḍā gives as his own by prefixing them with "I say"). The commentary as reproduced from the text of the journal issues is, in its final form, twelve volumes in length, ending with verse twenty-five of sūrah twelve.

Unlike much modern Qur'ān commentary, the Tafsīr al-manār is traditional at least in its form as interlinear tafsīr. It is not, however, heavily reliant on the traditional material of exegesis that we have seen repeated so frequently in the preceding works, although the asbāb al-nuzūl are occasionally mentioned. The commentary of Riḍā does make greater use of collections of ḥadīths than did Muḥammad ᶜAbduh, who generally was more skeptical of tradition than his successor.[15] Riḍā relies mainly on al-Ṭabarī for what traditions he does cite, and frequently discusses the commentaries of al-Zamakhsharī, al-Rāzī and others. Yet for the most part, as will be evident, we are on essentially new ground in this fourteenth/twentieth century work of exegesis and will find that usually we are reading the ideas of ᶜAbduh and Riḍā rather than those of centuries of their predecessors as has been so largely the case from the time of al-Bayḍāwī on.

So much has been written about ᶜAbduh's ideas, and so easy is it to come to at least a superficial understanding of the dominant themes of his writings, that there is a great temptation here to attempt to balance the Manār commentary against the general framework of his thought as expressed in his other writings. In the Risālat al-tawḥīd, for example, he devotes an

---

[14] Amin ("The modernist movement", p. 165) comments that this title, al-ustādh al-imām [the master and guide], is rarely awarded and its consistent use in reference to ᶜAbduh is a good indication of the esteem in which he was held by his contemporaries.

[15] Riḍā refers to ᶜAbduh as a "qāḍī mujtahid", one who comes to independent decisions rather than relying on the conclusions formulated by earlier thinkers. (Ta'rīkh, III, 242).

entire chapter to what he calls "The Islamic Religion, or Islam [al-dīn al-islāmī aw-al-islām]" in which he clearly expresses his feelings on how Islam has become distorted from its original condition and intent.[16] Here as in numerous other places he develops the reasons for his fight against taqlīd, the acceptance of dogmas handed down by religious authorities without personal appraisal of them, and what he sees as the dangerous consequences of taqlīd. In al-Islām wa'l-naṣrānīyah is clearly enunciated his theme of Islam as the universal religion, the basis for the uniting of all Muslims. Here we see the Pan-Islamism so important to al-Afghānī translated in the thought of ᶜAbduh from a political orientation to a religious one. This is supported by Riḍā when he expounds ᶜAbduh's ideas in the biography Ta'rīkh in such sections as that entitled "al-Waḥdah al-islāmīyah". (II, 279-85)

It is the purpose of this essay, however, to consider what is developed within the confines of the structure of tafsīr. To the extent to which we may not find immediate evidence of the themes carried through in his other writings we can only wonder whether Riḍā has not been faithful to him or if the traditional structure of tafsīr does not permit even to the professedly liberal and liberated minds of the present century an understanding of the Qur'ān essentially divergent from that which has characterized the tafsīr of the preceding thirteen centuries. (Of course the recognition is presupposed that by limiting ourselves to the consideration of [in this case] only six verses, we are not in a position to assess the tafsīr as a whole.) We can approach the commentary, however, with the hope of finding many of the dominant themes of ᶜAbduh's work repeated, an expectation supported by Goldziher: "Es stellt die Konzentration der durch Dschemāl al-dīn und M. ᶜAbduh propagierten theologischen Lehre dar."[17]

---

[16]It is interesting to note immediately in this discussion a subtle change in emphasis from what has been seen in the tafsīr thus far considered. (This work, of course, is not a tafsīr and it may well be that we shall not find the same kind of instance in ᶜAbduh's commentary.) Where the general understanding has been that the Prophet (Prophets) brought islām which is tawḥīd, here we find ᶜAbduh saying: "The islamic religion came with (brought) tawḥīd of God . . . and it established the proof that the cosmos has one creator . . . [jā'a al-dīn al-islāmī bi-tawḥīd Allāh . . . fa-aqāma'l-adillah ᶜalá anna li'l-kawn khāliqan wāḥidan . . .] (Risālat, p. 141) The dīn itself established or showed the proof, a noteworthy variation on the general understanding that it was the Prophet and/or the Qur'ān that conveyed God's revelation.

[17]Richtungen, p. 325.

Fame tends to perpetuate itself, and the attention given to the person and doctrine of Shaykh Muḥammad ᶜAbduh of Egypt has served to make him one of the best-known of the leaders of the modern "reform" movement in Islam. Not all of his notice has been favorable, of course, and there are many who feel that he has been severely overrated and indeed that more noteworthy innovative approaches to the understanding of Islam in the modern world have come from sources other than the much-publicized Egyptian school.

One of the most incisive estimates of ᶜAbduh's theology is that of Max Horten[18] in which he indicates that the methods of the Egyptian thinker lacked scientific objectivity and thoroughness. He failed, according to Horten, to develop clear philosophical principles with which to deal with the problems of theology in the modern world. (Horten was certainly convinced of ᶜAbduh's contributions, however, and gave them ample credit.) Malcolm Kerr indicates that where ᶜAbduh and Riḍā fell short was in an unwillingness to go all the way in discarding the classical doctrines which they claimed were not adequate for the modern age. "The difficulty is that the teachings of ᶜAbduh and his circle rested on intellectual foundations that were, on the whole, vague and unsystematic. Their social and psychological impact was immense, but it was ambiguous . . . . ᶜAbduh's historical role was simply to fling open the doors and expose a musty tradition to fresh currents. His intention may have been more specific, but the effect was not."[19]

If some have criticized this reformer, and indeed the Muslim world in general, for not rising intellectually to the challenges of the modern age, these criticisms have certainly not overbalanced the appreciation expressed for ᶜAbduh and his school. In a work that was dominant for thirty years, C. C. Adams speaks of him as scholar, patriot, man of public affairs, one of the great leaders and reformers of Islam.[20] Muslims themselves, as

---

[18]"Muhammad Abduh" in Beiträge, XIV (1917), 74-128.

[19]Islamic Reform, p. 15. Even less charitable is the assessment of Elie Kedourie in his book Afghanī and ᶜAbduh in which he attempts to prove the latter's unorthodoxy, seeming to imply that he became a chief judge by flying under false colors: ". . . ᶜAbduh's remarkable history; heterodox in religion, radical in politics, he takes part in a rebellion, collaborates in the writing of a subversive print, but, in the end, breaking with Afghani and his past becomes . . . the eminent and respected Mufti . . . his renown and influence outstripping by far the seedy intellectuals and conspirators among whom his career began." (p. 37)

[20]Islam and Modernism, p. 103.

far afield as Indonesia (where he was particularly influential), have held him in the kind of esteem described by the words of a young Egyptian writer who calls his life a "mélange of the life of a prophet and that of a hero."[21] To West and East alike he probably remains the best known and in many ways the most important of those who have attempted to reform and/or reinterpret Islam in the late nineteenth and the twentieth centuries. As has been illustrated by the tafsīr examined in this essay, attempts at a new understanding of the role of dīn al-islām really did not begin until that time, and in the longer view history may find it difficult to be too harsh on those who were willing to take the first steps.

Were we to choose one statement as a kind of goal put forward by ᶜAbduh and Riḍā it might well be that given in the first volume of the journal al-Manār: ". . . the understanding of al-dīn according to the way of the ancestors of the community before the introduction of division, and a return in the acquisition of its knowledge to the earliest sources." (I, 892) Let us see, then, how this is expressed in the pages of the Tafsīr al-manār as Riḍā explains his understanding of al-islām.

* * *

Since Rashīd Riḍā was never able to complete the commentary past sūrah twelve, we do not have his tafsīr of 39:22 and 61:7. Fortunately he has included in a discussion of 3:85 some clear references to his interpretation of the meaning of 49:14. Thus with six out of the eight verses interpreted at some length, we should be able to ascertain without difficulty what he intends as the major considerations in an understanding of islām.

As might be anticipated from earlier commentaries, the tafsīr of 3:19 is the most lengthy and detailed of the six. While mentioning the preference of al-Kasā'ī for the reading anna, and giving the reasons for this choice, Riḍā does not take sides in the issue. However, there is not in his commentary any attempt made to connect verses 3:18-19 more than would follow from their natural sequence. That is, if he sees the second as completely dependent on the first, as did many of the earlier commentators, he does not say so. His first clear statement about the meaning of islām comes when he says:

---

[21]Quoted from Kāmil al-Shinnāwī by Osman Amin, "The modernist movement", p. 165.

> I say: al-dīn linguistically is recompense [al-jazā'] and obedience [al-ṭā^cah] and submission [al-khuḍū^c], i.e. the cause of recompense. And it is connected to the sum [total] of God's commandments [al-takālīf] by which the servants [al-^cibād] subject themselves [yadīnu] to God and [therefore] it has the meaning of al-millah and al-shar^c. And it is said that that with which God obligates the servants is called [a] shar^c from the point of view of God's postulating it [waḍ^cihi] and revealing it [bayānihi]; it is called [a] dīn from the point of view of [man's] submitting [to it] and obeying Him who speaks with authority [ṭā^cat al-shāri^c bihi]; and it is called [a] millah with respect to its being the complex of obligations [jumlat'l-takālīf]. (III, 207)

We have seen various instances of the incorporation into an understanding of islām of the dual aspects of man's action and God's being and deed. The idea has been expressed many times that not only does man act in response to what God is and does, but that these two facets are both part of one single act, stated particularly strongly in the understanding of tawḥīd given by al-Zamakhsharī and others. Here we find the term dīn given a similar interpretation by Rashīd Riḍā. Dīn, which in the context of the verse and by his own statement is al-islām, is at once the shar^c or commandment of God and the way in which man responds to that shar^c. In al-Zamakhsharī the emphasis was on islām as the response to God's being, i.e. unity. Here it is on dīn (al-islām) as the rejoinder to the commission of God, another facet of which is actually the re-response by God in terms of recompense to man. (It is also interesting to note here that while millah has sometimes carried a suggestion of reification in earlier tafsīrs, used in reference to the Muslim community, here in this modern commentary it is defined as the collectivity of God's commandments, a system of duties. The implication is still plural, but here seems to refer to the complex of Islamic injunctions as an ideal, not the actual Islam of history.)

Continuing with the definition of islām, Riḍā identifies it as the maṣdar of aslama with the meaning 'to submit' [khaḍa^ca] 'to surrender' [istaslama], and 'to fulfill or execute' [adá]. (III, 207) After affirming that islām is taken linguistically not only as submission but as entering into peace [salm] or reconciliation and soundness [silm], he says that the giving to dīn al-ḥaqq the name islām corresponds to all of the linguistic meanings of the word, particularly submission, in support of which he cites 4:125: "Who is more excellent in [terms of] dīn than the one who submits [aslama] his face to God, and he is beneficent, following the millah of Ibrāhīm ḥanīf." And leaving no doubt but that the millah of Ibrāhīm was indeed islām, he says:

> Ibrāhīm has been described by *al-islām* in a number of *surahs*, and others of the Prophets are described by it. It is made known by that, that the specification in his saying "Truly *al-dīn* with God is *al-islām* comprehends all of the *milal* that the Prophets brought, for that is their universal spirit [*rūḥuhā al-kullī*], the thing on which they all agree, despite the diversity of some of the obligations and forms of behavior in them, and with which they have been enjoined. (III, 207)

Here he seems to be using *milal* in distinction from *millah* the way we have seen *sharī^{c}ah* differentiated from *shar^{c}*. That is, while he stated above that *millah* is the collectivity of God's commandments, here in the plural it seems to refer to the different regulations expressed to the Peoples of the Book in different ages, probably best understood as a kind of progressive revelation. It is also clear that we have another expression of the dual implication of the term: in addition to God's revelation(s) it is at the same time the communities to which the revelation was made, as is made apparent in the following statement from ^{c}Abduh (see below) and in succeeding references. What is particularly interesting here, and characteristic of ^{c}Abduh's (and Riḍā's) emphasis on the universality of *islām*, is his discussion of the universal spirit of the *milal*. That in which they all participate is *al-islām*. This stress on harmony is in contrast to the often-repeated theme of earlier commentators that the other Peoples of the Book had distorted the true revelation and that *islām* would overcome, defeat and vanquish all other *adyān*. What Riḍā says is not in contradiction to that; is is rather that he places his emphasis on that in which they all share instead of the digressions and transgressions of the other peoples to whom God's revelation has come. He quotes al-Ustādh al-Imām as having continually asserted and repeated that

> . . . the true *muslim* in the judgment of the Qur'ān is he who is unblemished [*khāliṣan*] by the defects of associating others with God, sincere [*mukhliṣan*] in his actions and having faith, of whatever religious community [*millah*] he might be, and in whatever time and place he might be found. (III, 207)

This, he says, is what is meant also by Qur'ān 3:85.

So far we have certainly gotten little hint that *islām* for Riḍā has any other meaning than individual submission to God, based on and actually united in meaning with God's revelation and command. In an interesting passage on the purpose of *al-dīn*, however, we get a suggestion of what he will later clarify as *islām* in a more reified form. Here he says that God has prescribed *al-dīn* for two basic concerns:

> (The first) is the purification [*taṣfīyah*] of the souls [*al-arwāḥ*] and liberation of the intellects from taints

> of conviction [i^c^tiqād] in [or involvement with] the hidden power of creatures and their control over the action of existing things [al-kā'ināt], that they be free from surrender [al-khuḍū^c^] to and worship [al-^c^ibādah] of those who are like themselves or less than themselves in their preparation and perfection.
>
> (The second) is improvement of the hearts by excellence of the intention in all deeds and purification [ikhlāṣ] of the intention toward God and man; and whenever these two matters occur [man's] nature is set free from the bonds hindering it from reaching its perfection [kamāliha] individually and in society. (III, 257-8)

In the first of these concerns we have a preview of what Riḍā (and here the ideas are clearly based on ^c^Abduh) sees as the cause of diversity and division in Islam. In the second comes the emphasis, suggested by some of the earlier commentators[22] and developed much more fully by the modern writers, on the perfectibility of the nature of man. Not only is man individually perfectible, but men living together can, by the right intent, achieve a perfect society. He concludes the two points by saying that "these two matters are the spirit of the intention of the word al-islām." (III, 258)

In this passage Riḍā is pointing to a concept of islām which has not been developed by the other tafsīrs that we have read. The stress here is not on islām as submission (although this is explicitly included) so much as on islām as perfection, and individual perfection naturally carries with it the implication of a perfect society. This is spelled out even more explicitly in his next few sentences:

> As for acts of worship [a^c^māl al-^c^ibādāt], they are prescribed for the education [tarbīyah] of this command spirit into the creation spirit.[23] And toward that end intention [al-nīyah] and sincerity [al-ikhlāṣ] are made a condition in it; and when it is educated, for its possessor are facilitated the performance of the rest of the commands of discipline (morality) [al-adabīyah] and politics (civilization) [al-madanīyah] by which one is connected to the virtuous city [al-madīnah al-fāḍilah] and realization of the hopes of the philosophers [al-ḥukamā']. (III, 258)

---

[22] In the commentaries we have examined al-Bayḍāwī was the first to use the phrase "al-fiṭrah al-salīmah" [the perfect (or perfectible) nature of man], (although al-Rāzī did refer to the fiṭrat al-nafs), in his usage confining its meaning to the innate disposition in terms of which man is naturally accepting of al-islām. (Anwār al-tanzīl, I, 317)

[23] See Qur'ān 7:54, "His truly is all creation and commandment." (Arberry translation)

The created or natural spirit of man [al-rūḥ al-khalqī] needs discipline and training in order to reach its ideal state of perfection. This is provided by the commandments of God, the specifics of how man should respond to and worship his Lord, accomplished by the inculcation of what Riḍā calls the commanded spirit [al-rūḥ al-amrī] into this created spirit. Then he immediately makes the transition from individual discipline to social discipline [al-madanīyah] and indicates that when the individuals are personally educated to a condition of morality they will join together to realize the ideal state of society envisioned by the philosophers, a kind of Platonic state which is termed al-madīnah al-fāḍilah. If this is the intention of the word islām, we see developed clearly and in a way distinct from the preceding tafsīr the relationship between the individual act of submission -- with its stress on individual perfection -- and the perfect state resultant from that.

Returning to the first of the two basic concerns that he outlined above, Riḍā exclaims, "How great is the negligence of people away from the truth of al-islām! What happiness for people surpasses the knowledge of every individual that he has been given the capacity that has been given to those described as saints [bi'l-wilāyah] and holy ones -- and [yet] they pride themselves in leadership and eminence." (III, 258) Even when men realize their natural capacity for spiritual perfection they succumb to the temptations of power. He continues by saying that man binds his fellow in both a spiritual enslavement and a political enslavement. The essence [ḥaqīqah] of the spirit of islām is hidden from some by practical laws and legal conventions, and from others by theoretical (evil) inclinations [nazaghāt] and lowly conventions, for the former claim kufr or bid^c^ah [innovation] to all who differ from their ways and the others shout ignorance and bigotry of those who do not agree with them. But whenever there is a large number of sincere and devoted muslimūn among the ancients or moderns they become God's proof against them.

Although the Manār commentary is interlinear, one senses, as was observed above, a real difference in approach from the earlier commentaries. While those of previous centuries quite clearly took the lines of the Qur'ān as their points of departure, sometimes at the expense of clear continuity from one passage of exegesis to the next, the tafsīr of Riḍā seems to be using the āyahs as a proof for the point(s) he is making. Thus the verse ❬And those to whom the Book has been given did not differ until after knowledge came to them❟ fits, as it were, into the middle of his discussion of those who have succumbed to the lures of religious and political power. It is these, he says, who have caused the departure from the true islām of the Prophets by the creation of schools and groups fighting with one another, "although al-dīn is one with no division [tafarruq] in it and no cause for diversity, let alone fighting." Mentioning verse 2:212 ❛The people are one community❜ he talks about the formation of different schools in every religious community [millah]. (III, 258-59) (It is apparent that by millah he does not intend the understanding expressed in his earlier definition, i.e. the collectivity of the commandments of God. Here it is more specifically the group(s) who have accepted the commandments, once revealed.)

He classifies the leaders of the political and religious communities as ru'asā' al-dīn wa'l-dunyā, indicating that because the leaders have helped to separate one faction from another, al-dīn itself has disintegrated into the differing doctrines of sects and parties. Clearly while dīn in its ideal state is al-islām in a pure and unblemished manifestation, through the centuries it has become subject to all the forces of disintegration. Here he is discussing dīn not as the individual response to God but in its reified forms of sects and groups. Both as the ideal in its perfect state and as the actual in its perverted manifestations the dīn al-islām is presented in a form substantially different from what we have seen before. Formerly the differing has generally been expressed as a negation of tawḥīd by calling God a trinity or saying ᶜUzayr was the son of God; here the differing is described, as we have seen, as the division into sects destroying the unity of true dīn al-islām. Riḍā does not indicate, as have the other mufassirūn, that only the Jews and Christians have differed; writing from the perspective of the fourteenth/twentieth century he says that "it is necessary that we not forget ourselves -- it is not hidden from us with what difference and division we have been afflicted." (III, 259)

Yet despite this theme which dominates his discussion of 3:19 and following, Riḍā never divorces his understanding of ideal islām (and its perversion) from the meaning of the surrender of the individual to God. Discussing the call of the Prophet to the Jews in Madīnah to return to the true essence of al-dīn [ḥaqīqatihi], he says, "and this is submission [islām] of the face to God and sincere devotion to Him in every deed. . ." (III, 260) The strength of his emphasis has been on islām as a kind of entity, essential and developmental, but it is absolutely clear that talking about islām as that in which the universal spirits of all the milal participate is meaningless apart from the understanding of personal, individual surrender to God and his commandments. In giving this as a basic meaning of the term, Riḍā is very much one with all of those who have commented on this 3:19 āyah of the Qur'ān.

Having thus laid the foundations for his understanding of dīn al-islām and its development in the tafsīr of 3:19, Riḍā enlarges upon it in a most interesting way when he comes to consider 3:84-85. The last passage of 3:84 ❬and we are submitters unto Him❭ has elicited some commentary worth quoting in full:

> . . . yielding with pleasure and sincerity, turning from our passions and cravings in al-dīn, not taking it [al-dīn] in a spirit of partisanship [jinsīyatan] for the sake of worldly fortunes [ḥuẓūẓ al-dunyā], but only seeking through it to come close to God by the improvement of [our] souls and the sincerity of [our] hearts and the ascending of [our] spirits to the height of nobility and well-being [al-karāmah wa'l-falāḥ]. The āyah opens with mention of al-īmān [❬Say: We have faith in God❭] and it closes with al-islām [the succeeding verse] which in its perfection [kamālihi] is the fruit and the objective [of al-īmān], and this is religious islām [al-islām al-dīnī] with which all the Prophets have had to do. (III, 357-58)

Several points stand out immediately as worthy of note. First we have the use of the term jinsīyah. This he will refer to and clarify in the succeding commentary; its understanding is most important to the development of his ideas. Here we have the interesting suggestion that indeed it is possible to take dīn as a communal affiliation for the sake of worldly gain. Secondly, we might note again the emphasis on islām as perfection, albeit here specifically the perfection of individual submission with reference to al-īmān. Then we have the very interesting expression al-islām al-dīnī. One can only suppose that there must be a non-religious islām, a totally new concept in the context of Qur'ān commentary, and indeed this seems to be the import of his ensuing discussion which we shall examine in detail. He goes on to say:

> ❬If anyone seeks other than al-islām as [a] dīn, it will not be accepted from him and he will be a loser in the hereafter.❭ For al-dīn, if it is not the islām the meaning of which we expounded earlier, is nothing but formalities [rusūm] and imitative traditions [taqālīd] which people adopt as a bond for ethnic identity [al-jinsīyah], and an instrument of partisanship, and a means of worldly gain. And that is the kind of thing that increases the hearts in corruption and the spirits in evil, for in this world the people are increased only in hostility, and in the hereafter only in hopelessness. . . . (III, 358)

In other words, he is saying that if one's religion is any other kind of islām than he has described in the earlier passages, i.e. if it is the reified Islam of the commonality, then one is lost. What a stunning denunciation of the external forms (without inner substance) of reified religious systems!

At this point in his discussion of 3:85 Riḍā presents what almost seems to be an interruption in the text, a digression into an area unrelated to the theme that he has been developing. Closer examination shows it to be very much a part of this theme, however, and quite important to his explanation of the difference between al-islām al-dīnī and al-islām al-jinsī. First he quotes a long section from the Mafātīḥ al-ghayb of al-Rāzī. This is a portion familiar to us in which al-Rāzī discusses the relation of islām and īmān, the former being more general and the latter more specific, although the two are really one.[24] Riḍā feels that such distinctions as al-Rāzī makes are confusing, and the cause of confusion is the joining together [tazāḥum] in his mind of theological [al-kalāmīyah] and linguistic applications.

Actually, Riḍā says, the understandings of al-islām and al-īmān linguistically are dissimilar, "for al-islām is entering into peace [al-silm] and it applies to the opposite of war and to security or wholeness [al-salāmah] . . . while al-īmān is conviction [al-taṣdīq] and it is of the heart as though someone says something and you believe [ya^{c}taqidu] in its veracity [ṣidq]." (III, 359) He then goes on to make his important point: in the Qur'ān, which we take to be what he calls the "theological" application, islām and īmān apply to what he terms an īmān khāṣṣ, specialized faith, that which is the factor of salvation in God's sight and which is the dīn acceptable to Him. Tying together the two terms, he says:

> [al-īmān] is certain confirmation [taṣdīq] of the oneness of God and His perfection and of the revelation and the Messengers and the last day, in as much as it has effective priority over the will, and consciousness, so that good works spring from it . . . . And as for [al-islām] it is sincerity [ikhlāṣ] towards Him in al-tawḥīd and servanthood and in letting oneself be led towards that to which He has guided by the tongues of the Messengers. And it [al-islām], in this meaning, is the dīn of all the Prophets with which He sent them for the guidance of His servants. And al-īmān and al-islām according to this converge upon a single reality [ḥaqīqah], which each of them attains on a [from its own] standpoint. (III, 359-60)

Riḍā refers to 49:14-17 throughout this discussion, thus giving us the benefit of what would probably have been the gist

---

[24] See above, pp. 115-16.

of his commentary on that passage had he reached that far. The point of this particular section seems to be not too different from what we have seen in many of the classical tafsīrs, perhaps best expressed in the understanding of al-Ṭabarī. Islām and īmān are sometimes used for the external part of them both [qad yuṭlaq . . . ᶜalá mā yakūnu min-huma ẓāhiran] regardless of whether that be out of certainty or out of an ignorance or out of an hypocrisy. This is not, however, true islām (or true īmān). The submission of these Arabs was for the purpose of conciliating the mu'minūn after having been at war with them (this being the linguistic definition he gave to islām earlier). But, he says, "this does not have the meaning of sincere devotion and being led [inqiyād] with submission [idhᶜān]." (III, 360) In other words, external islām is not true [al-ṣaḥīḥ] islām, and the real meaning of it in its Qur'ānic usage is that in which islām and īmān converge in the dīn approved by and acceptable to God.

Now where does all this fit in with his discussion of jinsīyah? Without saying so explicitly, Riḍā seems to draw a parallel between the external islām of the Arabs of 49:14 and that by which the followers of taqlīd and ethnic islām are described. Neither, he appears to be saying, is true in the sense of the Qur'ānic faith discussed above. The conclusion of his comments on 3:85, in which he develops this theme, deserves full notice here:

> As for the usage of the term al-islām to mean the doctrines and traditions and practices of those people who are known as Muslims, it is a new usage based on the principle "religion is what the followers of a religion have" [al-dīn mā ᶜalayhi al-mutadayyinūn]; so that Buddhism [al-būdhīyah] is what the people have who are described as Buddhists and Judaism [al-yahūdīyah] is what people have to whom the name Jew is applied and Christianity [al-naṣrānīyah] is what those people have who say "we are Christians", and so forth. And this is al-dīn with the meaning of community (or ethnic identity) [al-jinsīyah], and whether it [jinsīyah] has a revealed or a positivist basis [aṣl samāwī aw-waḍᶜī], it undergoes change and alteration so that it is far from its source in its regulations and its goals. The significant thing is the situation of its adherence [at the moment], not the known or unknown origins [of that religion]. And the dīn of the People of the Book was transformed into "a" jinsīyah in this sense: it is that which prevented the People of the Book from following the Prophet in what He brought of the explanation of the spirit of the dīn Allāh which all the Prophets had along with the variation of their laws in application [al-furūᶜ], and this is al-islām. And al-islām is a meaning that the Qur'ān has clarified. Whoever follows it is according to the chosen dīn of God and whoever goes against it is desirous of other than the dīn of

> God. It is not the same in meaning as al-jinsīyah as we know it, which differs [from true religion] by the different things that happen to its people in the way of uncritical acceptance [al-taqālīd]: for true [al-haqīqī] islām is contrary to habitual [al-ᶜurfī] islām. Thus our course in this tafsīr has been a rejection of making al-islām a conventional ethnic identity [jinsīyah ᶜurfīyah] heedless of the fact that it is divine guidance. If it were taken up in accord with its original nature, and there followed thereby as a consequence the community link, then that link would be only for good for its people, without being harmful to others, because of its being based on the rules of justice and virtue and human mercy. But making al-jinsīyah the basis is corrosive of religion which is the repository [manāṭ] of the happiness of this world and the next. (III, 360-61)

He begins by admitting that the term has been applied to and is used with reference to those who simply accept the dogmas and traditions that have been handed down to them. Just as those who are born and raised in a situation where Buddhism prevails (and likewise with Christianity and Judaism) automatically become Buddhists, with acceptance of all that that tradition carries, so those raised in Islam follow blindly that which has come down to them. The phrase "religion is what the followers of a religion have" carries the double entendre of reified and non-reified dīn. By paralleling that by which the followers of Islam are described with the "-ism's" -- Judaism, Buddhism, Christianity -- he is clearly referring to the dīn al-islām in its reified form. Here, then, is the real meaning of jinsīyah for him. Because of one's particular ethnic identity, or circumstance of regional or national association, he automatically adopts the religion of that situation.[25]

Riḍā admits that such an identity need not dissociate the dīn [in its reified sense] from its fundamentals, or what he calls its revealed basis. That is, while one can be born into a group dīn, he may still understand and practise dīn as his personal response to God. The problem seems to come in Riḍā's (and ᶜAbduh's) old foe taqlīd, whereby people lose the sense of personal communication or relationship with God and merely accept and practice the doctrines and rituals of the religion because they are given. In the case of islām he makes it very clear that

---

[25] Riḍā has developed the idea of jinsīyah, based on ᶜAbduh, in a variety of places. In the Manār Journal (V, 687), for example, he states: ". . . al-islām for those muslims who describe themselves as modern has gone away from its essence as religious creed [ᶜaqīdah dīnīyah] to its form as ethnic and political [jinsīyah siyāsīyah]. Cf. Ta'rīkh, II, 231-35 entitled "Al-jinsīyah wa'l-diyānah al-islāmīyah".

its essential meaning is the spirit of the dīn Allāh brought by all the Prophets. This, as he has said frequently, is the dīn acceptable to God. The basic distinction he makes is between this true [al-ḥaqīqī] islām and that characterized by al-jinsīyah which he calls habitual [al-ᶜurfī]. While it is possible for one to experience islām as personal submission as well as to participate in conventional or ethnic Islam, the fact is that it is bacause islām has become reified, a sect with its established doctrines just like the other religions, that it is habitual for its adherents. Thus in his concluding sentence he states clearly that it is because al-jinsīyah is made the basis of dīn, its people so involved with the religion of a particular group and area, that dīn in its basic sense of that in which one finds the joy of this world and the next is destroyed.

From this point on, in the tafsīr of the three remaining verses, we find little that is different from the themes outlined above. It is interesting to note that beginning with 5:3 the commentary is much more traditional in content. This may be explainable in part by the fact that ᶜAbduh's lectures, on which Riḍā's commentary is based, went only to Qur'ān 4:125. We observed above that Riḍā was more of a traditionist (one who studies the ḥadīth) than his mentor; we see here that apparently he was also more of a traditionalist (one who accepts the traditional interpretations).

In the first of these passages, 5:3, Riḍā devotes himself entirely to a discussion of the ḥadīths related about this verse and to the commentaries of a number of mufassirūn. We have seen all of this material before: the traditions that the Prophet died eighty-one days after the descent of the āyah and that the Jews would have chosen this as a feast day, and that the completion of dīn means purification of the bayt al-ḥarām as well as the completion of duties and regulations, the prohibited and the permitted; particular reference is made to the tafsīrs of Ibn ᶜAbbās, al-Ṭabarī, al-Rāzī, al-Bayḍāwī and Abū Suᶜūd. (VI, 154-157) In all of this there is really no discussion of the meaning of islām itself, attention being centered on the understanding of the completion of dīn.

Riḍā follows this direct exegesis with a section entitled "The completion of al-dīn by the Qur'ān". As this does not deal explicitly with islām we shall not analyze it here. In fact there is only one mention of the term, although that mention itself is interesting. The discussion is based on al-Shāṭibī al-Gharnāṭi's al-Muwāfaqāt, the like of which, says Riḍā, "has not been written concerning the sources of islām [uṣūl al-islām] and and its wisdom [ḥikmatihi]." (VI, 157) This phrase is one that most likely would not have been used in earlier centuries, when one spoke rather of uṣūl al-fiqh or uṣūl al-dīn, etc. By uṣūl al-islām Riḍā would seem perhaps to suggest the sources or fundamentals of the religion in its reified sense, the wisdom which has characterized its development.

In 6:125, predictably, Riḍā returns to the understanding of islām in its strictly personal sense. His comments are interesting, however, as a kind of summary of what he has said earlier:

> ﴿Whomever God wills to guide, He expands his breast for al-islām﴾. This is a description of the condition of the one prepared for the guidance of al-islām by the soundness of his nature [bi-salāmat fiṭratihi] and the purity of his soul [ṭahārat nafsihi] from two natural tendencies keeping him from responding to the call of truth, and they are pride and envy, and by providing it -- i.e. his soul -- with the two guidances to the truth and to sound judgment in conduct [al-rashād]. And these latter two constitute the freedom of thought that overcomes blind subservience to the inherited tradition of the fathers and the ancestors, and the strength of will that [is able to] turn away from following leaders or conforming to peers. And whoever is like that is qualified, by the will of God Most High and [by] His ordaining, to receive the call to al-islām which is the dīn al-fiṭrah [the religion of the natural disposition] and the educator of it [al-fiṭrah]. (VIII, 42)

Man by creation is of a sound and pure soul or disposition, not succumbing to the temptations which have in reality led him away from this natural state and resultingly have made of the dīn al-islām a perversion. These temptations are the tendencies toward taqlīd and jinsīyah (and siyāsīyah [political power]). The one whose heart is expanded is he who is free of these inclinations, returned to his natural pure state in which he is receptive of al-islām, the dīn that by creation he innately accepts. Riḍā makes the interesting statement that islām is the educator of this fiṭrah, implying that man's disposition is by nature not perfect but perfectible. He apparently does not mean Islam in its reified sense, and yet it seems that there may be an indication of something beyond the pure response of man to God which has been the predominant understanding of dīn al-islām in the succeeding tafsīrs, particularly of this verse. In other words, islām is not "educating" (an act), or "education" (an experience), but the "educator", the agent of the process of education. This could well be interpreted to mean that it has a pattern of its own which in some sense can be considered apart from any man's participation in it (see above, p. 188, n. 16). This idea of islām as the educator -- ambiguous in Riḍā's writing insofar as the question of its independence of man is concerned -- is to be expressed in greater detail by our other fourteenth/twentieth century commentator, Sayyid Quṭb.

The last āyah mentioning islām on which Riḍā has given commentary is 9:74 ﴾. . . they rejected [Him] after their islām﴿. In earlier tafsīr there has been some question in connection with this verse as to whether or not "they" changed their minds after a sincere islām, or if they were never sincere at all. Here it is clear that the latter is intended, for Riḍā says, "They used to swear to the believers in order to please them [li-yuraḍḍūhum] . . ." (X, 552) In the case of the situation described by this verse, however, it is even worse, for the kufr attributed to them "contradicts external submission [yunāfī al-islām al-ẓāhir], to say nothing of internal faith [faḍlan ᶜan al-īmān al-bāṭin]." (X, 552) This is coordinate with his explanation given of 49:14 (in the tafsīr of 3:85), external submission distinct from al-islām al-ṣaḥīḥ. The rest of the commentary on this verse is dealing with the circumstances of its revelation, most of which is already familiar to us.

What, then, can we conclude about Riḍā's (and ᶜAbduh's) understanding of islām? There can be no question but that the true [ḥaqīqī] meaning is the individual, personal surrender to God so clearly outlined in the discussion of 3:19. Yet it is apparent in the several sections considered, that having once expressed this meaning in terms of the kind of definition common to classical tafsīrs, he continues to point it up by means of comparison with what he draws as the opposite, namely conventional religion. Rather than illustrating by his own usage that the term islām has come to have a reified reference, he emphasizes the fact by a very precise and damning attack on such a development. The object of his attack is al-islām al-ᶜurfī, the conventional religion characterized by taqlīd and jinsīyah, which he denounces as inauthentic, corrupt, and a new usage. While we have seen earlier that true islām has been contrasted with the kind of external submission of those in fear of the Prophet or desiring alms, here religious islām [al-islām al-dīnī] is contrasted with non-religious, or jinsī islām, that by which one identifies with the religious tradition into which he is born.

In addition to this negative illustration of reification, Riḍā himself gives us the suggestion of an understanding of islām dissimilar to what we have seen in earlier tafsīrs. This is islām as the universal spirit [al-rūḥ al-kullī] in which all of the religions of the world share in essence. It is this islām (which, of course, he considers al-islām al-ḥaqīqī) that he describes as the educator of the fiṭrah. In earlier commentary (based mainly on al-Bayḍāwī) it was exclusively the fiṭrah that was disposed toward islām. Here the emphasis is also on islām as the educator of the natural disposition. This idea of islām as universal spirit finds even fuller expression in some of the more recent modern commentaries, as we shall see in Sayyid Quṭb's writing.

We have noted above that there has been a recurring emphasis, based particularly on the commentary and traditions of the early centuries after the Prophet, on the two meanings of personal submission and the group of those who have submitted, incorporated into the one term islām. In these cases the identity has been between the deed and the group, individual surrender and the actual community of muslims. Here in Riḍā we find that in his stress on the perfectability of men and society he uses islām to refer both to the true submission of the man of faith and as a description of the ideal society attainable if men could only lose the bonds of jinsīyah. The identity of singular and plural in one term still pertains, but while in the former it was descriptive of what was, in this modern commentary it refers to what could be. The overriding conception of existing communal Islam for Riḍā is a negative one, characterized by all the elements preventing one from true submission to God.

XIV (b)

Among those who listened to the teachings of Rashīd Riḍā at the Dār al-ᶜUlūm in Cairo was Ḥasan al-Bannā', founder of the Ikhwān al-Muslimūn. Many of the doctrines basic to this controversial organization were developed out of principles already laid down by al-Afghānī, ᶜAbduh and Riḍā.[26] But Ḥasan al-Bannā's movement was really a movement of the common people, and in the attempt at a regeneration of Islam it became a powerful, militant and fundamentalist organization. While the school of ᶜAbduh and Riḍā continued to work through and value the formal processes of education, the Ikhwān eventually became a party of revolution,[27] finally banned by the Egyptian government.

---

[26]See Bertier, "L'ideologie politique des frères musulmans" in Orient, VIII (1958), 43-57.

[27]The question of the Ikhwān as a political party is an interesting one, for in actuality they have stood for an abolition of all political parties and divisions in favor of an overriding Islamic unity.

Notoriety given to the political activities of the Ikhwān has tended to overshadow the fact that it has been a deeply pious movement, strenuously opposed to the taqlīd and partisanship against which ᶜAbduh and Riḍā wrote so vigorously, and striving for religious renewal and for an increased interest in the social welfare of the masses. Adherents strictly observe the injunctions of religious law, and one of the basic aims of the movement is the harmonizing of the duties of Islam with the requirements of modern life.[28] The supreme frustration of the Ikhwān has been the failure to have its program -- which it considers the embodiment of the ideal of Islamic life -- accepted by the political authority. This has forced it, ironically, into a position of opposition, when its basic premise is the unity of all Muslims.

One of the leaders of the Ikhwān al-Muslimūn until his recent death was Sayyid Quṭb, author of the last commentary to be considered in this essay. A journalist and author of wide repute, he was implicated in the conspiracy to assassinate Jamal ᶜAbd al-Nāṣir in November of 1954,[29] and spent the rest of his life in and out of prison. His writings, ranging from children's literature and songs to novels, social tracts and theological works, have been translated into Persian, Turkish, Urdu, English and some Indonesian languages.

Born in 1324/1906 in Asyūṭ, Egypt, Sayyid Quṭb was the oldest of five children, all of whom are known in their own right as authors and scholars.[30] His family, originally from the Arabian Peninsula, has been an influential one, and several of its members were also later involved in the Ikhwān. (His sister's son was executed for his affiliation.) After receiving a

---

[28]Richard P. Mitchell (The Society of Muslim Brothers, p. ix) summarizes their situation as follows: "Although sharing in some areas the relatively catholic Muhammad ᶜAbduh tradition, the Society also reflected the progressive change in the character of that movement to more rigidity and thus intolerance. Yet, we conclude, that the movement, although conservative in spirit and quantitative membership, attracted as activists largely lay and urban people, most of whom in varying degrees had already accepted the premises of modernization."

[29]See Nuseibeh, Ideas of Arab Nationalism, pp. 166-67.

[30]Details of Sayyid Quṭb's life have been given to me in a personal interview with Muzammil Husayn Siddīqī (Nadwa Islamic Seminary, Medinah Islamic University), based on biographical data from the following Urdu translation: Sayyid Quṭb Shahīd, Jādah wa-manzil tarjamah-i maᶜālim fī al-ṭarīq. Khalīl Aḥmad Ḥāmidī, transl. Lāhor: Islāmik Pablikeshanz Limiṭaḍ, [1968].

traditional education Sayyid Quṭb entered Dār al-ʿUlūm, from which he graduated in 1933. He became a lecturer at the same institution. Then as Inspector of Schools for the Ministry of Education[31] he visited the United States for two years; on his return to Egypt in 1945 he joined the Ikhwān. At that time the society was extremely popular, boasting over two and one-half million members.

By the late 1940's, the Egyptian political scene had polarized into two camps following the parties of the Ikhwān and the Wafd.[32] Ḥasan al-Bannā' was assassinated in 1948, and by 1952 Sayyid Quṭb had become one of the three leaders of his movement. Particularly active in the area of journalism, which was always his first love, Quṭb had edited a weekly journal for a brief period (1947-48)[33] and in early 1954 became editor of _Majallat al-Ikhwān al-Muslimīn_, a magazine devoted to expounding the principles of the Ikhwān.[34] This was also short-lived, however, censored out of existence by the government in only a few months. After his implication in the attempt on ʿAbd al-Nāṣir's life in October of 1954 (for which six other brethren were hanged), he was sentenced to fifteen years in prison, of which he served nine. Continuing to work and write actively for the Ikhwān, he was back in prison within a year.

Sayyid Quṭb's real troubles began with the publication of a book called _Maʿālim al-ṭarīq_, which was particularly critical of the current regime. It was considered a crime merely to have read this work, and it is for its authorship, as well as for his other political activities, that Sayyid Quṭb was executed (along with six other members of the Ikhwān) in 1386/1966.

Not all of Sayyid Quṭb's writings are considered revolutionary, of course, and many of them are widely accepted as thoughtful and appropriate statements of the principles of Islam. Among these is his _tafsīr_ of the Qur'ān, _Fī ẓilāl al-Qur'ān_.[35] It was through association with some friends of Ṭāhā Ḥusayn (for

---

[31] He was later offered the position of head of the Ministry of Education, a post he refused on the grounds that education in Egypt was not truly Islamic.

[32] Mitchell, _Society_, p. viii.

[33] Heyworth-Dunne, _Religious and Political Trends in Modern Egypt_, pp. 97-98.

[34] Husaini, _The Moslem Brethren_, p. 24.

[35] Cairo: Dār Iḥyā' al-Kutub al-ʿArabīyah, 137?-1379 [195?-1959], 30 voll. in 7.

whom Quṭb was private secretary earlier in his career) that he really became interested in Qur'ānic science. His *tafsīr* was some time in writing, and was finally redone in its present form in 1955. This work is now available in Turkish and Persian, and is being translated into Urdu.

That for which Sayyid Quṭb is probably best known in the West is his *al-ʿAdālah al-ijtimāʿīyah fī'l-islām*.[36] Called by Christina Phelps Harris "a reasoned defense of Muslim conservatism",[37] it was written as an expression of the Islamic theory of life, a statement of the comprehensive and unified system by which Islam governs the affairs of men in society. We shall see this theme predominant in the *tafsīr* of Sayyid Quṭb, in which he places a major emphasis on the role of *islām* in coordinating individual and corporate life.

In 1947 Franz Rosenthal translated a pamphlet,[38] published by the Ikhwān, that states the principles by which the brethren attempt to understand the role of *islām* (Islam) in present-day political life. The following is a quotation from that translation:

> Our aims include everything that the word *Islām* stands for. The term *Islām* has a very wide meaning and is not adequately defined by that narrow interpretation which is given to it by many people. We believe that Islām comprises and regulates all human affairs and does not shrink from new problems and necessary reforms. It is not restricted to religious and spiritual matters.
>
> We understand, however, the word *Islām* in a different sense. We understand it in a very wide sense, as regulating all the affairs of this world and the next. This interpretation of *Islām* is not of our making, but is derived from the study of the Qur'ān and the manner of life (*sīrah*) of the first Muslims. If the reader desires to understand how it is possible for the Ikhwān to claim that they promote an idea which, it would seem, has a wider meaning than that implied in the term *Islām*, let him take his Qur'ān and strip his soul from desire (*hawā*) and purposefulness (*ghāyah*). Then he will understand the actual meaning of the Qur'ān, and he will recognize its identity with the propaganda aims of the Ikhwān. (p. 283)

---

[36]Translated by John B. Hardie as *Social Justice in Islam*. Washington, D.C.: American Council of Learned Studies, 1953.

[37]*Nationalism and Revolution in Egypt*, p. 139. Cf. Nuseibeh, *Ideas of Arab Nationalism*, pp. 166-67.

[38]"Daʿwatunā", in *Rasā'il al-Ikhwān al-Muslimīn* (Cairo: Maṭbaʿat al-Ikhwān al-Muslimīn, 1943 or 1944). Published by Rosenthal as "The 'Muslim Brethren' in Egypt" in *MW*, XXXVII (1947), 278-91.

These words were not written by Sayyid Quṭb (as far as we know). They do, however, apparently represent the theories that he helped to propagate as head of press propaganda of the Ikhwān, a position he held for many years. Keeping this in mind as an official statement by that group for whose principles Sayyid Quṭb lost his life, let us see what he himself says about *islām* in his *tafsīr* of the Qur'ān.

* * *

> «Say: We have faith in God, and what was revealed to us, and what was revealed to Ibrāhīm and Ismā^{c}īl and Isḥāq and Ya^{c}qūb and al-Asbāṭ, and what came to Mūsá and ^{c}Īsá, and what came to the Prophets from their Lord. We do not distinguish between any of them, and we are *muslimūn* to Him.» This great unity [*al-wahdah al-kubrá*] amongst all the revelations [*risālāt*], and all the Messengers, is the foundation of the Islamic idea [*al-taṣawwur al-islāmī*], and is that which makes the Muslim community [*al-ummah al-muslimah*] the community inheriting the legacy of the creed [^{c}*aqīdah*] based on the *dīn* of God on the earth, bound to this deep-rooted source, remaining on the pathway of guidance and light. And it is that which makes the Islamic system [*al-niẓām al-islāmī*] the universal system ruling all people living under its protection, without partisanship [*ta^{c}aṣṣub*] or oppression [*iḍṭihād*]. And it is that which makes of the Islamic society [*al-mujtama^{c} al-islāmī*] a society open to all people gathered in love and peace. (I, 161-62)

These words, spoken in exegesis of 2:135 of the Qur'ān, offer an excellent introduction to what we shall find to be the main thrust of Sayyid Quṭb's understanding of *islām*. He is not only particularly interested in its communal form, but as we shall see below he feels that *islām* is not fulfilled apart from the context of the group. Interwoven in his commentary are the two strands of the real and the ideal, the Islamic community as it exists in its actual form and in its perfect form, and it will soon become clear that unlike Riḍā (and ^{c}Abduh), Sayyid Quṭb does not distinguish in his writing between these two aspects.

Interestingly enough, there is very little in the *tafsīr* of verse 3:19, «Truly *al-dīn* with God is *al-islām*», that betrays in itself any difference in understanding between Sayyid Quṭb and the classical *tafsīrs*. He begins by saying that it is "one way of believing [^{c}*aqīdah*] and one reality [*ḥaqīqah*], by which God gives as *dīn* to His servants absolute submission [*istislām*] to God. *Islām* of the heart and the conscience and *islām* of action [*al-ḥarakah*] and deed [*al-^{c}amal*] -- there is no direction for people except toward Him, and there is no objective for them except Him, and no rule among them except by His sharīᶜah." (III, 62) We are given a hint of what his primary concern is to be when he describes islām as having a comprehensive [al-shāmil] meaning, "one islām and one doctrine with which all the Messengers have come . . ." (III, 62) Still, one can easily imagine this having been said by any of the traditional writers, the understanding being that, in general, islām means individual submission.

However, he follows this with a passage that gives a strong suggestion of the new direction his thought takes. Commenting on ❴and if anyone rejects the signs of God . . .❵ he says:

> And then He commanded His Messenger -- blessings and peace be upon him -- to abridge the way of controversy with those to whom the Book had come and the kuffār alike, and to call them all to this one dīn -- to islām with its comprehensive meaning, and to the final form of this islām as brought by the seal of the Messengers. (III, 62-63)

Islām is a continuation of what has been brought earlier, but now it is in its final form. This idea is picked up again in the commentary on 3:83 ❴. . . when to Him has submitted whoever is in the heavens and the earth, willingly or unwillingly, and to Him they will be made to return?❵:

> Truly dīn of God is one, upon which all the Prophets agreed, and the obligation to God is one, enjoined on all of the Messengers. And faith in the new religion [al-īmān bi'l-dīn al-jadīd] is the fulfillment of this obligation, and al-islām is the last dīn [hādha'l-dīn al-akhīr], and he who turns his back on it has turned away from the dīn of God which He enjoined upon all those having faith in God, that they might respond to Him. Truly it is al-islām. And al-islām is the law of existence [nāmūs al-wujūd] in response to which all existence participates. (III, 90)

Two things stand out here as somewhat different from the tafsīr of earlier centuries. The first is that he sees [this form of] islām as having begun at a particular point in time after the revelations to the other Prophets. Thus he refers to the new dīn, the last dīn, identifying it specifically as islām. We have seen in almost all of the earlier commentaries frequent references to the fact that the other peoples to whom God revealed His message did participate in islām. Quṭb does not deny this, but here he also identifies islām specifically as the final revelation. What he seems to be saying is that true dīn, islām, is of universal validity for all peoples, but that it is only the final revealed form, Islam, that truly recognizes this.

Secondly, we have the statement that al-islām is the law of existence. He uses this term nāmūs for islām throughout his commentary, with some telling examples to be cited later. Here is another instance of the stress on what Riḍā called the universal spirit [al-rūḥ al-kullī]. We shall see later in this commentary that even more than Riḍā, Sayyid Quṭb gives the impression that for him islām in this meaning seems to have a kind of ideal existence.

A passage succeeding that quoted above supports these two understandings of islām as new and as law:

> And because the muslim community is the community cognizant of that law, familiar with the unity of the Messengers and the messages, God commanded its Prophet -- blessings and peace be upon him -- to make known in detail and definition īmān of his community in all of the revelations before al-islām, and in all the Messengers before Muḥammad, in order to explain by that the limits of al-islām such as its revelation was concerned with. (III, 90)

Again we see the idea expressed that the other revelations came before al-islām.[39] Following this passage with verse 3:85, he says that "this is al-islām in its comprehensiveness and its inclusion of all of the revelations before it, and in its esteem for all of the Messengers before it, and in its uniting [tawḥīd] of all of the dīn of God, and its returning of all of the calls and all of the revelations to that one source, and al-īmān is in them altogether as God desired them for His servants." (III, 91) The very use of "it" here is indicative of an interpretation different from those of earlier commentators. While they might have said that all of the Prophets before Muḥammad (and, of course, including him) were concerned with islām, Sayyid Quṭb is saying that islām (Islam) is concerned with all of the earlier revelations. Particularly striking is the statement that islām (which in other commentaries has been defined quite consistently as tawḥīd) is itself that which unites or proclaims oneness, a proclamation not of the oneness of God, but of the unity of the dīn of God.[40] Islām (Islam) in its uniting of all of the revelations has subsumed them all under one form, and the implication

---

[39] This phrase "qabla al-islām" is used in other places in Sayyid Quṭb's tafsīr; cf. XXVIII, 81, where he speaks of stories told of the divine way "before al-islām".

[40] Cf. another modern commentator, ᶜAbd Allāh Yūsuf ᶜAlī (The Holy Qur'an, I, 137) who says that ". . . all Religion is one, and it is being renewed in Islam", and later talks of "the light of eternal Unity and Harmony which is Islam". (II, 1541) The traditional commentaries were also primarily concerned with unity, but for them the focus was clearly on God's unity, acknowledged by man in tawḥīd. Here the stress has moved to the idea of the unity of religion.

is that Islam supersedes by incorporating. Here we have moved from the idea of personal submission to the apparently reified concept of Islam as a comprehensive unit.

We saw in Riḍā the reference to islām as the educator of the natural disposition of man. This idea is brought out even more clearly in Sayyid Quṭb's discussion of Q 5:3 when he says the following concerning the completion of dīn:

> There will be no further occasion for elaboration. For in its principles and its universals there is sufficient basis for individual consciences [al-ḍamā'ir] and for human societies [al-mujtama^c^āt]. As for separate and new requirements -- about which no text has appeared -- in the intelligence that al-islām builds [yabnīhi] and protects [yaḥrusu] from mistakes is sufficiency for confronting them with new solutions under the protection of the great principles and universals. (VI, 30)

A constantly recurring theme in this tafsīr is the link between the individual and society. He generally refers to these in terms of the individual heart or mind or conscience [ḍamīr, pl. ḍamā'ir] and the collectivities of these individuals [al-mujtami^c^āt]. (We shall see later some striking statements concerning their interrelationship.) In this passage the real point of interest is that it is al-islām that builds intelligence and oversees conduct. Although the passage admittedly is ambiguous, the implication may well be of something beyond the strictly individual submission of the muslim, an entity (or law [nāmūs]) which in itself directs and controls. This is expressed again in the commentary on sūrah 61 in which, in discussing the phrase "when fighting was prescribed for them" (2:246; 4:77), he says

> Truly al-islām does not desire fighting, and does not wish it out of love for it. But it orders it because the event necessitates it and because the objective that lies (beyond) it is great. For al-islām directs humanity to the divine way in its last, enduring form. (XXVIII, 79)

Here we see an objectification of islām as that which desires (or rather does not desire) and orders and directs. It is interesting to note that previous commentators most probably would have said that God orders and directs; here islām becomes the subject.

In the second clause of 5:3 ❛. . . and I have fulfilled for you My blessing❜ he describes the vigilant Muslim community established by the sharī^c^ah in leadership over the earth [^c^alá khilāfat al-^c^arḍ], equitable in this leadership and fulfilling its covenants with God and man in all conditions. (VI, 30) In contrast to Riḍā, who was acutely aware of the errors into which the Muslim community could fall (and had fallen!), Sayyid Quṭb here gives us a sense of the infallibility of the community. The followers of this guidance do not err and the group is continuously responsible to its duty to be khilāfah. We shall find repeated references to the community, which can be no other than the Muslim community as established through Muḥammad, as the concrete embodiment of God's law for mankind. It is interesting that concerning the last passage, 'and I have chosen for you al-islām as [a] dīn', Sayyid Quṭb does not say "it is His choice of this ummah" (which would indicate that Islam is the name of the community) but rather says "it is His choice for this ummah." (VI, 30) Nevertheless, the general expression he uses for the community is al-mujtama^{c} al-islāmī, and it hardly seems likely that he has in mind in these numerous references anything other than the ummah he here describes as vicegerent over the earth.

In his discussion of 6:125, Sayyid Quṭb never uses the term islām, making the immediate identification of the islām of the verse with īmān. Representative of his commentary on this verse is this passage:

> Truly al-kufr is a [kind of] death, and al-īmān is a life; truly al-kufr is a darkness, and al-īmān is a light; truly al-kufr is a narrowness and destruction and fear, and al-īmān is a breadth and an ease and a peace within the hearts. (VIII, 16)

Yet interestingly enough, only a few pages earlier, in connection with 6:117, he does use islām with the obvious understanding of something beyond the personal act of faith. The verse warns against obeying those on earth who lead one astray from the way of God. Sayyid Quṭb says, "And because of that, al-islām sets up its system according to the fixed sharī^{c}ah of God that does not follow the inclinations of man . . ." (VIII, 12)

Similarly in the tafsīr of 9:74, like so many of his predecessors, Sayyid Quṭb does not discuss the meaning of islām. In fact he does not use it at all; his commentary on this passage is very traditional in form, giving the familiar stories such as that of Jallās. However, here again we do not have to look far to find some very revealing statements in which he uses islām with a clearly reified reference. Qur'ān 9:71 discusses al-zakāt, the alms-tax, as one of the duties of the mu'minūn. Following are some of the comments that Quṭb offers on this verse:

> And by that al-zakāt takes its place in the sharī^{c}ah of God, and its place in the Islamic system . . . . The proper support [qawām] of life in the Islamic system is work . . . . Al-zakāt is one of the branches of the system of group solidarity in al-islām . . . (X, 80)

Warning that work is essential to the well-being of the group, Sayyid Quṭb makes it clear that al-zakāt should not be incorrectly used.

> For al-zakāt is a system of social protection and security for designated groups within the community; it is not a foundation of the economic system in the Islamic state [al-dawlah al-islāmīyah] . . . (X, 81)

> For al-islām is a system of joint responsibility in which respectable people do not lower themselves, and in which a trustee does not squander, and some people do not consume others in the form of systematic regulations such as occurs in the laws of the earth and the laws of the jungle! (X, 82)[41]

The need for caring for the poor is great, however, and should not be ignored. This is expressed in a bitter passage about the current refugee problem in the Middle East. Describing the displaced person, whom he calls "Ibn al-Sabīl", he says:

> He is a traveller cut off from his possessions -- even if he has wealth in his homeland -- and among us today are many of these refugees displaced from Palestine or other places within the community of islām [bilād al-islām], polluted by imperialist tyranny. The imperialist states have taken possession of their security in order to consume their virility and their manhood and leave them weakened beggars, so that they are unmindful of lost homeland [waṭan] or wounded honor. And they devastate them with an organized devastation in the name of assistance [ighāthah]. And if they had a portion of al-zakāt in the great Islamic homeland [al-waṭan al-islāmī al-kabīr], this terrible development that has happened to the refugees of Palestine and other refugees would not have occurred to them. (X, 83)

Interesting as these statements are in themselves, their obvious relevance for our study lies in their usage of Islam. It is the name of a system, a state, a community and a homeland, explicit and clear examples of what we have described as reification.

Moving on to the tafsīr of 39:22, we find, not surprisingly, that Sayyid Quṭb again deals specifically in the realm of personal heartfelt submission. God makes hearts from which He knows good will come wide for al-islām and bestows the light

---

[41] In contrast to this, for example, al-Ṭabarī in Jāmiᶜ al-bayān uses the term islām only once in his tafsīr of 9:71, and that in opposition to polytheism [shirk]. (XIV, 347-48) In considering the use of islām in the other commentaries used in this study, in almost every case I have perused the material immediately before and after the eight verses with which I am specifically dealing. Where islām was discussed I have mentioned it in the preceding analyses. The fact is, however, that while I have seldom found it used, or certainly defined, in these peripheral verses in the other tafsīrs, in Sayyid Quṭb it is very often used in such ways as are evidenced here.

on them so that they shine in it. The expanded heart is one open for acceptance and joy, light and radiance. (XXIV, 26) We find no hint whatsoever of the reified usage so dominant in the preceding passages.

We have seen in earlier sections of this work that some of the most interesting (in the sense of their distinction from previous tafsīr material) comments have been made in the passages immediately preceding the verses in which islām is used. This is also true with 49:14-17. Considering 49:12, which enjoins the faithful not to be suspicious of, or spiteful toward, each other, he says that "the matter does not stop in al-islām with this noble and pure horizon in the instruction [tarbīyah] of the consciences and the hearts", but it goes on to establish a principle of cooperation among people. (XXVI, 139) Again we see islām as the educator, the guiding force. Then discussing freedom and the rights of man he says that the Islamic community [al-mujtama^{c} al-islāmī] sees to this in deed, actualizing it in the daily events of life just as it actualized it in the conscience of individuals. (XXVI, 140) Proper ethical and moral behavior, he says, "is one of the leading principles of Islam in its social system and in what it initiates through legislation and implementation." (XXVI, 140) References to Islam as a system and a community are too numerous to be cited in entirety here; they leave no doubt but that the author sees Islam in these instances in its reified understanding.

Sayyid Quṭb then gives a passage that is particularly notable in the light of Riḍā's great emphasis on jinsīyah. Speaking of the bond of love and mutual assistance that God has enjoined on all men, he says that this is

> . . . the flag that al-islām raises in order to save mankind from the fetters of partisanship to al-jins [nationality], and to the world, and to clan, and to family. All of this is a part of the time of ignorance [al-jāhilīyah], obscured in different ways and called by different names. And all of this is ignorance, apart from al-islām! (XXVI, 143)

Both Riḍā (and ^{c}Abduh) and Quṭb are concerned with allegiance to groups and sects, but the way they relate this concern to islām is strikingly different. While the former decries the fact that islām itself in its conventional usage (Islam) has become characterized by jinsīyah, Sayyid Quṭb indicates that such bondage is part of ignorance and not a part of islām. This is not to say that they are actually in disagreement; the point is that while for Riḍā there is a clear distinction between the actual (al-islām al-^{c}urfī) and the ideal or essential (al-islām al-ḥaqīqī), Sayyid Quṭb does not include political and regional affiliations -- insofar as they lead to division and partisanship -- in his understanding of islām. Islām for him is described as it is in its ideal or real form, and he goes on to say:

> Al-islām has struggled with this ignorant partisanship in all its forms and all its manifestations, in order to set up its universal human system under the protection of one banner: the banner of God -- not the banner of patriotism. And not the banner of nationalism. And not the banner of family. And not the banner of jins. All of these are false banners which al-islām does not know. (XXVI, 144)

About the 49:14-17 verses themselves Sayyid Quṭb offers an interpretation very much in line with what we have seen in the other commentaries. Here, rather than as an expression of the real and the ideal, he uses islām as both individual act and group in much the same way as did the earlier writers. "This descended to the Arabs of Bani Asad. They said: We have faith. [This was when] they first entered into al-islām." (XXVI, 144) Despite the many evidences of an understanding of islām that seems almost unrelated to the individual act of surrender, the personal submission of the muslim is still very much a part of the whole picture for Sayyid Quṭb (as expressed particularly in his tafsīr of 3:19). That this apparently is not his primary concern, however, is clear in the light of the proportionately little attention he has given to it in terms of specific usage. This is not to imply that he does not appreciate the depth of the act of islām and its importance in understanding the basic message of the Qur'ān. It seems, rather, that his primary interest is in developing an understanding of the role and function of the community to which he so often refers with the nisbah adjective "islāmī".

In no place is this clearer than in his commentary on 61:7. Actually he uses the entire chapter 61 -- only 14 verses long -- as the basis for a very interesting discussion of the relationship of the individual to the community and the meaning of islām in terms of this relationship. Because it is so representative of Sayyid Quṭb's thought, and because in its approach it is explicitly different from what other commentators have expressed, we shall consider the passage in its entirety.

> Truly the Qur'ān -- as we said on numerous occasions in this section -- was such as to establish an ummah. It established it in order that it take on the responsibility [amānah][42] of His dīn on the earth, and His

---

[42]The idea of amānah (which might be translated trusteeship, although no English word adequately expresses its meaning for

procedures in life and His system among people. And it was inevitable that it would establish its [the community's] individual members as individuals and establish it as a group, as an actual entity -- all of that at one time -- for the muslim is not established as an individual except in a group. And al-islām is inconceivable as existent except in the context of an intra-dependent organized group, having organization, and having a collective purpose, conditional in time, dependent simultaneously on every individual within it. It [al-islām] is the setting up of this divine program in the [individual] conscience and in actuality with its establishment on the earth. And it is not set up on earth except in a group living and moving and working and proceeding within the limits of that divine way.

And al-islām, despite the emphasis on what concerns the individual conscience and individual responsibility, is not a religion of isolated individuals, each one worshipping God in a hermitage. This does not even fulfill al-islām in the conscience of the individual [it is not sufficient for one's personal inner life], nor does it fulfill it, by the nature of the case, in his [overt] life. Al-islām did not come in order to be isolated with this [kind of] isolation; it came only to regulate the life of mankind and direct it. And it watches over every individual and group activity in every direction. Humanity does not live individually but lives in groups and communities. Al-islām comes in order to regulate it [humanity], and it is like that. And it is based on the principle that mankind lives thus. Therefore all of its customs and its rules and its systems are shaped according to this basis. And when its concern is directed toward the conscience of the individual it therefore molds this conscience according to the principle that it lives in a group. And it and the group in which they [individuals] live are directed toward God, and take on, in it, the responsibility [amānah] of His dīn on the earth, and His way in life, and His system among men.

And since the first day the call was to set up an islāmic society [mujtama^{c} islāmī] or a muslim community [jamā^{c}ah muslimah] -- with leadership to be obeyed which is the leadership of the Messenger of God - blessings and peace be upon him - and with communal requirements among its individuals, and with an essence [kiyān] distinguishing it from the rest of the communities around it, and with customs related to the conscience of man, consideration being given in them, at the same time, to the life of this group. And all of that was before the muslim state was set up in Madīnah. Indeed the establishing of that community was itself the means for the establishment of the state in Madīnah. (XXVIII, 77)

Muslims) is a very profound one in Islamic thought. The implication is that man has taken on the responsibility for obeying God's laws in response to the continuing promise of His guidance. See Qur'ān 33:72: "We offered the trust to the heavens and the earth and the mountains, but they refused to carry it and were afraid of it; and man carried it." (Arberry translation).

The import of these paragraphs is so clear that it is scarcely necessary to elaborate here. We might, however, make special note of the fact that in this statement Sayyid Quṭb really covers all of the various usages of islām as we have seen them in the preceding commentaries. It is discussed in terms of individual dīn, although he makes it abundantly clear that this interpretation of islām is meaningless apart from the context of the group. It is certainly used as reified, with the discussion of organization and collectivity. We see again the emphasis on islām as the regulator of individual and group life, that which directs and oversees. (As we observed above, earlier commentators probably would have said that it is God who regulates and directs.) Finally, a clear line of development is drawn from the establishment of the community of the Prophet to its real beginnings as a political state at Madīnah.

It is interesting to see that our attempts to distinguish between islām and Islam (according to the differentiation made in the introduction) really break down here. The muslim state and the Muslim state, at least insofar as their usage here indicates, apparently are indistinguishable for Sayyid Quṭb, as in fact they would have been for all of the commentators had the others discussed the state. The point is that most of the rest of the writers of tafsīr did not specifically and explicitly talk about islām in this context. That which really marks the pcint of difference between this writer and the rest is to be found in the beginning of the last paragraph quoted above. While traditional commentators have spoken of "the call to islām" (in Riḍā's case, "the call to true islām"), with the primary emphasis falling on the individual act of submission, Sayyid Quṭb speaks instead of the call to set up an islāmic society, a muslim community. We cannot say that islām in its communal understanding is more important to Sayyid Quṭb than islām as personal response to the act and being of God; what we can say is that it is this aspect to which in his commentary he gives primary attention. And herein lies the basic mark of distinction between his tafsīr and that representing the previous thirteen centuries, even including that of ᶜAbduh and Riḍā.

In this emphasis on community, however, different as it may be from the approach of the earlier commentators, are some interesting parallels with the understanding of islām as expressed particularly in the tafsīr and tradition of the first few Islamic centuries. In the following summary and concluding statements, we shall attempt to draw the lines of relationship through the historical analyses of the eight Qur'ān verses in their understanding of <u>islām</u> as individual and as communal, that which binds man to man, and man to God.

FIVE: CONCLUSION

In attempting to summarize the several interpretations of islām given in these fourteen centuries of commentary, one is reminded of the words of the Prophet that al-islām began as a stem, then doubles, then quadruples, then is made six-fold, then splits into many branches.[1] The common stem remains, however, as the point of departure from which various levels of interpretation and differences in meaning have sprung, and in which they all continue to share. In order to organize the conclusions of the commentators analyzed in the preceding essay, and to bring into focus the exact nature of their common understanding, we shall review briefly the major points that they have been making.

We have observed that in most cases verse 3:19 of the Qur'ān, ﴾Truly al-dīn with God is al-islām﴿, has served as the occasion for the most thorough and representative definition of islām presented by each commentator. This may be because it is the first instance in which the maṣdar is used in the Qur'ān; on the other hand it very well may be because the simple and straightforward structure of the verse itself gives a better opportunity for a clearly definitive analysis than do most of the other verses. In some instances, however, additional and illuminating insights have been presented in the tafsīr of the later verses, particularly in the case of the modern writer Sayyid Quṭb. In order to gather into one representative statement the different interpretations of islām given by each writer, I propose here a restating of 3:19 in terms of the commentary given on all of the eight verses in question; material taken from the other seven sets of commentary is used to augment the original tafsīr given of the first verse. Hopefully by this means we shall be able to perceive the various elements that have combined to determine the general understanding of islām as presented by the writers of tafsīr.

Ibn ᶜAbbās: God has witnessed that there is no God but He and that man's acceptable response to Him, his dīn, is the affirmation of that unity as expressed by all the Prophets from the time of Ibrāhīm. By this response one becomes a member of the community of those who have submitted, both the individual

[1] Ibn Ḥanbal, Musnad, III, 363.

expression of tawḥīd and the group of submitters having the name islām.

Muqātil ibn Sulaymān: The only true dīn, the only valid and acceptable response of man to God, is the recognition of God's oneness and the affirmation of it, the act of submission through which one earns the name muslim, expressed particularly by the observance of those regulations by which one enters the community of islām.

Al-Ṭabarī: Truly al-dīn with God is al-islām, His guidance toward the understanding of reality which is at once the means whereby man can respond to that reality and the response itself. On one level islām implies both the act of joining the group of muslims and the name of that group, and on another level means the deeper personal surrender of the heart in the fullest sense of which it is understood as īmān.

Al-Qummī: Al-dīn is submission through internal affirmation and self-dedication to God and to the saints, related to īmān in terms of degree and manifested through individual performance of God's commands.

Al-Ṭūsī: Al-dīn, which is obedience to God as well as requital by God in terms of man's obedience, is surrender to the guidance and command of God, distinguishable from īmān only in its inclusion of the performance of the specific requirements as outlined by the Prophet.

Al-Zamakhsharī: Truly al-dīn, the response of man acceptable to God from all eternity, is al-islām, the recognition of God's unity and justice and the expression of that unity and justice through living a life of moral integrity. At once the mutual relationship between the attitude and deed of the servant and the being of God, it alone of all the milal and adyān is approved by God.

Al-Rāzī: Islām, which is al-dīn with God, is (1) submitting, becoming muslim; (2) entering into wholeness or peacefulness; and (3) expressing sincerity of devotion to God by the discharging of the requirements of divinity and servanthood. In the fullest understanding of that which it is necessary to do once one has accepted the state of being muslim, islām is synonymous with _īmān_, both of which terms carry the implication of external affirmation and internal confirmation.

Al-Bayḍāwī: Truly _al-dīn_ with God is man's affirmation of God's oneness and his acceptance of the revelation of sacred law brought by Muḥammad from God, through the recognition of which one expresses that affirmation; on another level _islām_ is expressed as submission to the Prophet by which one declares his intention to cease opposing those of the Prophet's community.

Ibn Kathīr: _Al-dīn_ with God is (1) primarily and basically recognition of the oneness of God and acting in terms of it through sincere devotion, and (2) secondarily and by implication the community of Muḥammad, understood in terms of his regulations as transmitted by God.

Al-Suyūṭī: Truly the _dīn_ which is approved by God is _al-tawḥīd_, the revelation of which has been received by all the Peoples of the Book, i.e. the testimony that there is no God but He and the affirmation of what the Messengers brought from God, as well as the group of those who have made this testimony.

Abū'l-Su^cūd: _Al-dīn_ with God is affirmation that there is no God but He and embracing the noble _sharī^cah_, those specific regulations enunciated by the Prophet by which one carries out the will of God; it is the religion that God has made to predominate over all of the other religions.

Al-Kāshānī: Truly _al-dīn_ with God is the affirmation of God's oneness (the realization of which is achieved by some through intuitive knowledge and by others through proofs and the guidance of His signs), and accepting the ordinance of God as revealed through the Prophet and his successors designated through the ^cAlawī line; it is also the group into which one is born and according to whose regulations one carries out the basic legal procedures such as inheritance and marriage.

Shāh Walī Allāh: _Al-dīn_ with God is the original source on which the different communities [_milal_] have been based and from which they have diverged, the archetype of human response to God specifying for man the good and the evil. It is realized now in the _millah_ of the Prophet which is like a tree with some strong branches and some weaker ones. This is the group of those who through the guidance that came to all the Prophets express their personal submission through the five arkān or acts of devotion, in the performance of which is the joy of al-īmān.

Al-Shawkānī and al-Ālūsī: Truly that which God has enjoined upon man as a set of regulations and at once as the acceptance of those regulations, that which will remain to the end of the days of the world, is the testimony and affirmation that there is no God but God. As the guidance through which one is led to the sharīᶜah, it is closely related to īmān on one level, yet distinguished from it on another level by the possibility of its actualization without conviction and confirmation.

Rashīd Riḍā (Muḥammad ᶜAbduh): Truly al-dīn, which is at once the commandment of God and the way in which man responds to that commandment, is al-islām al-ḥaqīqī. In absolute contrast to al-islām al-ᶜurfī, the conventional religion characterized by taqlīd and jinsīyah, true islām is the personal submission of the individual to God and the universal spirit in which all religions share, the educator of the natural disposition and the ideal society attainable when the dīn of all men is perfected.

Sayyid Quṭb: Truly al-dīn with God is submission of the heart in conscience, action and deed; it is the new and final religion, the universal law of existence which builds up, protects and guides individuals within society; and it is the collectivity whose system governs specific geographical units, but which as the universal community is open to all who are gathered in love and peace.

A most fascinating study of the history of Islamic thought can be centered on the many ramifications of the idea of unity, oneness. It has been made very clear in the above tafsīr that this concept is absolutely basic to the Muslim orientation of the universe: all else is of secondary importance to the overriding fact that God is one, that He alone is God and that nothing can be likened unto Him. The greater the awareness of this fact, the stronger has been the concurrent emphasis on man's essential difference from God; some have received the penalty of death for claiming participation in the being of God. Yet the strand of understanding that apprehends the oneness of the universe, of all nature and with it of man and God Himself, has come to be very much a part of the total picture of Muslim piety.

The emphasis on unity is shown in a different dimension in this study of the meaning of islām. We observed in the introduction that for the most part academic studies of islām have revolved around the historical development of the community of Muslims, Islam, and around the linguistic analysis of the various forms of the verb aslama. It was at the intersection of these two studies, we said, that we hoped to focus our attention, i.e. on the point of interaction between the verbal and the nominal elements in islām. Here metaphors fail, however, for while we have certainly encountered interaction, it cannot be described in any case as having come at a single point. Rather, individual discussions of islām (and the totality resulting from the contributions of each writer), have been presented in such a manner that the resulting understandings have been integrated and unified.

While we insist that a division in understanding is foreign to the Qur'ān commentators (particularly up to the modern period), we must nevertheless distinguish for our own clarification the ways in which their analyses have been developed. Basically they have proceeded along two "axes" of investigation: (1) the relation between the external and the internal aspects of surrender, i.e. between islām as taṣdīq and islām as external conformity; and (2) between the individual and the group aspects of islām. What we have observed is that each writer, when dealing with these several constituent elements, has reflected a remarkable unity of understanding, although there has been a change in the expression of this unity.

In summarizing the conclusions of some orientalists concerning the meaning of islām, we noted, on the whole, a failure to give adequate presentation of some of the breadth and depth of its meaning for those of the muslim faith. Their various presentations did cover a great many of the points we have seen treated by the commentators themselves, but no one of the orientalists was completely successful, I feel, in showing how several interpretations can hold at the same time. In addition, their great stress on linguistic usage and Qur'ānic intention seems to have precluded an adequate understanding -- or at least an adequate presentation -- of how the meaning of islām has developed and broadened historically. In their attempts to analyze what the term means in the Qur'ān they have often overlooked the historical flow, involving both movement and continuity, that takes us from what islām "meant" to what it "has meant" and what it "means". In effect, the definitions they have given, in most cases, are static ones, whereas the appreciation we have gained from the commentaries is of an *islām* that is dynamic both within the understandings of the individual writers and as expressed by the historical development of the concept from one age to another. We shall consider in more detail what were called the two axes (or foci) of the study of *islām*, attempting to show both what the conclusions of the writers of *tafsīr* have been and how, in the light of such conclusions, orientalists generally have fallen short of presenting an adequate picture of its meaning for Muslims.

To subdivide further, we find that the understanding of *islām* as external/internal brings us into the area of the bond between man and God as well as of the different forms, or motivations, of man's submission. In both of these areas, the relationship of internal and external submission, and the relationship of the act and being of man to the act and being of God, we find first that they take the clear form of an expression of unity, and second that there has *not* been what could be called a change or development in their consideration historically.

The interpretation of *islām* as the internal affirmation and confirmation of the unity of God, the heartfelt response of man to His revelation, has perhaps been given more adequate treatment by Western analysts of the term than any other aspect of its understanding. We saw in the introduction that most of these Western writers have emphasized some element of submission, usually in relation to God's initiative. There has been, of course, no Qur'ānic commentator considered in this essay who has not laid a primary stress on this aspect. They have all made it clear that *islām* and *īmān* (the specific act of faith most commonly defined as *taṣdīq* and *iqrār* of God's revelation) have at least some areas of identification. The degree to which they have chosen to equate these terms has, of course, varied considerably. Al-Rāzī has been most conspicuous in his attempt to indicate that while different in generality, they are one in existence. For him *islām* must always be of the heart -- if not, it cannot be called *islām*. Rashīd Riḍā gives a similar interpretation when he says that both *islām* (in its true meaning) and *īmān* are considered to be *īmān khaṣṣ*, specialized faith, the only *dīn* acceptable to God and the only means of man's salvation.

Most of the other commentators, however, have indicated that they understand some basic difference between *islām* and *īmān*, or at least that *islām* can have a purely external meaning while *īmān* always refers to internal confirmation and faith. They have differed, of course, in their attempts to reconcile the islām used to characterize the submission of the Arabs (described in Q 49:14) with the islām so clearly indicated to be internal in such verses as 6:125 and 39:22. In no case, however, have they indicated that the two are irreconcilable. We have found the very careful analysis of al-Ṭabarī to be among the most illuminating in dealing with this relationship. He expresses a kind of two-leveled islām, on the one level as the verbal submission by which one enters the community of muslims (we shall consider this aspect of his understanding below) and on the other as it is coordinate with īmān and involving total surrender of the heart, mind and body. Expressly or by implication, most of the commentators, like him, have been concerned not with what might be interpreted to be contradictions within the verses in question, but with the presentation of an islām in which various meanings are incorporated into a unified understanding.

(An interpretation of īmān, both in itself and as it relates to islām, has been one of several concerns in this essay. Its investigation has been almost a side benefit of the whole study, providing tempting glimpses into an area deserving of far more specific attention and consideration. In future work done on this concept, extremely important to an understanding of muslim piety, I strongly recommend the tafsīr of the Qur'ān as a very fruitful area of research.)

We have said that involved in the question of the internal-external nature of man's submission is the issue of his relationship to God. Submission to the Prophet purely for means of self-protection or self-aggrandizement, given only as a superficial understanding of islām, has been of little interest to the Qur'ān commentators. They have, rather, been supremely interested in islām as submission to God, done in response to His command and involving the fulfillment of His injunctions. Beginning with Ibn ᶜAbbās, in practically every instance the expression of the meaning of islām has been absolutely coordinate with the expression of tawḥīd, recognition of the unity of God. In other words, we cannot begin to describe or understand what man's islām is without seeing it in the light of God's being, which is one and apart from any other being, and of His command to man to respond to the recognition of that being.

Only a few of the orientalists have suggested the idea of islām as a reciprocal relationship between man and God, the most notable being David Künstlinger. But even in his case, what he describes is a give and take with the idea of a covenant relationship in which two parties act and react in two separate functions.

The description of islām in the tafsīrs, however, particularly exemplified in the understanding of tawḥīd, seems to indicate rather that the two functions of what God is and what man does are dimensions of the whole. Künstlinger says that rather than submitting to God, man accepts the conditions of the duties which God has laid upon him, for which he is rewarded. The implication here is of two parties negotiating with each other. Yet the overwhelming feeling one gets from the tafsīrs is that man does [testify to the unity of God in tawḥīd] precisely because God is [one], and that tawḥīd encompasses at once God's unity and man's response to that unity. Man recognizes and proclaims God's unity, and incorporates into his own existence the integrity that is based on God's divine oneness.

This idea is expressed particularly forcefully in the writing of al-Zamakhsharī, who presents the same kind of unified understanding of justice, ᶜadl. God is both just and justice, and because He acts justly man is commanded to act in a just manner, his actions equivalent to his islām which is his recognition in word and deed of the justice of God. Another term with which the writers of tafsīr have been very concerned, and in which we can see additional illustration of the unity of the man-God relationship, is dīn (in its personalist, non-reified usage). A number of writers have illustrated this unity, one of the clearest statements coming with al-Ṭūsī, who drew a circle of continuity around God's command, man's dīn in response, and God's requital done in terms of man's response. This same idea is brought out by Riḍā when he relates sharᶜ [God's commanding] to dīn [man's submitting] to recompense by God [al-jazā']. All of this is done, of course, in explanation of the full understanding of islām.

Again, there have been a variety of interpretations given to the term nūr, light, especially as described by Qur'ān 39:22 and 61:8. Basically the understanding has been that the light is from God, while islām is something that man does. Yet in several instances we have seen it clearly stated that islām is the light, illustrating once more the unmistakable bond between God and the manifestations of His guidance, and man and the modes of his response. In no instance has there been a suggestion of the association of man with God in this stress on unity; the consistent theme has rather been that in the description of all those elements making up man's response, their understanding is clear not by a focus on what man himself does, but on the presence and being of Him in terms of whom the response is made.

Thus far we have considered the expression of unity in the understanding of *islām* strictly as it is conceived as the personal act of submission. Within this usage we have looked at the consideration of *islām* on what we might call a vertical plane:

God
↕
man

In this area, as we noted, there has been a remarkable continuity of thought in the *tafsīrs*, fluctuations apparently coming more as a result of individual interpretation (such as in the case of al-Rāzī considering *islām* and *īmān*) than of historical development. It is in this realm that most of the orientalists have concentrated their study. However, there is another dimension of *islām* that must be given very careful consideration if we are to take seriously the intentions of the writers of *tafsīr*. This is the horizontal plane on which *islām* is seen both as the expression of individual submission and as the name of the group of those who have submitted: individual ⟷ community. It is in this area that we can point to some changes in understanding, or at least in usage.

In the light of most of the writing of Western orientalists (and, indeed, modern Muslims writing in English), it is interesting to consider again the necessity of rendering *islām* in English either in italics or as Islam. As we have had to do in this essay, they naturally use Islam when referring to the historical Muslim community with its objectified systematization of beliefs and practices. When this is done, it is frequently without reference to the fact that the term has another meaning, and yet it is this other meaning -- usually given in terms of personal submission -- with which the orientalists are most often concerned when they attempt to analyze and define *islām*. That is, while most of their stress in giving specific definitions has been on the "true" meaning of *islām* given in terms of the individual, their most common usage in writing is a clear reference to the group or historical community. (This is also characteristic of modern Muslim commentary, particularly as seen in Sayyid Quṭb.) I feel that the preceding study of *tafsīr* has shown quite clearly that the "original" meaning of *islām*, that for which the orientalists have been seeking, is to be found precisely in a fusion of the individual and group interpretations. This dual usage exemplified by the orientalists perhaps is understandable because it is here that a change seems to have occurred in the understanding of *islām* by Muslims, as is shown in this study of *tafsīr*. While once it was inclusive of both elements, the individual and the group, it is now used much more as one or the other, and it has come to be applied in the communal sense in a way somewhat different from (or additional to) the way it was used by the early commentators.

We have pointed again and again to references in the tafsīrs in which the apparent intention has been this "unified" meaning of islām as both individual act and plural condition. This is particularly evident in the commentaries from the first several centuries; in the places in which it occurs in later works it is usually in reference to a tradition whose origin was also in these early centuries. Ibn ᶜAbbās says clearly that islām is tawḥīd, yet cites the understanding that one can be born into al-islām. From the very beginning there was no conscious or intellectual distinction made between the individual responsibility to carry out the specific commandments of God and the fact that these regulations are incumbent on all the members of the community and thus characterize that group itself. In a number of places in the tafsīr of Muqātil ibn Sulaymān there is no clear indication whether he is using islām as a personal response to God's revelation or as the community itself, the implication being quite evident that he himself did not conceive of such a distinction.

When we get to al-Ṭabarī we can begin to discern another "state" in the understanding of islām, reflecting to a great extent the continuing development of the process of tafsīr writing. By this time commentary on the Qur'ān had become more acceptable, and traditionalist though he was, we have noted that al-Ṭabarī organized his great collections of traditional material in terms of his own understanding of its relative acceptability and augmented it with his own thoughtful analysis. Thus we find that in his very outlining of the relationship of islām as īmān and islām as external submission, he provides a general understanding of where the group meaning of islām fits into this structure. The two aspects of singular and plural apparently are still one concept for him, but it is only in his discussion of islām as the joining of the group of muslims that it is also used as the name of that group. As the personal surrender of the heart it is equivalent only to īmān.

It is interesting to note that in these instances in which there seems to be no distinction between the act of submission and the community of the Prophet, the reference is always to the historical group of muslimūn at the time of Muḥammad rather than to the particular group existing and fully organized at the time of the writing of each mufassir. Thus al-Ṭūsī talks about the entry of all the Arabs into al-islām at the time of the Ḥajj al-Wadā[c], but gives nothing that could be taken as a reference to the Muslim community of the fourth century hijrī. We see again that Ibn Kathīr leaves open to question whether the dīn he is discussing is the personal islām of the individual or the group of followers of the Prophet. But he, too, refers only to the historical community, giving the impression that he sees no need to make a clear distinction. Similar instances are to be found in al-Suyūṭī and others of the later writers, including al-Kāshānī and particularly Shāh Walī Allāh.

These later writers have been characterized again and again as belonging to that extended period in which there was a resurgence and a solidification of traditionalism (see p. 119, note 2 on al-Ṭūsī). Their material was based primarily on the early period of Qur'ān commentary and it is not surprising that in a variety of instances their interpretation of islām reflected this unified understanding of its individual and communal aspects. (In none of these traditional commentaries do we find the discussion of the political or social situation of their own time as is true of the commentary of Riḍā in his attack on jinsīyah or Sayyid Quṭb in his concern for the Palestinian refugees.) Shāh Walī Allāh, despite his anticipation of some modern interpretation, was decidedly concerned with traditions, and it is particularly in the discussion of these traditions that we see examples of the double meaning of islām described here. We do not, however, find much of any reference to this kind of expression in the writings of al-Zamakhsharī and al-Rāzī. The distinct impression one gets from these commentaries is that they have taken up where al-Ṭabarī left off; while he gave us the beginnings of a carefully structured presentation with the distinct contribution of his own judgments on the material, his successors made even greater use of the prerogative of personal opinion. Thus al-Zamakhsharī employs few of the traditional interpretations in which the dual understanding we have described seems to have been so often expressed, and al-Rāzī devotes practically his entire discussion of islām as based on these eight passages to illustrating its identity with īmān.

If al-Zamakhsharī does not provide us with these references, however, he does make use of a term that continues to be prominent in almost all of the succeeding tafsīrs. This is the plural of dīn, al-adyān. We observed the use of this term once in Ibn [c]Abbās, with the notation that it may well have been a later addition. Its usage is certainly negligible before the fifth century, but from that time on it becomes almost standard in the interpretation of such verses as 61:9. It has been made quite clear in the study of all of the tafsīrs that the interpretations of dīn and islām are very closely intertwined. We have made only preliminary forays into the understanding of this very common but often very ambiguous word dīn, and as with īmān it becomes clear that we need a much more exacting and particular study of its origins and continued usage in the various branches of Muslim writing. We can say here that its primary understanding is of the individual personal response to the revelation of God which is, in the terms of 3:19, called islām. To see this word in the plural, then, presents the immediate problem of deciding if the writer means the several responses of several individuals, or if he intends a plurality of religious systems. It is striking that its usage in the later commentaries has mainly been in connection with 61:9, a verse which itself has the singular dīn. The evidence gained from these readings is not so definitive that one is able to come to a clear conclusion about the intention of the various writers in using adyān: in a number of cases, however, it seems most likely that the writers intended a contrast between the religion of Islam and the other religious communities or milal. As we noted in connection with al-Zamakhsharī earlier, the Qur'ānic promise that the dīn al-islām would be victorious over all other religion can be easily understood in terms of a political and social dominance at a time (extending for a number of centuries) when the Islamic state was clearly in a position of flourishing power.

We can see, then, that in the understanding of islām on the horizontal plane of the relationship of individual and group there have been several developments. At first there seems to have been another expression of the unity that we have seen as so characteristic of Muslim thought in the intention of both personal submission and communal reference without distinction. Next there was the stage in which it appears that a form of self-conscious definition took the place of the earlier unconscious, or automatic, association of two elements in one term, and islām was specifically and clearly defined in terms of personal response to the revelation of God. Then came the prolonged period characterized both by references to the earlier understanding of personal and group in one expression in repetition of the early traditional materials, and by what seem to have been occasional indications of a more reified understanding of islām, particularly as indicated by the use of adyān. These latter were, of course, only incidental to the dominant expression of islām as individual submission. These changes, if they can indeed be called such, are subtle and clearly to be assumed by inference rather than by the direct expression of the tafsīr writers themselves.

When we come to the modern period of commentary, however, the situation becomes markedly different. Here we find the very specific reference to islām as something distinct from personal submission. This could not be stated more clearly than by Rashīd Riḍā when he contrasts al-islām al-dīnī with al-islām al-ᶜurfī, indicating that it is the association by ethnic identity with the religion of one's own nationality or cultural surroundings that actually can prevent one from the true submission to God which he has described in terms of īmān. Rather than emphasizing, or trying to harmonize, internal and external islām as descriptions of heartfelt vs. expedient submission, he draws a clear line of distinction between islām of the heart and Islam as conventional reified religion characterized by blind uncritical acceptance of the ways of the ancestors. Here is a vivid illustration of the change from the unity of individual deed and group entity to a firm distinction between the two. While many earlier commentators from Ibn ᶜAbbās to al-Kāshānī have talked about being born into al-islām without attempting to indicate how this differs from the act of submission (and certainly with no negative implication), Riḍā expressly contrasts al-islām al-jinsī, that of group affiliation by accident of birth, as it were, with al-islām al-ḥaqīqī.

There is another sense, however, in which for Rashīd Riḍā islām does intend the unity of two meanings in one term. This is in the understanding of what society could be if only individuals were freed of mere communal affiliations to the point of experiencing true personal islām. As we noted in the conclusion to the discussion of ᶜAbduh and Riḍā, while the unity expressed by the early generations was of individual and actual, here it is of individual and ideal. We saw that within this concept of an ideal islām there is a stress on universality, the emphasis of which is somewhat different from what has preceded. Seen first in the writing of Shāh Walī Allāh, this universal dīn, which is al-islām, is developed by Riḍā as the rūḥ al-kullī, in which all of the religions of the world share, and as the educator of the natural disposition of man, who possesses the possibility of perfection.

This theme of universality is echoed strongly in the writing of Sayyid Quṭb when he speaks of the great unity that joins together all of the revelations and all of the Messengers. But while Rashīd Riḍā is generally careful to maintain a distinction between this ideal islām (even insofar as it may have represented something beyond the purely individual surrender of the muslim) and the reified Islam by which he is so repelled, this is not the case with Sayyid Quṭb. For the latter there is no explicit distinction between what the muslim community is in actuality and what it is ideally. That is, it is impossible to determine in many cases whether he is discussing the particular community existing at the time of his writing, the ummah with its political and regional specifications, or if he is referring to that universal community theoretically open and available to all. The important difference between Sayyid Quṭb and all of the commentators preceding him, of course, is that often he does use islām in its reified and concrete sense, as a system and an organization and as the name of a political entity. Unlike instances in the early tafsīrs in which islām is at once individual and communal, these particular references in Sayyid Quṭb can only be to the specific organized group. At the same time, even more clearly than Riḍā, he often seems to speak of islām in what we have called the "ideal" sense, as that law or force guiding and directing the lives of men in community.

Thus for the traditional commentators (representing what we characterized above as the first of four periods or developments in the understanding of islām on its individual-communal axis), islām is used at once as the individual act of submission and as the group of those who have submitted, but with the overriding emphasis being on the former personal aspect. There is no reference in their writing to the "ideal" interpretation. In the next two periods this is modified only slightly, as we have seen. With ᶜAbduh and Riḍā, there is still a primary stress on the submission of the individual, but this submission is unified with the group in its ideal rather than its concrete understanding. True islām is both sincere individual submission and the community, but in its ḥaqīqī rather than its ᶜurfī meaning. With Sayyid Quṭb, however, the emphasis has moved from individual surrender to a primary focus on the organized community. Here we again see a unity or identification, but it is mainly of the actual -- both in the sense of the original ummah as was intended by the early commentators and as the contemporary Islamic state -- and the ideal, the universal guiding nāmūs. For Sayyid Quṭb there is little specific discussion of islām in its relationship to īmān; the identity in the personalist usage is assumed. He is basically interested in elucidating the absolute necessity of understanding the social aspect of islām, the community apart from which individual submission does not reach fulfillment.

In the briefest summary, then, we can conclude three things about the historical understanding of islām from this study of tafsīr:

1. Sectarian differences, insofar as we have been able to observe them, for the most part have not been significant. The patterns emerging from this study do not seem to be related to geographical or doctrinal affiliations.

2. On the level of individual islām as internal and/or external, including the area of the relationship of man's response to God's act and being, such differences as we have seen have been both insignificant and apparently unrelated to the factor of time. The possible exception to this is Sayyid Quṭb, who probably places less emphasis on this aspect because of his concern with communal organization.

3. On the level of the relationship of individual and group, there have been some significant changes in the way the term islām has been used, which are specifically related to time. In the traditional commentaries islām is both individual submission and the name of the group, but with primary emphasis on the former, and with the dual usage generally by implication. By the fourteenth/twentieth century the term is used in (at least) two distinct ways in both the Manār commentary and in the tafsīr of Sayyid Quṭb, and in the latter the communal is given the major emphasis.

What, then, is al-islām? The rich ambiguity of the word has permitted the expression of its meaning in a variety of ways and through a series of relationships. We have seen that in certain forms of interpretation, its understanding -- or certainly its usage -- has changed from what it was in traditional commentary to what it is today. And yet the theme of unity that we have seen illustrated so frequently throughout the expressions of the meaning of islām again holds sway, and it is with a strong feeling of an essential oneness of understanding that I see the totality of these passages of Qur'ān tafsīr. As single rays of light illuminate single facets of a many-sided gem, these writers have stressed individually the various elements that make up the totality of islām. Working with what has been specifically said, we can only guess at what has been omitted, and we are left with this intriguing but finally unanswerable question: Would the traditional writers actually have disagreed with the interpretations put forward by the modern commentators, particularly Sayyid Quṭb, or did they simply emphasize one aspect over another because they wrote out of a radically different set of circumstances?

The strong feeling I receive from reading these passages of tafsīr is that Rashīd Riḍā and Sayyid Quṭb, because of the exigencies of the situation of the Muslim community in the modern world, have been forced to make explicit certain things that earlier were so naturally understood as to have been taken simply as a matter of course. The two aspects of islām they have chosen to emphasize combine to reconstruct what I have suggested above as the two primary axes of the understanding of islām. Rashīd Riḍā is particularly concerned with a return to an appreciation of the meaning of true submission, sincere personal response to God's being and command. In the explication of this he has had to point up what have become real alternatives in the modern situation. Sayyid Quṭb is interested in determining the position of the Islamic community in present global society, and thus places explicit stress on the communal aspect which always has been implicit in the understanding of islām.

This is not to make the overly simplictic assumption that the early traditional writers of tafsīr would have accepted all of the interpretations of the modern writers without qualification. It is, however, to point once more to the basic depth and breadth of the term islām, in which can be (and have been) found the elements of a wide latitude of understanding, and in which differing interpretations contribute to the richness of the whole. More interesting than the changes in usage as we have seen them in this study is the strong thread of continuity that has continued throughout the fourteen centuries. This might be partly explained by the fact that tafsīr of the Qur'ān always has been a fairly rigid science, perpetuation of previous exegesis being more highly valued than originality. I think we must also assume, however, that basic themes have been continually repeated by many centuries of commentators, writing out of many different contexts, precisely because these various understandings are inherent in the religious experience to which apparently the Islamic system has continually conduced.

Islām begins as a stem, then doubles, then divides into many branches. But the common stem remains, that which holds together all of the differing interpretations and emphases given to it, and this common stem is the recognition of and response to the nature and will of God. Whether seen as the individual submission of the servant with acceptance of the heart and obedience of the limbs, or as the community open to all people united in love and peace, *islām* is the only *dīn* acceptable to God precisely because it owes its being to Him and Him alone. To Him everything returns -- everyone who participates in *islām* and every understanding of the meaning of *islām* -- and in this is the great unity to which all of the Qur'ān commentators, despite their differences, have pointed.

BIBLIOGRAPHY

I. Tafāsīr of the Qur'ān:

Abū'l-Su^c^ūd, Muḥammad b. Muḥammad al-^c^Imādī. Irshād al-^c^aql al-salīm. On the margin of Fakhr al-Dīn Rāzī's Mafātīh al-ghayb. Istanbūl: al-Maṭba^c^ah al-^c^Āmirah, 1307 [1891], 8 voll.

al-Ālūsī, Abū'l-Thanā'. Ruḥ al-ma^c^ānī fī tafsīr al-Qur'ān al-^c^aẓīm. Būlāq: al-Maṭba^c^ah al-Kubrá al-Amīrīyah, 1301-10 [1883/4-1892], 9 voll.

Azad, Mawlana Abū'l-Kalām. The Tarjumān al-Qur'ān. Syed Abdul Latif, ed. and transl. New York: Asia Publishing House, 1383- [1963-], 1 vol.

al-Bayḍāwī, ^c^Abd Allāh b. ^c^Umar. Anwār al-tanzīl wa-asrār al-ta'wīl. Istanbūl, 1285 [1868], 2 voll.

al-Dihlawī, Abū ^c^Abd al-^c^Azīz Aḥmad Walī Allāh. Hujjat Allāh al-bālighah. Cairo: Idārat al-Ṭibā^c^ah al-Munīrīyah, 1352 [1933], 2 voll. in 1.

al-Gharnāṭī, Abū Ḥayyān Muḥammad b. Yūsuf. al-Bahr al-muhīṭ. Cairo: Maṭba^c^at al-Sa^c^ādah, 1328-29 [1910-11], 8 voll.

Ibn ^c^Abbās, ^c^Abd Allāh. Tanwīr al-miqbās. On the margin of Jalāl al-Dīn Suyūṭī's al-Durr al-manthūr fī'l-tafsīr bi'l-ma'thūr. Teheran: al-Maktabah al-Islāmīyah, 1377 [1957], 6 voll.

Ibn Kathīr, Ismā^c^īl ibn ^c^Umar. Tafsīr al-Qur'ān al-^c^aẓīm. Beirut: Dār al-Andalus, 1386 [1966], 7 voll.

al-Kāshānī, Muḥammad b. Murtaḍá Fayḍ. al-Ṣāfī fī tafsīr kalām Allāh al-wāfī. Teheran, 1266 [1850].

Muqātil b. Sulaymān. Tafsīr khams mi'ah āyah min al-Qur'ān. OR. 6333, British Museum Photographic Service, London.

al-Qummī, ^c^Alī b. Ibrāhīm. Tafsīr al-Qummī. Najaf, 1386-87 [1967], 2 voll.

Quṭb, Sayyid. Fī ẓilāl al-Qur'ān. Cairo: Dār Iḥyā' al-Kutub al-^c^Arabīyah, 137?-1379 [195?-1959], 30 voll. in 7.

al-Rāzī, Fakhr al-Dīn. Mafātīḥ al-ghayb al-mushtahar bi'l-tafsīr al-kabīr. Istanbūl: al-Maṭba^c^at al-^c^Āmirah, 1307 [1891], 8 voll.

Riḍā, Muḥammad Rashīd. Tafsīr al-Qur'ān al-karīm, tafsīr al-manār. Cairo: Dār al-Manār, 1367-1375 [1948-1956], 12 voll.

al-Shawkānī, Muḥammad b. ^c^Alī. Fath al-qadīr al-jāmi^c^. Cairo: Muṣṭafá al-Bābī al-Ḥalabī, 1384-5 [1964-5], 5 voll.

al-Suyūṭī, Jalāl al-Dīn. al-Durr al-manthūr fī'l-tafsīr bi'l-ma'thūr. Teheran: al-Maktabat al-Islāmīyah, 1377 [1957], 6 voll.

al-Suyūtī, Jalāl al-Dīn, and Jalāl al-Dīn Muḥammad b. Ahmad al-Maḥallī. *Tafsīr al-Qur'ān al-karīm, tafsīr al-Jalālayn.* Damascus: al-Maṭba^{c}at al-Hāshimīyah, 1378 [i.e. 1379 (1959/60)].

al-Ṭabarī, Abū Ja^{c}far Muhammad b. Jarīr. *Jāmi^{c} al-bayān ^{c}an ta'wīl āyāt al-Qur'ān.* Maḥmūd Muḥammad Shākir and Aḥmad Muḥammad Shākir, edd. Cairo: Dār al-Ma^{c}ārif, 1374- [1954-], several voll. Also: *Jāmi^{c} al-bayān fī tafsīr al-Qur'ān.* Cairo: al-Maṭba^{c}at al-Kubrá al-Amīrīyah, 1323-1329 [1900-1911], 30 voll. in 9.

al-Ṭūsī, Abū Ja^{c}far Muhammad ibn Ḥasan. *al-Tibyān fī tafsīr al-Qur'ān.* Najaf: al-Maṭba^{c}at al-^{c}Ilmīyah, 1377-82 [1957-63], 10 voll.

Yusuf Ali, Abdallah. *The Holy Qur-an.* Text, translation and commentary. Lahore: Sh. Muhammad Ashraf, [1967, c1938], 3 voll.

al-Zamakhsharī, Maḥmūd b. ^{c}Umar. *al-Kashshāf ^{c}an ḥaqā'iq ghawāmiḍ al-tanzīl.* Beirut: Dār al-Kitāb al-^{c}Arabī, 1386 [1966], 4 voll.

II. Other Works in Arabic:

^{c}Abd al-Bāqī, Muhammad Fu'ād. *al-Mu^{c}jam al-mufahras li-alfāẓ al-Qur'ān al-karīm.* Cairo, 1364 [1945].

^{c}Abd al-Rāziq, Muṣṭafá. *al-Dīn wa'l-waḥy wa'l-islām.* Cairo: Dār Iḥyā' al-Kutub al-^{c}Arabīyah, 1365 [1945]. (Translation by L. H. Kenny presented to the School of Oriental Studies of the American University at Cairo, June, 1967.)

^{c}Abduh, Muḥammad. *al-Islām wa'l-naṣrānīyah.* Egypt: Dār al-Manār, 1373 [1953].

--------. *al-Muslimūn wa'l-islām.* Cairo: Dār al-Hilāl, 1383 [1963].

--------. *Risālat al-tawḥīd.* Egypt: Dār al-Ma^{c}ārif, 1386 [1966].

Abū Dā'ūd al-Sijistānī. *Sunan Abī Dā^{c}ūd.* Cairo: Maṭba^{c}at Muṣṭafá al-Bābī al-Ḥalabī, 1382 [1952], 2 voll.

al-^{c}Alāyilī, ^{c}Abd Allāh. *al-Marji^{c}, mu^{c}jam wasīt ^{c}ilmī lughawī fannī.* Beirut: Dār al-Mu^{c}jam al-^{c}Arabī, 1383- [1963-], 1 vol.

al-Astarābādī, Fakhr al-Dīn Muḥammad b. ^{c}Alī. *Manhaj al-maqāl fī taḥqīq aḥwāl al-rijāl.* Teheran, 1307 [1890].

al-Atharī, Muḥammad Bahjat. *A^{c}lām al-^{c}Irāq.* Cairo: al-Maṭba^{c}ah al-Salafīyah, 1345 [1926].

al-Azharī, Muhammad b. Aḥmad. *Tahdhīb al-lughah.* Cairo: al-Mu'assasah al-Miṣrīyah al-^{c}Āmmah, 1384 [1964].

al-Baḥrānī, Yūsuf. *Lu'lu'at al-Baḥrayn fī'l-ijāzāt wa-tarājim rijāl al-ḥadīth.* Najaf: Maṭba^{c}at al-Nu^{c}mān, 1386 [1966].

al-Bukhārī, Abū ^{c}Abd Allāh Muḥammad b. Ismā^{c}īl. *al-Jāmi^{c} al-ṣaḥīḥ*. Cairo: Dār Iḥyā' Kutub al-Sunnah, 1386 [1966], 4 voll.

al-Bustānī, Buṭrus. *Muḥīṭ al-muḥīṭ*. Beirut: 1284-1287 [1867-1870], 2 voll.

al-Dārimī, Abū Muḥammad ^{c}Abd Allāh b. ^{c}Abd al-Raḥmān. *Sunan al-Dārimī*. Damascus: al-I^{c}tidāl, 1349 [1931], 2 voll.

al-Dasūqī, ^{c}Umar. *Fī'l-adab al-ḥadīth*. Cairo: Dār al-Fikr al-^{c}Arabī, 1384 [1964], 2 voll.

al-Dhahabī, Muḥammad Ḥusayn. *al-Tafsīr wa'l-mufassirūn*. Cairo: Dār al-Kutub al-Ḥadīthah, 1381 [1961-2], 3 voll.

al-Dhahabī, Shams al-Dīn Muḥammad b. Aḥmad. *Mīzān al-i^{c}tidāl fī naqd al-rijāl*. Egypt, 1325 [1907], 3 voll.

----------. *Ta'rīkh al-islām wa'ṭabaqāt al-mashāhīr wa'l-a^{c}lām*. Cairo: Maṭba^{c}at al-Maqdisī, 1367 [1947], 1 vol. in 2.

al-Fayyūmī, Aḥmad b. Muḥammad b. ^{c}Alī al-Muqrī. *al-Miṣbāḥ al-munīr fī gharīb al-sharḥ al-kabīr*. Cairo, 1310 [1893].

Ḥājjī Khalīfah, Muṣṭafá b. ^{c}Abd Allāh. *Kashf al-ẓunūn ^{c}an asāmī'l-kutub wa'l-funūn*. Gustaf Flügel, ed. Leipzig: Oriental Translation Fund, 1251 [1835], 7 voll.

al-Ḥurr al-^{c}Āmilī, Muḥammad b. al-Ḥasan. *Amal al-āmil*. Baghdad: Maktabat al-Andalus, 1385 [1965], 2 voll. in 1.

Ibn al-Anbārī, ^{c}Abd al-Raḥman b. Muḥammad. *Nuzhat al-alibbā' fī ṭabaqāt al-udabā'*. Åttia Amer, ed. Stockholm: Almquist & Wiksell, 1383 [1963].

Ibn al-Athīr al-Jazarī, ^{c}Izz al-Dīn. *Usd al-ghābah fī ma^{c}rifat al-ṣaḥābah*. Cairo: al-Maṭba^{c}ah al-Wahhābīyah, 1280 [1863], 5 voll.

Ibn al-^{c}Imād, Abū al-Falāḥ. *Shadharāt al-dhahab fī akhbār man dhahab*. Cairo: Maktabat al-Qudsī, 1350-51 [1931-32], 8 voll. in 4.

Ibn al-Nadīm, Muḥammad b. Isḥāq. *al-Fihrist li-Ibn al-Nadīm*. Cairo: al-Maktabah al-Tijārīyah, 1348 [1929].

Ibn al-Qifṭī, ^{c}Alī b. Yūsuf. *Akhbār al-ḥukamā'*. Egypt: Maṭba^{c}at al-Sa^{c}ādah, 1326 [1908].

Ibn Abī Usaybi^{c}ah [Aḥmad b. Yūnus]. *^{c}Uyūn al-anbā' fī ṭabaqāt al-aṭibbā'*. Cairo: al-Maṭba^{c}ah al-Wahhābīyah, 1300 [1882]. 2 voll.

Ibn Ḥajar al-^{c}Asqalānī, Abū'l-Faḍl. *al-Durar al-kāminah fī a^{c}yān al-mi'ah al-thāminah*. Ḥaydarābād: Maṭba^{c}at Majlis Dā'irat al-Ma^{c}ārif al-^{c}Uthmānīyah, 1348-1350 [1929-1931], 4 voll.

----------. *al-Iṣābah fī tamyīz al-ṣaḥābah*. Calcutta: Maṭba^{c}at Madrasah al-Āsquf, 1273-1306 [1856-1888], 4 voll.

----------. *Tahdhīb al-tahdhīb*. Ḥaydarābād: Maṭba^{c}at Majlis Dā'irat al-Ma^{c}ārif al-Niẓāmīyah, 1325-1327 [1908-1910], 12 voll. in 6.

Ibn Ḥanbal, Aḥmad b. Muḥammad. Musnad. Egypt: al-Maṭba^{c}ah al-Maymanīyah, 1313 [1895], 6. voll.

Ibn Khaldūn, ^{c}Abd al-Raḥman. The Muqaddimah. Franz Rosenthal, transl. New York: Pantheon Books, Inc., 1958, 2 voll.

Ibn Khallikān, Aḥmad b. Muḥammad. Wafayāt al-a^{c}yān wa-anbā' abnā' al-zamān. Wm. MacGuckin de Slane, transl. Paris: Oriental Translation Fund of G.-B. and Ireland, 1259-1278 [1843-1861], 4 voll.

Ibn Mājah, Muḥammad b. Yazīd. al-Sunan. Cairo: Dār Iḥyā' al-Kutub al-^{c}Arabīyah, 1372 [1952].

Ibn Manẓūr, Abū'l-Faḍl Muḥammad b. Mukarram. Lisān al-^{c}arab. Cairo: al-Mu'assasah al-Miṣrīyah al-^{c}Āmmah, 1308 [1890], 20 voll.

Ibn Taghri Birdí, Jamāl al-Dīn. al-Manhal al-ṣāfī wa'l-mustawfī ba^{c}d al-wāfī. Cairo: Dār al-Kutub al-Miṣrīyah, 1375 [1956], 20 voll.

al-Jamal, Sulaymān ibn ^{c}Umar. al-Futūḥāt al-ilāhīyah. Cairo: al-Maktabah al-Tijārīyah al-Kubrá, 1378 [1958], 4. voll.

al-Jawharī, Ismā^{c}īl b. Ḥammād. Tāj al-lughah wa-ṣiḥāḥ al-^{c}arabīyah. Egypt: Maṭābi^{c} Dār al-Kitāb al-^{c}Arabī, 1377 [1957], 2 voll.

al-Kanturī, I^{c}jaz Ḥusayn. Kashf al-ḥujub wa'l-astār ^{c}an asmā' al-kutub wa'l-asfār. M. Hidayat Hosain, ed. Calcutta: Asiatic Society, 1331-54 [1912-35], 2 voll. in 1.

al-Kattānī, Muḥammad b. ^{c}Abd al-Hayy. Fihris al-fahāris. Fās: al-Maṭba^{c}ah al-Jadīdah, 1346-47 [1928-29], 2 voll.

al-Khaṭīb al-Baghdādī, Aḥmad b. ^{c}Alī. Ta'rīkh Baghdād aw-madīnat al-salām. Beirut: Dār al-Kitāb al-^{c}Arabī, 1386 [1966], 14 voll.

al-Khwānsārī, Muḥammad Bāqir. Rawḍāt al-jannāt fī aḥwāl al-^{c}ulamā' wa'l-sādāt. Teheran: Dār al-Kutub al-Islāmīyah, 1382 [1962].

al-Malaṭī, Muḥammad b. Aḥmad. al-Tanbīh wa'l-radd ^{c}alá ahl al-ahwā'. İstanbūl: Maṭba^{c}at al-Dawlah, 1300 [1936].

Mālik b. Anas. al-Muwaṭṭa'. Cairo: Dār Iḥyā' al-Kutub al-^{c}Arabīyah, 1371 [1951], 2 voll.

Ma^{c}lūf, Luwīs. al-Munjid. Beirut: al-Maṭba^{c}ah al-Kāthūlīkah, 1908. Second edition in Beirut: Dār al-Mashriq, 1967.

Manuq, ^{c}Alī b. Bālī. al-^{c}Iqd al-manẓūm fī dhikr afāḍil al-rūm. On the margin of Ibn Khallikān's Wafayāt al-a^{c}yān. Egypt: al-Ṭab^{c}ah al-Maymanīyah, 1310 [1894], 2 voll.

al-Maqqarī, Aḥmad b. Muḥammad. Kitāb nafḥ al-ṭīb min ghuṣn al-andalus al-raṭīb. Leiden: E.J. Brill, 1272-77 [1855-60].

Mas^{c}ūd, Jibrān. al-Rā'id. Beirut: Dār al-^{c}Ilm li'l-Malāyīn, 1384 [1964].

al-Maydānī, ^{c}Abd al-Raḥmān Ḥabannakah. al-^{c}Aqīdah al-islāmīyah wa-ususuhā. Damascus: Maṭba^{c}at al-Inshā', 1341 [1922].

Mubārak, ᶜAlī. al-Khiṭaṭ al-tawfīqīyah al-jadīdah. Būlāq: al-Maṭbaᶜah al-Amīrīyah, 1306 [1888], 20 voll. in 5.

al-Murtaḍá al-Zabīdī, Muḥammad b. Muḥammad. Sharḥ al-qāmūs al-musammá tāj al-ᶜarūs min jawāhir al-qāmūs. Egypt: al-Maṭbaᶜah al-Khayrīyah, 1306 [1888], 10 voll.

Muslim b. al-Ḥajjāj, Abū'l-Ḥusayn. Ṣaḥīḥ Muslim. Cairo: Dār Iḥyā' al-Kutub al-ᶜArabīyah, 1375-76 [1955-56], 5 voll.

al-Najāshī, Aḥmad b. ᶜAlī. Kitāb al-rijāl. Teheran: Markaz Nashr Kitāb, n. d.

al-Nasā'ī, Abū ᶜAbd al-Raḥmān. al-Sunan al-musammá bi'l-mujtabá. Egypt: al-Maṭbaᶜah al-Maymanīyah, 1312 [1894], 2 voll.

Quṭb, Sayyid. al-ᶜAdālah al-ijtimāᶜīyah fī'l-islām. Cairo: al-Bābī, 1326 [1908].

----------. Maᶜālim al-ṭarīq. Cairo: Maktabah Wahbah, 1384 [1964].

al-Rāghib al-Iṣfahānī, Abū'l-Qāsim al-Ḥusayn b. Muḥammad. al-Mufradāt fī gharīb al-Qur'ān. Egypt: Muṣṭafá al-Bābī al-Ḥalabī, 1381 [1961].

Riḍā, Aḥmad. Muᶜjam matn al-lughah. Beirut: Dār Maktabat al-Ḥayāt, 1378-1381 [1958-1961], 25 voll. in 5.

Riḍā, Rashīd. al-Manār. Cairo: Maṭbaᶜat al-Manār, 1315-1352 [1897-1933], 34 voll.

----------. Ta'rīkh al-ustādh al-imām al-shaykh Muḥammad ᶜAbduh. Cairo: Maṭbaᶜat al-Manār, 1324-1350 [1906-1931], 3 voll. in 2.

al-Ṣafadī, Khalīl. al-Wāfī bi'l-wafayāt. Damascus: al-Maṭbaᶜah al-Hāshimīyah, 1379 [1959].

al-Shaᶜrānī, ᶜAbd al-Wahhāb b. Aḥmad. al-Yawāqīt wa'l-jawāhir. Egypt: al-Maṭbaᶜah al-Maymanīyah, 1306 [1889].

al-Shartūnī, Saᶜīd. Aqrab al-mawārid fī fuṣuḥ al-ᶜarabīyah wa'l-shawārid. Beirut: Maṭbaᶜat Mursalī al-Yasūᶜīyah, 1307-1312 [1889-1893], 3 voll.

al-Shawkānī, Muḥammad b. ᶜAlī. al-Badr al-ṭāliᶜ bi-maḥāsin baᶜd al-qarn al-sābiᶜ. Cairo: Maṭbaᶜat al-Saᶜādah, 1348 [1929], 2 voll.

----------. Itḥāf al-akābir bi-isnād al-dafātir. Ḥaydarābād: Majlis Dā'irat al-Maᶜārif al-Niẓāmīyah, 1328 [1910].

Sibṭ ibn al-Jawzī. Mir'āt al-zamān fī ta'rīkh al-aᶜyān. Ḥaydarābād: Dā'irat al-Maᶜārif al-ᶜUthmānīyah, 1371-72 [1951-52], 8 voll. in 2.

Ṣiddīq Ḥasan, Muḥammad. Abjad al-ᶜulūm. Bhopāl: Maṭbaᶜ al-Ṣiddīqī, 1296 [1879], 2 voll. in 3.

Subkī, Tāj al-Dīn ᶜAbd al-Wahhāb b. ᶜAlī. Ṭabaqāt al-Shāfiᶜīyah al-Kubrá. Cairo: ᶜĪsá al-Bābī al-Ḥalabī, 1384-87 [1964-67], 8 voll.

al-Suyūṭī, Jalāl al-Dīn. *Bughyat al-wu^{c}āt fī ṭabaqāt al-lughawiyīn wa'l-nuḥāt*. Cairo: Maṭba^{c}at al-Sa^{c}ādah, 1326 (1908].

----------. *Dhayl ṭabaqāt al-ḥuffāẓ li'l-Dhahabī*. Damascus, 1347 [1929].

----------. *Ḥusn al-muḥāḍarah*. Cairo: Sharafīyah Press, 1327 [1909].

----------. *al-Itqān fī ^{c}ulūm al-Qur'ān*. Cairo: Maṭba^{c}ah Ḥijāzī, 1328 [1950], 2 voll. in 1.

al-Tahānawī, Muḥammad A^{c}lá b. ^{c}Alī. *Kashshāf iṣṭillāḥāt al-funūn*. A. Sprenger, ed. Calcutta: Lee's Press, 1279 [1862], 2 voll.

Tashköpruzade, Aḥmad. *Miftaḥ al-sa^{c}ādah*. Ḥaydarābād: Dā'irat al-Ma^{c}ārif, 1329-56 [1911-37].

al-Ṭayālisī, Muḥammad b. Ja^{c}far. *Musnad Abī Dā'ūd al-Ṭayālisī*. Ḥaydarābād: Maṭba^{c}at Majlis Dā'irat al-Ma^{c}ārif al-Niẓāmīyah, 1321 [1904].

al-Tirmidhī, Abū ^{c}Īsá Muḥammad b. ^{c}Īsá. *al-Jāmi^{c} al-ṣaḥīḥ*. Cairo: Maṭba^{c}at al-Ḥalabī, 1356 [1937], 2 voll.

al-Ṭūsī, Abū Ja^{c}far Muḥammad b. Ḥasan. *Fihrist kutub al-shī^{c}ah*. A. Sprenger, ed. Calcutta: Baptist Mission Press, 1272 [1855].

Wensinck, A. J. *Concordance et indices de la Tradition Musulmane*. Leiden: E.J. Brill, 1936-43, 14 voll. in 2.

al-Yāfi^{c}ī, Abū Muḥammad ^{c}Abd Allāh b. As^{c}ad. *Mir'āt al-janān wa-^{c}ibrat al-yaqẓān*. Ḥaydarābād: Maṭba^{c}at Dā'irat al-Ma^{c}ārif al-Niẓāmīyah, 1337 [1919].

Yāqūt (1179-1229 hijrī?). *Irshād al-arīb ilá ma^{c}rifat al-adīb*. D. S. Margoliouth, ed. Leiden: E. J. Brill, 1325-1345 [1907-1926], 7 voll.

Zabārah al-Yamanī, Muḥammad b. Muḥammad. *Nayl al-waṭar min tarājim rijāl al-Yaman*. Cairo: al-Maṭba^{c}ah al-Salafīyah, 1348/9-50/51 [1929/30-31/32], 2 voll.

Zayd b. ^{c}Alī. *Majmū^{c} al-fiqh*. E. Griffini, ed. Milan, 1338 [1919].

Zaydān, Jurjī. *Tarājim mashāhīr al-sharq fī'l-qarn al-tāsi^{c} ^{c}ashar*. Cairo: Maṭba^{c}at al-Hilāl, 1341 [1922].

III. Other Works in Western Languages:

Abbott, Nabia. *The Rise of the North Arabic Script and its Kur'ānic Development*. Chicago: University of Chicago Press, 1939.

----------. *Studies in Arabic Literary Papyri*. II: Qur'ānic Commentary and Tradition. Chicago: University of Chicago Press, 1967.

Adams, C. C. *Islam and Modernism in Egypt*. London: Oxford University Press, 1933.

Ahmad, Aziz. Islamic Modernism in India and Pakistan 1857-1964. London: Oxford University Press, 1967.

Ameer Ali, Syed. Islam. Karachi: Ismailia Association of Pakistan, 195-.

----------. The Spirit of Islām. Revised edition. London: Christophers, 1922.

Andrae, Tor. Mohammed, the Man and His Faith. Theophil Menzel, transl. First issued in 1936. New York: Harper Torchbooks, 1960.

Antonius, George. The Arab Awakening. London: Hamish Hamilton, 1938.

Baljon, J. M. S. Modern Muslim Koran Interpretation 1880-1960. Leiden: E. J. Brill, 1961.

Berkes, Niyazi. The Development of Secularism in Turkey. Montreal: McGill University Press, 1964.

Blachère, Regis. Introduction au Coran. Second edition. Paris: Éditions Besson & Chantemerle, 1959.

----------. L'Islam: Croyances et Institutions. Beyrouth: Imp. Catholique, 1943.

Boer, T. J. De. The History of Philosophy in Islam. Edward R. Jones, transl. First edition 1903. London: Luzac & Co., 1961.

Brockelmann, Carl. Geschichte der arabischen Litteratur. Zweite den Supplementbaenden angepasste Auflage. Leiden: E. J. Brill, 1943-1949, 2 voll. Erster-dritter Supplementband. Leiden: E. J. Brill, 1937-1942, 3 voll.

Browne, Edward G. A Literary History of Persia. Cambridge: University Press, 1930.

Carra de Vaux, Bernard. Les Penseurs de l'Islam. Paris: Geuthner, 1921-26, 5 voll.

Corbin, Henry. Terre Céleste et Corps de Résurrection de l'Iran Mazdéen à l'Iran Shī'ite. Paris: Corrêa, 1960.

Cragg, Kenneth. Counsels in Contemporary Islam. Edinburgh: University Press, 1965.

----------. The House of Islam. Belmont, California: Dickenson Publ. Co., 1969.

Donaldson, Dwight M. The Shi^c^ite Religion. London: Luzac & Co., 1933.

Dozy, Reinhart. Supplément aux Dictionnaires arabes. Leiden: E. J. Brill, 1881, 2 voll.

Elliot, Sir H. M. The History of India. London: Trübner & Co., 1867-1877, 8 voll.

Gardet, Louis. Dieu et la Destinée de l'Homme. Paris: Librarie Philosophique J. Vrin, 1967.

Gardet, Louis, and M.-M. Anawati. Introduction à la Théologie Musulmane. Paris: Librarie Philosophique J. Vrin, 1948.

Gibb, Hamilton A. R., and Harold Bowen. Islamic Society and the West. London: Oxford University Press, 1962-63, 1 vol. in 2

Goldziher, Ignaz. Le Dogme et la Loi de l'Islam. Félix Arin, transl. Paris: Librarie Paul Geuthner, 1920.

----------. Muhammedanische Studien. First edition 1888. Hildesheim: Georg Olms Verlagsbuchhandlung, 1961, 2 voll. in 1.

----------. Die Richtungen der Islamischen Koranauslegung. Second edition. Leiden: E. J. Brill, 1952.

----------. Vorlesungen über den Islam. Third edition. Heidelberg: Carl Winter Universitätsverlag, 1963.

Grimme, Hubert. Mohammed. Münster: Aschendorff, 1892-95.

Hammer, Joseph de. Histoire de l'Empire Ottoman. J.-J. Hellert, transl. Paris: Barthès, Dufour et Lowell, 1836.

Harris, Christina Phelps. Nationalism and Revolution in Egypt. The Hague: Mouton and Co., 1964.

Heyworth-Dunne, J. An Introduction to the History of Education Egypt. London: Luzac and Co., n.d.

----------. Religious and Political Trends in Modern Egypt. Washington D.C.: Published by the author, 1950.

Hirschfeld, Hartwig. New Researches into the Composition and Exegesis of the Qoran. London: Royal Asiatic Society, 1902.

Horovitz, Josef. Koranische Untersuchungen. Berlin-Leipzig, 1926.

Horster, Paul. Zur Anwendung des islamischen Rechts im 16. Jahrhundert. Stuttgart: W. Kohlhammer, 1935.

Horten, Max. Die philosophischen Ansichten von Rāzi und Tusi. Bonn: Peter Hanstein, 1910.

----------. Die spekulative und positive Theologie des Islam. Hildesheim: Georg Olms Verlagsbuchhandlung, 1967.

Hughes, Thomas Patrick. A Dictionary of Islam. Revised Edition. Lahore: Premier Book House, 1964.

Husaini, Ishak Musa. The Moslem Brethren. John F. Brown and John Racy, transls. Beirut: Khayat's, 1956.

Isḥāq, Muhammad. India's Contribution to the Study of Hadith Literature. Dacca: University of Dacca, 1955.

Izutsu, Toshihiko. The Concept of Belief in Islamic Theology. Tokyo: The Keio Institute of Cultural and Linguistic Studies, 1965.

----------. Ethico-Religious Concepts in the Qur'ān. Montreal: McGill University Press, 1966.

----------. God and Man in the Koran. Tokyo: The Keio Institute of Cultural and Linguistic Studies, 1964.

----------. The Structure of the Ethical Terms in the Koran. Tokyo: Keio University Studies in the Humanities and Social Sciences, 1957, 2 voll.

Jeffery, Arthur. Materials for the History of the Text of the Qur'ān. E. J. Brill, 1937.

Jomier, J. Le Commentaire Coranique du Manâr. Paris: Éditions G.-P. Maisonneuve, 1954.

Kedourie, Elie. Afghani and ^{c}Abduh. London: Frank Cass & Co., 1966.

Kerr, Malcolm. Islamic Reform. Berkeley: University of California Press, 1966.

Klein, F. A. The Religion of Islām. London: Kegan Paul, 1906.

Lammens, Henri. Études sur le règne du Calife Omaiyade Mo^{c}āwia 1er. Paris: Paul Guethner, 1908.

----------. L'islam: Croyances et Institutions. Beyrouth: Imp. Catholique, 1943.

Lane, E. W. An Arabic-English Lexicon. Parts 6-8 edited by Stanley Lane-Poole. London: Williams and Norgate, 1863-93, 1 vol. in 8.

Laoust, Henri. Essai sur les doctrines sociales et politiques de Takid-Dīn Aḥmad b. Taimīya. Cairo: Imprimerie de l'institute Français d'archéologie orientale, 1939.

MacDonald, Duncan B. Aspects of Islam. New York: The Macmillan Co., n.d.

Makdisi, George. Ash^{c}arī and the Ash^{c}arites. Paris: G.-P. Maisonneuve, 1962.

----------. Ibn Qudāma's Censure of Speculative Theology. London: Luzac and Co., 1962.

Margoliouth, D. S. Chrestomathia Baidawiana. London: Luzac and Co., 1894.

Massignon, Louis. Opera Minora. Liban: Dar al-Maaref, [1963-], 3 voll.

Mitchell, Richard P. The Society of the Muslim Brothers. London: Oxford University Press, 1969.

Nasr, Seyyed Hossein. Three Muslim Sages. Cambridge, Mass.: Harvard University Press, 1964.

Nicholson, Reynold. A Literary History of the Arabs. First issued in 1907. Cambridge: University Press, 1962.

Nöldeke, Theodor. Geschichte des Qorans. Revised edition. Leipzig: Dieterich'sche Verlagsbuchhandlung, 1909, 2 voll.

----------. Sketches from Eastern History. John S. Black, transl. Revised edition. Beirut: Khayat's, 1963. 1st ed. 1892.

Nuseibeh, Hazem Zaki. The Ideas of Arab Nationalism. Ithaca, N. Y.: Cornell University Press, 1956.

Penrice, John. A Dictionary and Glossary of the Ḳor-ān. London: Henry S. King, 1873.

Rahbar, Daud. Indices to the Verses of the Qur'an in the Commentaries of al-Ṭabarī and al-Rāzī. Hartford: Hartford Seminary Fdn., 1962.

Ringgren, Helmer. Islam, 'aslama, and Muslim. Uppsala, 1949.

Sabbagh, T. La Métaphore dans le Coran. Paris: Adrien-Maisonneuve, 1943.

Sauvaget, Jean. Introduction to the History of the Muslim East. Berkeley: University of California Press, 1965.

Smith, W. C. Islam in Modern History. Princeton: Princeton University Press, 1957.

----------. The Meaning and End of Religion. New York: Macmillan, 1963.

----------. Modern Islam in India. First issued in 1943. Lahore: Sh. Muhammad Ashraf, 1963.

----------. Orientalism and Truth, A Public Lecture in Honor of T. Cuyler Young. Delivered May 9, 1969. Printed for private distribution by the Program in Near Eastern Studies, Princeton University.

Sprenger, Aloys. Das Leben und die Lehre des Mohammad. Second edition. Berlin: Nicolaische Verlagsbuchhandlung, 1869, 3 voll.

Strothmann, R. Die Zwölfer-Schīʿa. Leipzig: Otto Harrassowitz, 1926.

Torrey, C. C. The Commercial-Theological Terms in the Koran. Leyden, 1892.

----------. The Jewish Foundation of Islam. New York: Jewish Institute of Religion Press, 1933.

Ülken, Hilmi Ziya. La Pensée de l'islam. Gauthier Dubois, Max Bilen and the author, transls. Istanbul: Fakülteler Matbaasi, 1953.

Von Grunebaum, Gustave E. Medieval Islam. Second edition. Chicago: University of Chicago Press, 1962.

Watt, Montgomery. Islamic Philosophy and Theology. Edinburgh: University Press, 1962.

Webster's Third New International Dictionary. Philip Babcock Gove, ed. First edition in 1909. Springfield, Mass.: G. and C. Merriam Co., 1961.

Weijers, H. E. Orientalia. Amsterdam: Apud Johannam Müller, 1846.

Wellhausen, J. The Arab Kingdom and its Fall. Calcutta: Calcutta University Press, 1927.

Wensinck, A. J. A Handbook of Early Muhammadan Tradition. First issued in 1927. Leiden: E. J. Brill, 1960.

----------. The Muslim Creed. Cambridge: University Press, 1932.

Wüstenfeld, F. Die Geschichtschreiber der Araber. Göttingen: Dieterichsche Verlags-Buchhandlung, 1882.

IV. Articles and Parts of Books:

Abbot, Freeland K. "Maulānā Maudūdī on Quranic interpretation". MW, XXXVIII (1958), 6-19.

Ahmad, Rashid (Jullandri). "Qur'ānic exegesis and classical tafsīr". IQ, XII (1968), 71-119.

Ahrens, Karl. "Muhammed als religionsstifler". Abh. K. M., XIX (1935), 1-207.

Amin, Osman. "The modernist movement in Egypt". Richard N. Frye, ed., Islam and the West. 'S-Gravenhage: Mouton & Co., 1957.

Anawati, Georges. "Un traité des noms divins de Fakhr al-Dīn al-Rāzī". George Makdisi, ed., Arabic and Islamic Studies in Honor of Hamilton A. R. Gibb. Cambridge: Harvard University Press, 1965.

Baneth, D. H. "The original meaning of islām as a religious term; a renewal of a medieval interpretation". Proceedings of the Twenty-Third International Congress of Orientalists, Cambridge 1954. London, n. d. [sc. 1955?].

Barth, J. "Studien zur kritik und exegese des Qorāns". Isl., VI (1915-16), 113-148.

Bazmee Ansari, A. S. "Al-Dihlawī Shāh Walī Allāh". EI_2, II (1965), 254-55.

Bertier, Francis. "L'ideologie politique des frères musulmans". Orient, VIII (1958), 43-57.

Birkeland, Harris. "The Lord guideth: studies on primitive islam". Skrifter [of the Oslo Academy], Part II (1956), 1-140.

----------. "Old muslim opposition against interpretation of the Koran". Avhandlinger [of the Oslo Academy], Part II (1955), 1-42.

Brockelmann, Carl. "Al-Baiḍāwī". SEI, (1953), p. 58.

----------. "Ibn Kathīr". EI, II (1927), 393-94.

----------. "Al-Suyūṭī". EI, IV (1934), 573-75.

----------. "Al-Zamakhsharī". EI, IV (1934), 1205-07.

Cragg, Kenneth. "The modernist movement in Egypt". Richard N. Frye, ed., Islam and the West. 'S-Gravenhage: Mouton & Co., 1957.

Goldziher, Ignaz. "Aus der theologie des Fachr al-dīn al-Rāzī". Isl., III (1912), 213-47.

----------. "Zur charakteristik Ǵelāl ud-dīn us-Sujūṭī's und seiner literarischen thätigkeit". SBKais. Ak., LXIX (1871), 7-28.

Hartmann, M. "Die osmanische 'Zeitschrift der Nationale Forschungen'". Isl., VIII (1918), 304-26.

Hasanal-Ma^csūmī, M. S. "An appreciation of Shāh Walīullah al-Muḥaddith al-Dihlawī". IC, XXI (1947), 340-52.

Hidayet Hosain, M. "Al-Ṭūsī". EI, IV (1934), 982.

Horst, Heribert. "Zur überlieferung im Koran-kommentar aṭ-Ṭabarīs" ZDMG, CIII (1953), 290-307.

Horten, Max. "Muhammed Abduh". Beiträge, XIV (1917), 74-128.

Husain, Mawlavi M. "The Persian autobiography of Shāh Walīullah bin ᶜAbd al-Raḥīm al-Dihlavī: its English translation and a list of his works". JASB, VIII (1912), 161-75.

Jeffery, Arthur. "The present status of Qur'anic studies". Report on Current Research on the Middle East. Washington, D. C.: The Middle East Institute, Spring 1957.

Kramers, J. H. "Al-Rāzī". SEI, (1953), pp. 470-71.

----------. "Shaikh al-Islām". EI, IV (1934), 275-79.

Kraus, Paul. "The 'controversies' of Fakhr al-Dīn Rāzī". IC, XII (1938), 131-53.

Künstlinger, David. "'Islām', 'muslim', 'aslama' im Kurān". RO, XI (1935), 128-37.

Lidzbarski, Mark. "Salām und islām". ZS, I (1922), 85-96.

Loth, O. "Ṭabarī's Korankommentar". ZDMG, XXXV (1881), 588-628.

Margoliouth, D.S. "On the origin and import of the names muslim and ḥanīf". JRAS, XXXV (1903), 467-483.

Nasr, Seyyed Hossein. "Fakhr al-Dīn Rāzī". M. M. Sharif, ed., A History of Muslim Philosophy. Wiesbaden: Otto Harrassowitz, 1963, vol. II.

----------. "Ithnā ᶜasharī Shīᶜism and Iranian islam". A. J. Arberry, ed., Religion in the Middle East, vol. II.

Paret, R. "Al-Ṭabarī". EI, IV (1934), 578-79.

Péres, H. "Al-Ālūsī". EI_2, I (1960), 425.

Rahbar, Daud. "Reflections on the tradition of Qur'anic exegesis". MW, LII (1962), 296-307.

----------. "Shāh Walī Ullāh and ijtihād". MW, XLV (1955), 346-58.

----------. "Sir Sayyid Aḥmad Khān's principles of exegesis". MW, XLVI (1956), 104-112, 324-335.

Ringgren, Helmer. "The conception of faith in the Koran". Oriens, IV (1951), 1-20.

----------. "The pure religion". Oriens, XV (1962), 93-96.

Robson, James. "'Islam' as a term". MW, XLIV (1954), 101-109.

Rosenthal, Franz. "The 'Muslim Brethren' in Egypt". *MW*, XXXVIII (1947), 278-91.

Schacht, J. "Abu'l-Su^{c}ūd". *EI*$_2$, I (1960), 152.

----------. "Muḥammad ^{c}Abduh". *EI*, III (1936), 678-80.

Sell, Edward. "Islām". *ERE*, VII (1915), 437-38.

Shahid, Irfan. "A contribution to Koranic exegesis". George Makdisi, ed., *Arabic and Islamic Studies in Honor of Hamilton A. R. Gibb*. Cambridge: Harvard University Press, 1965.

Smith, Wilfred Cantwell. "The concept of shari^{c}a among some mutakallimun". George Makdisi, ed., *Arabic and Islamic Studies in Honor of Hamilton A. R. Gibb*. Cambridge: Harvard University Press, 1965.

----------. "The historical development in Islam of the concept of Islam as an historical development". Bernard Lewis and P. M. Holt, eds., *Historians of the Middle East*. London: Oxford University Press, 1962.

Strothmann, R. "Shī^{c}a". *EI*, IV (1934), 350-58.

Veccia Vaglieri, L. "^{c}Abd Allāh b. al-^{c}Abbās". *EI*$_2$, I (1960), 40-41.

Yahuda, A. S. "A contribution to Qur'ān and ḥadīth interpretation". Samuel Löwinger and Joseph Somogyu, eds., *Goldziher Memorial Volume I*. Budapest, 1948.